Supply Chain Management
Best Practices

Supply Chain Management
Best Practices

Second Edition

DAVID BLANCHARD

WILEY

John Wiley & Sons, Inc.

Published by John Wiley & Sons, Inc., Hoboken, New Jersey.
Published simultaneously in Canada.

For general information on our other products and services or for technical support, please contact our Customer Care Department within the United States at (800) 762-2974, outside the United States at (317) 572-3993 or fax (317) 572-4002.

Wiley also publishes its books in a variety of electronic formats. Some content that appears in print may not be available in electronic books. For more information about Wiley products, visit our web site at www.wiley.com.

Library of Congress Cataloging-in-Publication Data:

Blanchard, David, 1958–
  Supply chain management : best practices / David Blanchard. – 2nd ed.
      p. cm.
  Includes bibliographical references and index.
  ISBN 978-0-470-53188-4 (cloth)
  1. Business logistics. I. Title.
  HD38.5.B476 2010
  658.5–dc22

                                                          2009043705

Printed in the United States of America

10 9 8 7 6 5 4 3 2 1

To Nancy, Julia, and Grace

Contents

Preface to the
Second Edition

A s noted in the first edition, when you give a book a title like *Supply Chain Management Best Practices*, there's not much mystery in what it's going to be about. Throughout its 18 chapters, this book will identify some of the best supply chains in the world, describe in detail what it means to have a "best-in-class" supply chain, and offer suggestions—in the form of best practices—on how to build a world-class supply chain.

This book is largely told through the experiences of supply chain practitioners and experts. The companies and the people referred to in this book are real, as are their accomplishments (and, in some cases, their failures). What sets this book apart from other supply chain books is that I have taken a journalist's approach to the subject rather than an academic's or a consultant's. As the editorial director of Penton Media's supply chain group of publications, I've had access to supply chain professionals at companies of all sizes, in dozens of different industries. So in writing this book, I have set out to tell the story of supply chain management through the eyes of the people who know it best.

In the United States alone, companies spend more than $1 trillion every year on transportation, warehousing, distribution, and associated inventory management. The responsibility for managing that spending falls squarely on the shoulders of supply chain professionals. Their roles may differ from company to company, but their goals are generally the same: develop and position their companies' supply chains so that they can compete and win in today's global marketplace. Many of these professionals work for companies that consider supply chain management and its many subdivisions (e.g., planning, purchasing, logistics, trade management) as little more than necessary evils and cost centers. Yet it's an inescapable fact that many of the biggest and best-run companies got to where they are thanks to their adoption of best practices to manage their world-class supply chains.

This book, then, is designed to help you figure out how you can get your own company on the "best practices" track. It will explain why there is so much interest in supply chain management today by offering numerous examples of companies that have found success by focusing on specific processes within their supply chains. Through anecdotes, interviews, case studies, research, and analysis, the book will explore the development of supply chain management by looking at some of the people and the businesses largely responsible for its momentum.

For most of the three years since the first edition was published, I was editor-in-chief of *IndustryWeek*, the leading magazine for manufacturing management, and in that role I had the opportunity to visit manufacturing plants, distribution centers, major ports, third-party logistics operations, and various government offices throughout North America, Europe, and Asia. In preparing this second edition, I have added a significant amount of new material and additional best practices to each chapter, with the goal of producing as timely and relevant a book as possible. This current edition also includes two entirely new chapters devoted to perhaps the two hottest buzzwords in supply chain and manufacturing circles today: green and lean.

The book is organized into three sections. Part I opens with a brief introduction to supply chain management (Chapter 1), looks at examples of some best-in-class supply chains in a number of different industries (Chapter 2), and discusses ways to measure the performance of a supply chain (Chapter 3). (For those readers who are interested in an entire book devoted to supply chain basics, I recommend Michael Hugos's *Essentials of Supply Chain Management, Second Edition*, also published by John Wiley & Sons.)

Part II presents the traditional core processes of supply chain management. Chapters 4 through 11 follow the progression of plan, source, make, deliver, and return and related points in between, and discuss in detail the best practices being followed by specific trendsetting companies.

Part III looks at best practices in strategic areas that have become increasingly important to supply chain management since the turn of the millenium: outsourcing (Chapter 12), collaboration (Chapter 13), security (Chapter 14), radio frequency identification (Chapter 15), green supply chains (Chapter 16), and continuous improvement and lean management (Chapter 17). Finally, Chapter 18 focuses on the ultimate best practice: hiring and developing best-in-class supply chain personnel.

Acknowledgments

The genesis for writing this book came largely from a need to clean up my office. I've been writing about supply chain management for a long time, dating back to the days when nobody even used the words "supply chain," and being a pack rat, I have several filing cabinets' worth of notes, interview transcripts, research studies, surveys, press kits, and article clippings, as well as several shelves stuffed with reference books. One day, staring at my daunting collection of supply chain stuff, the thought occurred to me: "Surely, there's got to be a book somewhere in all of this." And indeed there was, eventually.

I mention this to dispel the myth that every book emerges fully formed from the divinely inspired mind of the author. Nothing could be further from the truth. This book evolved by fits and starts from the writing and editing I've done over two decades, most particularly the decade I've spent as chief editor or editorial director of Penton Media's supply chain group of publications, including *Supply Chain Technology News*, *Logistics Today*, *Material Handling Management*, and *IndustryWeek*.

This book also references the reporting of many fine journalists who have worked with me and for me, and many of the insights on the following pages originated with them (and are duly noted throughout the book). In alphabetical order, I'd like to acknowledge and publicly thank Mary Aichlmayr, Dan Jacobs, Jill Jusko, Jonathan Katz, Brad Kenney, Jennifer Kuhel, Roger Morton, Traci Purdum, Helen Richardson, Adrienne Selko, Sarah Sphar, John Teresko, Perry Trunick, and Nick Zubko for their contributions.

It's always good to thank your bosses, so thanks to those I've worked for at Penton since the late 1990s, namely Newt Barrett, Dave Madonia, Teri Mollison, Ron Lowy, Steve Minter, and John DiPaola. And special thanks to Bob Rosenbaum, not only because he had the good sense to hire me, but because he showed me that it was possible to write a supply chain book in the evenings and on weekends without completely losing your mind.

Not to single anybody out, but I also have to thank Nick Lester, Dick Green, Craig Shutt, Andy Horn, Steve Kane, and Paul Beard—just because.

I'm especially indebted to all the supply chain professionals who shared their experiences and insights with me. And of course, this book wouldn't have been possible without the good graces of the fine folks at John Wiley & Sons, particularly Tim Burgard.

Finally, thanks to my friends and family, who supported me enormously throughout the writing process and offered endless encouragement. Special thanks go to my parents, Jack and Dottie Blanchard, for their lifelong support; to my daughters, Julia and Grace, for being the greatest kids a dad could ever want, who never complained about seeing only the back of my head on some weekends, and who celebrated with me every time I'd finish another chapter; and most of all, to Nancy, my wife and soulmate. WEATSIA!

Supply Chain Management
Best Practices

PART I

Introduction to Supply Chain Management

CHAPTER 1

If Supply Chain Is the Answer, Then What's the Question?

Flashpoints

A supply chain is the sequence of events that cover a product's entire life cycle, from conception to consumption.

A one-size-fits-all supply chain strategy is doomed to failure.

Although the modern concept of supply chain management dates back to the early 1980s, very few companies have fully embraced it.

Building a best-in-class supply chain requires money, time, talent, energy, focus, commitment, and guts.

You Knew This Job Was Dangerous When You Took It

Imagine, if you will, a typical day in the life of a supply chain professional. Your boss comes into your office with one of those looks you've come to dread—furrowed brow, deep-set eyes, concerned scowl. He looks you straight in the eye and asks you why it costs so much to transport your company's products to your customers. You can tell by the expression on his face that he doesn't want to hear about rising fuel costs or industry consolidation. It's *your* job to worry about that stuff, not his. And right now, even though your budget projections say you'll have to spend at least 5 percent more on transportation this year than you did last year, your boss tells you in no uncertain terms that he expects you to keep the increase down to 2 percent or less. Preferably less.

At the water cooler, your director of sales gives you a sheepish smile and asks if you can arrange for an extra 1,000 widgets to be made and shipped to a big customer by the end of the week. Actually, she doesn't really ask you so much as *tell* you, since she's already promised the customer that it will happen. She leaves before you get the chance to ask if she's charging the customer double the normal price since it'll cost you at least twice normal rates to source the parts used to make the widgets from your offshore supplier, plus the cost of expedited delivery. On top of that, production will have to schedule an extra shift to get that many widgets made that quickly.

Later in the morning, while you're patting yourself on the back because you managed to find a domestic source for most of the widget parts, your boss asks you to shepherd your company's radio frequency identification (RFID) initiative. The Department of Defense (DoD), another big customer, wants your company to put RFID tags on every case of widgets that you ship to them. It's part of the DoD's efforts to keep better track of its inventory. That's great for the military, but your boss wants you to figure out how RFID is going to help your company, particularly since industry estimates say you could incur start-up costs of more than $1 million. Your boss waves off the list of questions that immediately come to your mind; he wants you to answer those questions yourself, provide him with regular updates on your progress, and map out an implementation plan that results in a decent return on investment within a year.

For all his many faults, though, your boss is a fair man, and recognizing the extra burdens he's been laying on you, he invites you to lunch. Before your salad arrives, he's already launched into a harangue about outsourcing. Your competitors have been getting to market faster and are spending less money to do it, and he's convinced it's because they've contracted their distribution to third-party logistics providers (3PLs). So when you get back to the office, he wants you to figure out which 3PL can do it better, faster, and cheaper for you. Your customer service levels, needless to say, cannot change in the slightest, unless of course they actually improve.

Oh, and one more thing, your boss adds as you get up to leave the restaurant: He wants you to schedule another trip to China (your seventh trip there in three years). It's time, he says, to get serious about this globalization stuff, and you can start by lining up another low-cost supplier for your widget parts.

Most of your afternoon is spent trying to mend some fences down in the information technology department. Your chief information officer has made it clear that absolutely nobody is going home today until somebody can figure out why the supply chain planning system still isn't fully integrated with the inventory management system—and why manufacturing keeps making 12-inch widgets when the sales plan calls for 18-inch versions. Toward the end of the afternoon, your plant manager asks for "a little bit of help" calculating what the plant's carbon footprint is. You get the unmistakable feeling that he wouldn't mind one bit if you figured it out for him.

As you finally shut down your computer and get ready to call it a day, your head of human resources pops her head in your doorway and tells you she hasn't had a bit of luck yet finding a global trade expert, so it looks like you'll have to keep filling in for a while longer. Hearing the tail end of that conversation, your boss walks with you out to the parking lot and reminds you he still needs to see your contingency plan in the event of a work slowdown at a major West Coast port. Oh, and a big storm is developing in the South China Sea, and one of your key supplier's plants is right in the storm's path. Fortunately, you'll be able to monitor the situation from your home throughout the evening, thanks to modern technology and all the personal productivity gadgets your company has purchased for you.

At the end of the day, after you've kissed your spouse goodnight and laid your head on your pillow, you drift off to sleep secure in the knowledge that the distance between you and your supply chain is no further than the BlackBerry recharging on your nightstand.

The Big Picture

Admittedly, the preceding example represents a rather extreme and time-compressed scenario, but on any given day, a supply chain manager has to deal with numerous situations quite similar to those just described, with the expectation that costs will be minimized, disruptions will be avoided, and the profitability of the company will be enhanced. No pressure, right?

Maybe we're getting ahead of ourselves, though, so let's start at the beginning: What exactly is a supply chain? There are plenty of definitions for the term, and we'll look at a couple of them, but this question gets asked so often because the answer tends to change depending on who's doing the telling. It's like that old fable about the blind men who stumble on an elephant and try to tell each other what the elephant is like: The man holding the elephant's leg thinks the animal looks like a tree; the man holding the tail thinks an elephant resembles a rope; a third man who grabbed a tusk thinks the whole animal must look like a spear. Each of their answers is partly right, but anybody who has actually seen an elephant smiles at the story because they know these blind men are missing the big picture.

The funny thing is, those kinds of faulty assumptions are made all the time about supply chains. Since computer maker Dell's supply chain is based on a make-to-order model, for instance, it has been suggested that Dell's direct model is the best model for *all* high-tech companies or, for that matter, for *any company in any industry*. However, while rival computer maker Hewlett-Packard's sourcing processes might look a lot like Dell's, its transportation networks will be completely different from beef producer ConAgra's, which relies on refrigerated vehicles. So, the idea that "one supply chain strategy fits all" is as wrong-headed as thinking an elephant looks like a tree.

A *supply chain*, boiled down to its basic elements, is the sequence of events and processes that take a product from dirt to dirt, in some cases literally. It encompasses a series of activities that people have engaged in since the dawn of commerce. Consider the supply chain General Mills manages for every box of cornflakes it sells: A farmer plants a certain number of corn seeds, cultivates and harvests a crop, sells the corn to a processing facility, where it is baked into cornflakes, then is packaged, warehoused to a distributor, transported to a retail store, put on a store shelf, sold to a consumer, and ultimately eaten. If the cornflakes are not sold by the expiration date on the box, then they are removed from the retailer's shelf and disposed of.

A supply chain, in other words, extends from the original supplier or source (the farmer and the seed) to the ultimate customer (the consumer who eats the cornflakes). So whether you're talking about an Intel semiconductor that begins its life as a grain of sand or a Ford Explorer that ends its life in a junkyard where its remaining usable components (tires, seat belts, bumpers) are sold as parts, everything that happens in between those dirt-to-dirt milestones encompasses some aspect of the supply chain.

The Supply Chain Council, an organization that develops industry benchmarks and metrics, came up with a way to summarize the concept of supply chain management in just five words: *plan, source, make, deliver*, and *return*. While it's difficult to find a consensus in any field, let alone a field that intersects with so many disparate disciplines, that five-word definition has been accepted as the basic description of what a supply chain looks like and what its core functions are. (The Supply Chain Operations Reference, or SCOR, model is discussed in Chapter 3.)

For those who like a little sizzle with their steak, another industry group, the Council of Supply Chain Management Professionals (CSCMP), is a bit more descriptive with its definition: "Supply chain management encompasses the planning and management of all activities involved in sourcing and procurement, conversion, and all logistics management activities." That includes coordinating and collaborating with channel partners, including suppliers, intermediaries, third parties, and customers. In short: "Supply chain management integrates supply and demand management within and across companies."[1]

The Supply Chain's Back Story

As noted, the concept of working with suppliers and customers is as old as commerce itself, but the modern idea of a "supply chain" is fairly recent, probably dating back no farther than the late 1950s to the pioneering research conducted by Jay Forrester and his colleagues at the Massachusetts Institute of Technology. A half century ago, Forrester began studying supply pipelines and channel interrelationships between suppliers and customers, and he identified a phenomenon that later came to be known as the *bullwhip effect*.

Forrester noticed that inventories in a company's pipeline (i.e., supply chain) tend to fluctuate the further they are from the ultimate end user.[2] The idea of the bullwhip effect remained largely a curiosity until the 1990s, when computers were fast enough, powerful enough, and affordable enough that researchers could not only gain an understanding of the bullwhip effect, but also design software programs that could circumvent it. Supply chain management as a discipline basically evolved out of Forrester's quest to understand and ultimately control these increases in demand fluctuations. Although he didn't use the exact words "supply chain" to describe his findings, "Forrester and his group should really get the credit for supply chain management," asserts Edward Marien, longtime director of supply chain management programs at the University of Wisconsin.[3]

At some point in the early 1980s, the concepts of transportation, distribution, and materials management began to merge into a single, all-encompassing term: *supply chain management*. The term apparently first appeared in print in 1982, and is attributed to Keith Oliver, a consultant with Booz Allen. In any event, in 1985, Harvard professor Michael Porter's influential book, *Competitive Advantage*, illustrated how a company could become more profitable by strategically analyzing the five primary processes on which its supply chain framework is built:[4]

1. *Inbound logistics*. These are the activities associated with receiving, storing, and disseminating inputs to the product (material handling, warehousing, inventory control, transportation scheduling, and returns to suppliers).
2. *Operations*. This refers to the activities associated with transforming inputs into the final product form (machining, packaging, assembly, equipment maintenance, testing, printing, and facility operations).
3. *Outbound logistics*. These are the activities associated with collecting, storing, and physically distributing the product to buyers (finished goods warehousing, material handling, freight delivery, order processing, and scheduling).
4. *Sales and marketing*. Within a supply chain context, these are the activities that induce buyers to purchase a product and enable them to buy it (advertising, promotions, sales force, quoting, channel selection, channel relations, and pricing).

5. *Service*. This refers to the activities associated with providing service to enhance or maintain the value of the product (installation, repair, training, parts supply, and product adjustment).[5]

Like Forrester before him, Porter saw that companies could significantly improve their operations by focusing on interrelationships among business units. These interrelationships, he wrote, are "tangible opportunities to reduce costs or enhance differentiation in virtually any activity in the value chain. Moreover, the pursuit of interrelationships by some competitors is compelling others to follow suit or risk losing their competitive position." As a result, according to Porter, it is critically important for companies to focus on horizontal strategy—a coordinated set of goals and policies across distinct but interrelated business units. This horizontal strategy, which is a succinct way of describing supply chain management, represents the essence of corporate strategy.[6]

Although their work was separated by more than two decades, both Forrester and Porter saw that a vertical strategy—the idea of compartmentalizing every department and group into unconnected silos—was counterproductive to a company's long-term growth and health. Curiously, two decades after Porter's work, one of the popular buzzwords of the day—unsiloing—refers to the concept of managers cooperating across departments and functions, sharing resources, and cross-selling products to promote the entire company's bottom line.[7]

The terms may change throughout the years, but the underlying goal of supply chain management has remained constant:

- Articulate exactly what a company's supply chain looks like and what it encompasses.
- Identify specific bottlenecks that are slowing down the movement of information, goods, and services.
- Put the right processes in place to get the right products delivered to the right place on time.
- Empower the right people so they can accomplish all of the above.

Roadblocks on the Supply Chain Path

Although the concept of supply chain management entered the public consciousness nearly 30 years ago, to date only a very small percentage of companies have fully embraced the idea. Even though many of the best-known manufacturing and retail companies in the world are as celebrated for their supply chains as they are for their brands, relatively few companies even attempt full-scale supply chain projects, and of those that do, many are stymied by various roadblocks that make them question whether the end result will be worth the aggravation.

Consulting firm Accenture teamed up with Stanford University and global business school INSEAD to try to figure out why that should be.[8] Of the companies they studied, it turns out that more than half encountered unexpected problems in the course of their supply chain transformations. Exacerbating the situation is the fact that these problems aren't easily solved:

- *Technology implementations didn't work as promised.* The supply chain movement faced a moment of crisis when the Internet bubble burst, taking many supply chain technology vendors (and even more vaporware companies) with it. Companies that should have known better assumed that establishing a Web site was a ticket to instant riches, and they embraced the Internet with a giddy "gold rush" fervor. They spent millions on ill-advised end-to-end projects that had no timeline for deliverable payback, and they got badly burned in the process. To this day, many companies still remain extremely cautious about investing in any kind of supply chain solution.

- *Projects cost too much and never came close to meeting service targets.* This problem predates the supply chain. The list of unfinished and underimplemented enterprise resource planning projects is a lengthy one, and unfortunately there are plenty of similarly out-of-control supply chain projects to add to that list. Many of these enterprise-wide initiatives end up being a bottomless money pit of costs with no end in sight and no discernible benefits.

- *Supply chain projects were inconsistent with a company's current business strategy.* The unfortunate reality is that many companies don't have a well-defined business strategy. Trying to plug a supply chain initiative into an uncertain and continually shifting corporate plan can wear out even the most patient project managers.

- *It was too difficult to manage change internally and externally.* For a supply chain project to succeed, employees first need to be convinced that sharing product and transactional data between their own divisions is a good thing. Too often, companies will fail in their attempts at collaborating with key supply chain partners because their own internal groups don't cooperate with each other. You have to be able to trust your own people before you can hope to collaborate with other companies.

The Accenture study, incidentally, looked at companies that ultimately found a way to successfully launch and complete their supply chain initiatives. You can well imagine that at companies that have had far worse luck with their projects, many managers close and lock their doors behind them every time they see a supply chain project leader walking toward their offices.

Separating the Good from the Best

There's no getting around it: Supply chain management is just plain difficult. No single company has all the answers, and what's more, most companies ask virtually the same questions. So why are some companies celebrated for their supply chain successes, while other companies seem to be stuck in a rut? What distinguishes a best-in-class supply chain from every other supply chain?

As this book will illustrate, every top-performing company—no matter what industry it competes in—has aggressively attacked its inventory problems, committed resources to improving its customer service levels, and partnered with its key suppliers to take control of its supply chain. Every single one of them.

Top-performing supply chains, quite frankly, do things a little differently than everyone else. According to Debra Hofman, an analyst with AMR Research Inc., best-in-class companies share these three traits:

1. *They aim for balance*. These companies may not be the very best in every category, but they are consistently good enough in all areas that they add up to be best-in-class.
2. *They increase demand visibility*. Having a high level of forecast accuracy is the key to reaching perfect order fulfillment, which is the holy grail of customer service.
3. *They isolate high costs*. The best companies know where they hold their costs and why, so that's where they focus their best practices and technology investments.[9]

Karen Butner, global supply chain management leader for the IBM Institute for Business Value, boils it all down to one common factor: "Top supply chains all have the ability to respond quickly to shifts in demand with innovative products and services."[10]

When it comes to best practices, supply chain success requires commitment at the highest corporate levels. It should surely come as no surprise that the chief executive officer (CEO) of the biggest company in the world (Mike Duke of Wal-Mart) used to manage the company's logistics department, which is where the retail giant's strategic edge begins. Booz Allen, the consulting firm that first popularized the term *supply chain management*, reports that companies with CEO-level support for their supply chain projects have nearly twice the annual savings in customer service costs as companies where the responsibility is lower in the organization. In a survey of senior executives, Booz Allen concludes, "Without guidance and oversight from the CEO and the company's full leadership team, the supply chain's performance often does not live up to expectations."[11]

Best practices don't just happen by throwing a lot of money at your supply chain problems. Improvements come through strategies that identify and track key supply chain processes early and often. As J. Paul Dittmann, director of the University of Tennessee's Office of Corporate Partnership, has observed, very few companies actually have a documented supply chain strategy.[12] "Such a strategy," he suggests, "starts with assessing the future needs of their customers. The strategy development process then determines the new supply chain capabilities the company will need in the future to meet its customers' needs. Unfortunately, most supply chain organizations are so consumed with the daily battles of cutting cost, managing inventory, and delivering good customer service that they don't plan properly for the future, sometimes with disastrous results." Indeed, whenever companies experience the first hint of trouble, whether it's the onset of an economic recession or a new competitor that seemingly sprang up overnight, the supply chain strategy is shelved, where it often sits collecting dust for many years.

In short, building and maintaining an end-to-end supply chain organization takes money, but it also takes time, talent, energy, focus, commitment from senior management, and a lot of guts to pull it off successfully. However, those are the qualities that the best-run companies in the world share, and it's why they're on top. As Dittmann says, "Supply chain is the frontier of competition." In the next chapter, we'll look at specific examples of how some well-known companies in a number of different industries are managing their best-in-class supply chains.

CHAPTER 2

Anatomy of a Supply Chain

Flashpoints

Best-in-class supply chains share many common characteristics, no matter what industry they're in.

It takes a coordinated team effort to build, maintain, and sustain a well-run supply chain.

Best practices don't just happen. Somebody has to devise them and then apply them.

Supply chains are defined as much by their similarities as by their differences. While there may not appear to be much in common, say, between a multibillion-dollar big-box retailer and a single-site mom-and-pop shop, in fact both companies operate on the same principle: When you're out of stock, you're out of business. With out-of-stock rates averaging 10 percent (in some product categories, it can be considerably higher), having products on the shelves is the be-all and end-all of retail life. So retailers of all shapes and sizes—whether they're mass discounters the size of a small country like Wal-Mart or a modest chain of three comic book stores—are naturally inclined toward adopting best practices that will maximize their revenues (e.g., rapid replenishment) while minimizing their costs (e.g., demand planning).

The story is much the same for manufacturers, distributors, nonprofits, service industries—in short, any organization that makes or moves products, whether physical or digital, has common supply chain challenges. According to Jim Tompkins, chief executive officer (CEO) of supply chain consulting firm Tompkins Associates, top-performing supply chains share these seven characteristics:

1. They have a clear supply chain strategy as their foundation. This strategy is based on a deep understanding of the company's business strategy.
2. They are adaptable and quick, which allows them to compete in today's dynamic environment.
3. They are transparent, have clearly stated performance expectations, and have a culture of accountability to their customers.
4. They are focused on continuous improvement throughout the supply chain and aim at peak-to-peak performance.
5. They know their strengths and their weaknesses, and participate in benchmarking activities.
6. They have an end-to-end perspective, focusing on the supply chain activities of plan-buy-make-move-store-sell (Tompkins's tweak of the Supply Chain Council's basic definition of the supply chain as plan-source-make-deliver-return).
7. They have a global, rather than regional, focus.[1]

In short, the best-run organizations have developed world-class supply chains that extend from their customers' customers to their suppliers' suppliers, and all points in between. As this chapter illustrates, many of the best practices of one industry can be tweaked so that they'll work for another industry as well.

Best practices only tell part of the story, though. The not-so-dirty little secret is that behind every successful supply chain organization is a team of dedicated and influential change agents. Or, to put it more simply, a supply chain wins or loses based on the quality of the people who manage it. With that in mind, let's look at some of the most innovative efforts at supply chain management in several industries and at some of the people who have spearheaded their companies' best practices efforts.

Aerospace: Changing the Game, for Better or Worse

It's only fitting that we should start by looking at The Boeing Co., as the aerospace giant's 787 Dreamliner project is not only a game changer when it comes to pushing the boundaries of what's possible with a fully connected supply chain, but it's also an example of what can go wrong when a company's supply chain reach exceeds its grasp.

Boeing's goal with the Dreamliner was nothing short of evolutionary: Rather than merely talking about an extended enterprise that involved key partners in every step along the supply chain, Boeing would actually do it. Namely, Boeing the airplane maker would become Boeing the airplane assembler, outsourcing the entire production of its new aircraft to suppliers and then finishing the plane at the final assembly stage. On the face of it, that doesn't sound radically different from what the major automakers do, locating Tier 1 suppliers in close proximity to the assembly plants. However, while an automobile might be built with as many as 8,000 to 10,000 parts, an airplane might have 3 million parts or more.

In addition, while in the past Boeing had used outside suppliers to build roughly 50 percent of its planes, its plan for the Dreamliner was to outsource 70 percent of its fabrication, with much of the major components coming from outside the United States. Engines, for instance, would come from both Ohio and the United Kingdom; wingtips from Korea; trailing edges from Australia and Japan; center fuselages from Italy; cargo access doors from Sweden; and passenger entry doors from France. In fact, Boeing went so far as to develop a cargo plane—the Dreamlifter—to transport the larger parts, such as wings and fuselage, to the final assembly plant in Everett, Washington.[2]

The reason for outsourcing so much of the production work is the realization that the best process skills in aerospace oftentimes lie outside Boeing's factories, says Mike Bair, vice president of business strategy and marketing for commercial airplanes and former head of the Dreamliner program. The new plane would involve not only a new supply chain plan but also the development of lightweight composite materials and fuel-efficient engines, new production processes, and an interior architecture that would set new standards for passenger comfort. With a target delivery date of May 2008, the Dreamliner became the fastest-selling commercial aircraft in history, with more than 700 orders from 50 airlines by late 2007.[3]

Then cold reality set in: Due to numerous setbacks and supply chain problems, Boeing was not able to deliver any Dreamliners by 2008. Nor, as it turned out, was it able to fill any orders in 2009, either. As of summer 2009, Boeing was hopeful that the first order would be delivered by the fourth quarter of 2010. "It has simply proved to be more difficult than we anticipated to complete the structural work on the airplane out of sequence in our Everett factory," admits Scott Carson, Boeing's executive vice president of commercial airplanes.

As consultant Stephen C. Rogers explains, the never-ending delays weren't due to a flawed supply chain strategy; instead, it was the unprecedented nature of the project itself that led to the problems. "The supply chain structure for the Dreamliner took best-in-class supply chain thinking and applied it from the design phase through to production," he observes. However, "the scale and scope of the task was enormous when considering the sheer number of parts, amount of innovation, number of subcontracting tiers, and geographical dispersion of the contractors. No company ever managed such a project before." Since nearly three-quarters of the work was being done by suppliers, naturally most of the production problems were on the supplier end as well, and as Boeing quickly discovered, a game-changing initiative like the Dreamliner requires extreme supply chain management.

In response, Boeing has instituted a more intense supplier support and monitoring system to address breakdowns in the supply chain. Rogers points out, "The key [for Boeing] is to manage what counts and find ways to extend resources through the use of suppliers. This is easier said than done since many Tier 2 and Tier 3 suppliers have allegiance to the Tier 1 supplier, not the company that is buying the chain's combined output. Why? Because the relationship is typically tier to tier, not across multiple tiers."[4] In 2009, the aerospace giant acquired one of its key suppliers, Vought Aircraft Industries, increasing Boeing's involvement in the production stages by transforming one of its outsourcers into an in-house provider. Sometimes, then, even an old-fashioned best practice like buying out a supplier trumps a game-changing strategy.

Automotive: Building Customer Loyalty for the Long Term

Consumers may have been pleased when Korean automaker Hyundai started offering a 10-year warranty on its cars, but the policy has made life a bit more complicated for Tim Hess, manager of parts transportation at Hyundai's regional parts distribution center near Los Angeles. These distribution centers—Hyundai has three in the United States—have to keep more than 600 Hyundai dealers stocked with parts that now may be covered under warranty for a decade.

For most automakers, their principal parts distribution is through dealers, but dealers and other repair shops also have access to competitively priced parts through the aftermarket. Since Hyundai is relatively new to the U.S. market, there are almost no aftermarket parts available for its vehicles. For that reason, all parts are handled through Hyundai's dealer network.

According to Hess, the auto parts business falls into two categories: repairs that the original equipment manufacturer (OEM) has to cover under warranty and repairs that the customer has to pay for. Although it seemed risky at the time the program was launched, extending its warranty coverage to 10 years has paid off for Hyundai because, as Hess explains, the policy has generated stronger customer loyalty, which in turn has led to more customer-paid business.[5]

A crucial element to building that loyalty is keeping the dealers supplied with parts so they can meet customers' expectations. That requires having a distribution network set up to get the parts delivered as quickly as possible to keep the customers happy and as efficiently as possible to keep the dealers happy. To make these goals possible, Hess uses various strategies depending on where the parts are being shipped. Within California and to Las Vegas and Phoenix, he comingles shipments with four other automotive OEMs for runs with a dedicated truckload carrier. While conventional consolidation is priced on a volume basis, with charges for multiple stops, the dedicated carrier's services are priced on a per-shipment delivered cost. "You simply agree to a minimum number of stops per night," Hess explains.

For dealers located along main corridors in the rest of the United States, Hess arranges as many overnight—and often unattended—deliveries as possible. The parts are delivered to a secured area, and the carrier is able to deliver to the dealerships during off-peak hours.

Before the parts distribution centers can do their thing, though, the parts have to be available, which adds an extra wrinkle to the process since all parts are imported. "Supply chain visibility is a huge issue for us," says George Kurth, director of supply chain and logistics with Hyundai Motor America. The automaker imports its parts from Korea, and uses a third-party logistics provider (3PL) to track all inbound shipments. "We have visibility in every major point from Korea to our U.S. parts distribution centers," he notes. "We track milestones such as shipments to the ports, vessel sail dates, vessel arrival dates, entry into Customs, release by Customs, origin rail head, destination rail head, delivery to our parts distribution center, and putaway." Hyundai has comparable visibility into its air shipments as well.[6]

If a shipment is delayed and a milestone is missed, a message goes out to Hyundai's inventory managers, updating them on the revised estimated time of arrival (ETA). The new ETA is also automatically uploaded to Hyundai's inventory management system. "In addition to being able to operate with leaner inventory, we use the dependable ETA for dealer customer service," Kurth notes, adding that Hyundai has been able to reduce its inventory by two weeks. "You can run lean if you have confidence in the ETA."

Chemicals: Finding the Right Supply Chain Formula

The chemical industry has long been accustomed to maintaining large stocks and plenty of inventory in the pipeline. At Dow Corning Corp., though, a manufacturer of silicone-based products, that industrial legacy had to change. Because 95 percent of its product line—60,000 unique stock-keeping units—were make-to-stock, Dow Corning realized it had to adopt a new production model if it expected to significantly reduce its inventory levels. At the same time, the company was on a mission to improve its delivery times to customers.

According to Lori Schock, Dow Corning's site supply manager, the company began analyzing every element of its distribution process, including inventory levels, materials, distribution channels, and customer ordering patterns. "We asked ourselves, 'If a customer gives us adequate lead times, can we make- or assemble-to-order?' The answer is a resounding 'yes.' Moving away from make-to-stock would allow us to reduce inventory while improving delivery to the customer," Schock explains.

To achieve those goals, Dow Corning now allows its customers to order products directly from the Internet. Today, roughly one-third of the company's business comes through this self-service model, which has encouraged Dow Corning to make more of its product lines available over the Web-based system.

Delivery lead times to supply chain partners using the self-service model are guaranteed; if a customer needs a delivery faster than stated, the system will offer other scenarios as well as the costs for expedited service. Customers can immediately see the cost of an order and compare it with competitors, Schock notes. The self-service model includes competitive prices, updated several times a day. "The stronger we can make our customers in the market, the stronger we can become," she observes.

The company is also working to reduce the amount of inventory it has on ocean vessels at any given time. "With 25 percent to 35 percent of our inventory constantly in transit, supply chain management becomes more critical to ensure we optimize and streamline everything else that deals with inventory," says Schock. "Having visibility of where demand is generated is critical. Based on our business processes and the amount of inventory we have, we need to make huge fundamental changes to achieve significant inventory reductions."

To that end, Dow Corning is evaluating whether it should add or relocate its manufacturing capability in different parts of the world, as well as if it needs to rethink its sourcing strategy. One high-level goal to help control costs and reduce inventory levels is learning to identify how to link up demand visibility and production so the company can shift more of its production to make-to-order.[7]

Consumer Packaged Goods: The Moment of Truth

There is a defining moment of truth for every customer who enters a retail store, and it comes when the customer selects a specific product for purchase. If there is one thing retailers and their consumer packaged goods (CPG) suppliers fear more than anything else, it's the dreaded empty shelf. When you consider that the out-of-stock rate for retailers averages around 10 percent, there's a lot of money not being spent by frustrated consumers.

When Procter & Gamble Co. formed its Consumer-Driven Supply Network, it set some lofty goals for its supply chain transformation efforts: reduce inventory by 50 percent, trim out-of-stocks by 50 percent, and achieve 20 percent savings in logistics costs. Reaching those goals required addressing such key areas as product availability, shelf quality, and on-time delivery.

"Time is money—the longer and slower the supply chain, the more costly it is," points out Patrick Arlequeeuw, P&G's vice president, Consumer-Driven Supply Network Implementation. "When you take time and cost out of the supply network, you increase flexibility and responsiveness. Instead of a long, slow chain from raw materials to the finished product on the shelf, we are creating a network of suppliers, manufacturers, and retailers that facilitates real-time information flow between all these partners, starting with what's happening at the shelf."[8]

What that means is that P&G has moved from the traditional CPG model of producing to a forecast to producing according to demand, with the goal of replenishing products as soon as they're purchased. Part of that strategy depends on technology that can receive point-of-sale data from the retailer and convert that into a replenishment order. For instance, P&G synchronizes item data with key retail customers, which saves the company at least $25 million per year by eliminating unnecessary transcription work and reducing its out-of-stocks.

Equally important to that strategy is having an idea of what consumers want even before they enter the store. To that end, P&G regularly surveys its end consumers and works directly with its retailer customers to continuously improve its service levels.

The Consumer-Driven Supply Network is "based on a vision of using a consumer purchase to trigger real-time information movement throughout the supply network," explains Arlequeeuw. "This requires a fundamental change in how supply networks are designed. It means looking at the supply system from the shelf back and determining what is required to deliver the desired consumer experience."

The *direct-to-consumer model* pioneered by personal computer giant Dell (see Chapter 6) is very much on the minds of CPG manufacturers as well, Arlequeeuw observes. "We can deliver significant value to our retail customers and to consumers if we achieve a produce-to-demand system for our industry the way Dell has for the PC business."

To ensure that its version of the direct model is working, P&G collaborates closely with retail partners on in-store promotions and events. That collaboration also extends to all supply sources, where significant effort is going into making it easier to identify products in the back room. P&G is one of the CPG industry's leading proponents in developing and implementing radio frequency identification (RFID) technology (see Chapter 15).

For P&G, the value proposition in using RFID comes from having more of its products on retail shelves as well as reducing labor and inventory costs.

The strategy is paying off. "When we started the Consumer-Driven Supply Network journey, more than 20 percent of our product categories were plagued with high [more than 10 percent] out-of-stocks; now that number has dropped to below 5 percent," Arlequeeuw states. By focusing on its supply chain strategy, P&G has been able to drive consumer needs deeper into the supply network while increasing its responsiveness and flexibility.[9]

Food and Beverage: Cutting Out the Middleman

According to an industry study, 80 percent of the manufacturing companies in the United States are outsourcing their logistics operations to a 3PL. Be that as it may, dairy producer Land O'Lakes Inc. discovered it could gain a significant savings on its freight costs by bucking the 3PL trend. As a result of bringing its logistics operations back in-house as well as participating in a collaborative transportation network, the nation's leading butter producer shaved as much as 20 percent off its annual freight costs. (The company's total freight spend is estimated at $35 million.)

"First of all, we eliminated the administration fees the 3PL had been charging us—$15 to $20 a load—which, when you're talking about between 25,000 to 30,000 truckloads per year, is significant money," explains Pat Johnson, logistics manager for Land O'Lakes. "Second, we're now able to go directly to the motor carriers on these lanes and negotiate our own rates, without the 3PL taking its cut. By taking out the middleman, we're making logistics one of our core competencies."[10]

Third, Land O'Lakes' use of a Web-based collaborative network enables it and other participants—manufacturers, retailers, and carriers—to plan, execute, and settle their inbound and outbound truckload and less-than-truckload transportation. "There are three things you want to get from logistics: capacity—you want to be able to have the trucks when you need them; customer service—you want the drivers to be focused on getting to the docks on time, and to cooperate with the customers when they get to the docks; and third, of course, is [manageable] cost," Johnson states.

He further points out that the 3PL had been doing a pretty good job, but Land O'Lakes preferred to execute on its own freight strategy, which could happen only by bringing the transportation process back in-house.

The collaborative network consolidates and updates information about routes, loads, and schedules from all of the members' in-house logistics scheduling systems. One advantage to using a collaborative network, according to Johnson, is the ability to set up tours—sharing truckload capacity with other network participants. If, for instance, Land O'Lakes has several truckloads of refrigerated freight per week going from Wisconsin to Philadelphia, and another member of the network community, such as General Mills, has a similar number of weekly truckloads going from Philadelphia to Chicago, then both companies stand to benefit by sharing the available capacity and eliminating empty "deadhead" miles. General Mills, in fact, has reported saving as much as 7 percent of its own logistics costs using the network.

"Every tour that you can put together is worth about $10,000," Johnson explains. "It's a good thing for the driver, and it's a good thing for the shipper because you've got capacity and you can negotiate a lower rate." The collaborative network maintains anonymity among the community, so Land O'Lakes does not know who else is involved in the tours and vice versa. "We have visibility to freight going out, and our customer service people can see where the truck is," Johnson says. "We require the carriers to report to us every time there's a change in status. Whenever they arrive at a dock or leave a dock, they call their dispatch and tell them what's going on, and we get an update via e-mail if a problem comes up. It's a way to alert our customer service people that we've got a problem, so they can tell the customer before the customer tells us."

In the packaged foods industry, trucks are often empty as much as 25 percent of the time moving between stops, Johnson explains. By reducing the number of deadhead miles traveled—in effect, by using the collaborative network to ride share—Land O'Lakes was able to save $2 million in freight costs in the first year alone. "There are trucks that have the space on them to take 45,000 pounds of products to customers, yet they're getting only 34,000 or 35,000 pounds on them. If you could get somebody else on that truck with you, to fill it to capacity, it's gravy."[11]

High Tech/Electronics: Zero Latency

High-tech companies, particularly those involved in the telecommunications industry like Lucent Technologies (now known as Alcatel-Lucent), are especially susceptible to market fluctuations. Early in the 2000s, Lucent discovered rather belatedly that it had built way too many cell phones, a particularly acute problem since the shelf life of a new phone isn't much longer than that of a gallon of milk. Lucent, to put it succinctly, found itself in a supply chain crisis—over a 10-month period, the company wrote off a staggering $1 billion worth of inventory.

And yet, if you look at the situation from a glass-half-full point of view, that write-off initiated a remarkable turnaround. Concurrent with the creation of a Supply Chain Networks division in 2001, Lucent dropped its on-hand inventory from more than $7 billion down to less than $3 billion by 2002, and by 2003 inventory was just shy of $1 billion. Lucent took better control of its cash expenditures, dropping them from $2.2 billion per quarter to $130 million. The company also closed 400 production facilities as it adopted a virtual manufacturing model dependent on offshore suppliers to make its products. Over the same period of time, Lucent reduced its total number of suppliers in half—from roughly 3,000 to less than 1,500.[12]

"We had to determine how to best focus our resources, apply capital in the right areas, manage operating expenses with the variability in the market, and respond to changing customer needs in a smarter and more effective way," notes Joe Carson, Lucent's vice president of supplier management. "We gave up almost every bit of manufacturing but some final assembly and testing pieces." Most of Lucent's custom manufacturing is now done in China, with some work also taking place in Mexico and Eastern Europe. The company has also outsourced many of its supply chain functions to 3PLs.

Lucent has adopted a policy of "zero latency" when responding to end customer needs. "We have teams connected from our customers, through us, to our suppliers and our suppliers' suppliers," Carson explains. The company is focused on eliminating non-value-added time so that if a customer needs a quote, a cross-functional team can be assembled rapidly to respond. To that end, Lucent has cleared out the channel separating it from its customers so that it now has a better view of the customer's needs, while the customer has a better view of Lucent's capabilities.

The key, Carson points out, is to empower the suppliers so that they act as if they're on Lucent's board of directors, and vice versa. "Their success is our success, and our success is their success. That requires a different skill set in terms of how you manage your suppliers."

Since implementing the zero latency supply chain model, Lucent has reduced its number of warehouses in North America from 200 to 15. The company's quote-to-cash cycle has dropped by nearly 50 percent, and its overall logistics costs have been reduced by 20 percent.[13]

Pharmaceuticals: Fighting Counterfeiters with RFID

One of the greatest threats to the pharmaceutical industry is the proliferation of counterfeit drugs in the global marketplace. Although the industry is heavily regulated in the United States by the U.S. Food and Drug Administration (FDA), the thought that diluted, mislabeled, and completely faked products could enter the United States has led the FDA to prescribe preventive supply chain measures. RFID tags, for instance, have been suggested as a way to better secure the pharmaceutical pipeline. The expectation is that these tags, each of which carries a unique electronic product code, will eventually allow tracking and tracing capabilities of every packaged medical product.[14]

Some drug makers have been slow to apply the RFID tags themselves, leaving that task to healthcare distributors. However, since 2005, Pfizer Inc., maker of such prescription drugs as Lipitor and Zoloft, has shipped every package, case, and pallet of its Viagra product with the RFID tags, and since 2007 every case and pallet of its Celebrex product has been tagged. Pfizer's primary goal in adding the RFID tags is to enhance patient safety, explains Tom McPhillips, vice president of the company's U.S. Trade Group. "We are creating additional barriers for criminals who might attempt to counterfeit our products."[15]

Pfizer has also launched an e-pedigree program aimed at providing an electronic record capable of tracing every transaction involving its Viagra product. This program includes unique UPC (universal product code) numbers or electronic product codes that can be tracked online by pharmacists, who would be able to verify that the number had indeed been issued by Pfizer within the last 60 days, as well as access the item's chain of custody if necessary. If pharmacists' business practices are sound, "they can have a high level of confidence that the package they are authenticating is in fact a genuine Pfizer package," explains Peggy Staver, Pfizer's director of trade product integrity.[16]

These tracking initiatives highlight Pfizer's recognition that supply chain management is the primary link between its operations and customers. Three functional areas support the drug maker's supply chain activities. Its distribution/logistics team coordinates the movement of products between the company's global sites. Pfizer's supply chain planning team works closely with the sales and marketing areas. For long-range planning, the company uses mathematical optimization technology to evaluate its distribution network and create the best origin and destination routes, notes Tan Miller, Pfizer's director of logistics planning.

The company's procurement team focuses on everything from the purchase of raw materials and drug substances, to the securing of maintenance, repair, and operations supplies, to the hiring of freight transportation and other services for Pfizer's global manufacturing and logistics sites. The drug maker's order entry and material resource planning systems interface with a fulfillment management system to aid in the flow and staging of inventory with more than 50 worldwide manufacturing sites and distribution centers. The goal is to reduce Pfizer's reliance on supply-to-order by creating a supply chain replenishment model that can improve its service levels and inventory turnover while increasing visibility into the supply chain.[17]

Retail: Customer Centricity

Consumer electronics retailer Best Buy Co. Inc. once had a very unmerry Christmas. As Eric Morley, Best Buy's director of transportation, remembers, $15 million worth of personal computers were on the way to stores in time for the holidays when chip maker Intel Corp. unexpectedly announced it was going to introduce a new Pentium processor, which wouldn't be available until after the New Year.

"We were stuck," Morley says. It became the Christmas without a PC, because everybody decided to hold off on buying a new computer until models with the faster chips became available. "That's when we learned that you don't buy inventory just in case—you buy it just in time. That was Supply Chain 101."[18]

Best Buy began focusing on inventory optimization. On the demand side, for instance, the retailer employs analytical tools to optimize its pricing—determining, for instance, the best markdown prices. Best Buy also looks at the effectiveness of its advertising campaigns and what effect promotions have on the supply side of the business. The payoff has been an improvement in inventory turns of nearly 50 percent from 4.6 turns per year to 6.6.[19]

As a result of its supply chain programs, Best Buy now has high-level collaboration with selected vendors. The company recruits a key vendor in each retail department (e.g., computers, appliances, music) to undertake collaborative initiatives designed to deliver breakthrough results. One computer vendor, for instance, has increased its in-stock rate by 60 percent thanks to the program.

Whenever possible, Best Buy takes control of transportation at the supplier's back door. While that degree of involvement increases liability and administrative effort, over a five-year span the strategy has also raised delivery reliability, allowed a 70 percent reduction in average transit time, and facilitated a near doubling of inventory turns.

On the customer side, the company's best practices have been inspired in part by another major retailer, U.K.-based grocery supermarket chain Tesco, particularly in how Tesco gathers detailed transactional information on every customer, all of whom are then categorized based on their buying histories. Food products, somewhat like quickly obsolete electronics gadgets, have short shelf lives and are subject to very high demand spikes, observes Bob Willett, Best Buy's chief information officer and CEO of Best Buy International. Being able to recognize those spikes and then to take advantage of those sales opportunities have led the company to adopt a customer-centric supply chain transformation, based on the theory that knowing your customers' wants and catering to their specific buying patterns is a better strategy than merely competing on price.[20]

Following the Tesco model, Best Buy categorized five different customer groups: affluent professionals; young males preoccupied with owning the latest high-tech gadgets; fathers wanting to enhance their lifestyles; mothers wanting to enhance their children's lifestyles (so-called soccer moms); and small business owners. The company then redesigned more than 100 retail stores to appeal to these key customers (adding play areas for kids to appeal to the soccer moms, for instance, or staffing additional technical assistants for stores catering to small businesses). As retail consultant James Dion explains, "The strategy also includes giving employees closest to the customer some of the more important decision-making responsibilities. In addition, Best Buy store associates receive customer-centric training to be able to really deliver on the promise at the store level."[21]

"Every single employee, especially the ones that are in the communities where we operate, knows things about their local customers that nobody else can possibly know," points out Shari Ballard, Best Buy's executive vice president, retail channel management. "They're doing their part in figuring out how to bring the range of stuff we've got available as a company to that local customer to help them get the benefit of technology and use it in their lives."[22]

CHAPTER 3

Supply Chain Metrics

Measuring Up to High Standards

Flashpoints

Statistics are a vital part of managing a supply chain.

The smarter you are at measuring performance metrics, the better your supply chain will run.

Benchmarking lets you know exactly how good (or bad) your company is doing.

Keeping a supply chain scorecard will help you set and achieve attainable targets.

It's probably just a coincidence, but the rise in popularity of supply chain management occurred at the same time as the emergence of *sabermetrics*. No, you're not going to find that term defined in any business management journal; sabermetrics is the application of statistical analysis and research to the game of baseball. When personal computers became affordable in the early 1980s, supply chain analysts and sabermetricians alike fell in love with databases and spreadsheets that could crunch months' worth of product forecasts and decades' worth of box scores in minutes rather than days. These days, "keeping a scorecard" is as much a part of the supply chain language as it is sports talk.

To paraphrase John Thorn, coeditor of *Total Baseball*, statistics are not just a cold-blooded means of dissecting profit-and-loss reports in order to examine a company's performance; rather, statistics are a vital part of the supply chain. The supply chain may be appreciated without statistics, but it cannot be understood without them.[1]

To continue the sports analogy, in the spring of 2001, the only event in which athletic footwear and "Just Do It" icon Nike Inc. seemed to be excelling was poor planning. Philip Knight, Nike's chief executive officer (CEO), had to explain why the company's shoe sales were 24 percent less than expected, which led to an earnings shortfall of approximately $100 million. Much like a beleaguered baseball manager explains away a loss by pointing to a key player's failure to lay down a bunt in the late innings, so too did Knight point his finger at a convenient scapegoat: He blamed it on his supply chain plan.[2]

Specifically, Knight singled out the problems Nike had implementing a new supply chain planning system. Those implementation problems, he explained, were what led to unforeseen product shortages and excesses. The installation of the software had been rushed (Knight didn't dwell on his role in making that decision, much as a baseball manager tends to gloss over whether a player was rushed to the big leagues before he was ready), and that led to conflicts between Nike's legacy order management system and the new demand and supply planning software. As a result, the company made too many of one style of shoe and too few of another, building up inventories of shoes few people wanted while experiencing shortages of more popular brands.[3]

Simply put, Nike was having major league problems matching the right orders to the right customers. And Wall Street responded promptly, as Nike's share price dropped 19 percent when the glitch was announced.

How to Prevent a Supply Chain Heart Attack

Now, here's an example of how sabermetrics-style supply chain analysis can frame Nike's problems as part of a trend that goes far beyond the apparel industry. Two researchers—Vinod Singhal of the Georgia Institute of Technology and Kevin Hendricks of the University of Western Ontario—looked at more than 800 announcements of supply chain problems from public companies over an eight-year period (1992–1999).[4] These problems included things like inventory write-offs, parts shortages, shipping delays, and the like. The researchers then tracked the price of these companies' stocks one year before and two years after the announcement.

So what happened? After all the numbers were crunched, a clear trend emerged: Companies that experienced supply chain glitches over that time period saw their average operating income drop 107 percent, return on sales fall 114 percent, and return on assets decrease by 93 percent. And that's not all: These companies also typically saw 7 percent lower sales growth, 11 percent higher costs, and a 14 percent increase in inventories.

Exacerbating that already dismal situation is the fact that it takes a long time to recover from these disruptions.

"The supply chain disruption lowers the level of operating performance for a company, and then firms continue to perform at that lower level for the next couple of years," Singhal explains. He says a supply chain disruption can be compared to a heart attack because it cuts off the flow of information and supplies to a company, and it can have long-term—and sometimes fatal—effects on a company's health.

It doesn't really matter which industry the company is in, either, because any company reporting a supply chain glitch will see its shareholder value plummet. Process manufacturers (e.g., chemicals, food and beverage, textiles) tend to suffer the biggest hit to shareholder return, with a 51 percent drop. Retailers experience an average decrease of 42 percent, while high-tech manufacturers will see a 27 percent decline. Smaller companies are usually hit harder than large ones, although the drop in income is enormous for any size company: 150 percent for small companies, 86 percent for large.

"When people talk about supply chain management, they may agree that it's important, but they're not investing in solutions," Singhal points out. However, even when companies do spend on solutions, they're not necessarily spending wisely. "One reason supply chain problems occur is because there isn't enough slack in the system," Singhal notes. "As companies try to make their supply chains more efficient, they take away slack because it's expensive."

The answer, though, isn't to throw a lot of money at your supply chain problems. It's to get smarter at identifying and tracking key performance indicators that might signal potential glitches early on. That means developing better forecasts and plans, collaborating with suppliers and customers, ensuring real-time visibility, building flexibility into your supply chain, and other best practices.

What Makes a Supply Chain Leader?

Here's the good news: Whereas the Singhal/Hendricks study exposes the vulnerability of poorly managed supply chains, another study conducted by Accenture (in partnership with INSEAD and Stanford University) reveals that companies identified as supply chain leaders have a market cap up to 26 percentage points higher than the industry average.[5] That begs the question: What makes a supply chain leader, anyway?

That's where the statistical approach comes in. If you can measure the performance of your supply chain, then you'll be able to determine how close you are to being best in class. But how do you know exactly who is the best at supply chain management? When *Fortune* magazine identifies the top-performing companies in a given industry, it uses the straightforward standard of annual sales. When it comes to identifying the top supply chains, though, merely counting up dollars and cents won't get the job done. After all, a supply chain that is truly best in class will encompass numerous operations and processes that don't necessarily show up on a profit-and-loss sheet, such as planning and forecasting, procurement, transportation and logistics, warehousing and distribution, customer service, and other key factors in the overall supply chain equation.

Analyst firm AMR Research has attempted to quantify the qualities that define "best in class" with its annual ranking of the top supply chains. Part of this list is based on a vote from a community of supply chain practitioners and experts, and like most popularity votes, nobody will ever agree with every choice. However, the list also factors in three key metrics that AMR Research believes best indicate the overall effectiveness of a company's supply chain: three-year return on assets (net income/total assets), inventory turnover (cost of goods sold/quarterly average inventory), and three-year revenue growth. AMR assigns a score to the popular vote as well as to the metrics and then comes up with a composite score for all the companies (mostly manufacturers and retailers) under consideration.

Based on the final tally for 2009, inventory turns are perhaps the best indicator of a world-class supply chain. Three high-tech giants led the way with the most inventory turns: Dell had 46.2, Apple was close behind with 45.5, and IBM had 20.0 turns. Not coincidentally, Apple and Dell also finished at the top in the overall rankings, with IBM finishing in fourth (consumer products manufacturer Procter & Gamble claimed the third spot). It could be claimed that companies like Apple have an unfair inventory advantage, given that Apple's sales of digital iTunes songs alone represent more than $1 billion annually. Nevertheless, based on AMR's analysis, Apple's return on assets and revenue growth are also best in class, hence its number-one ranking.

According to AMR, the top 10 supply chains of 2009 are:

1. Apple Inc.
2. Dell Inc.
3. Procter & Gamble Co.
4. IBM Corp.
5. Cisco Systems Inc.
6. Nokia
7. Wal-Mart Stores Inc.
8. Samsung Electronics
9. PepsiCo Inc.
10. Toyota Motor[6]

Measure Satisfaction

When it comes to measuring overall supply chain performance, companies typically focus on benchmarking metrics, such as those established in the Supply Chain Council's Supply Chain Operations Reference (SCOR) model, which we'll look at in this chapter. Delivery performance, fill rates, perfect order fulfillment, cash-to-cash cycle time, inventory turns—these are some of the standards by which supply chains are judged, to determine whether they're best in class, fair to middling, or knocking on death's door. So let's take a look at how some top-performing companies are tracking their supply chains.

In Chapter 2, we saw how automaker Hyundai uses its parts distribution operation to build customer loyalty. The company's goal is to provide high levels of customer service while keeping its costs as low as possible. In this case the customers are Hyundai dealers, and through dealer satisfaction surveys the company has learned that order fill rate is the number-one driver of satisfaction. "If needed parts are available, our dealers are happy," explains George Kurth, director of supply chain and logistics with Hyundai Motor America.[7]

To ensure that it's keeping its dealers happy while keeping its costs down, Hyundai measures the facing fill rate, which is the order fill rate from the warehouse assigned to the dealer. "If we can keep that fill rate very, very high, it's good for dealer satisfaction and it reduces transportation costs," Kurth notes. "Shipping from the assigned warehouse on our dedicated delivery route is cheap. We pay for the truck no matter how full it is. If the part is not available from the assigned warehouse, we have to ship from another warehouse via an expedited carrier. We can satisfy the dealer and get the part there on time, but the cost soars."

Hyundai's facing fill rate on orders is about 96 percent, which is considered good for the automotive industry. The automaker also measures the fill rate for its entire warehouse network, which is 98 percent, also a high score for automakers. Kurth isn't satisfied with that score, though, because "that still means that 2 percent of the time, I have to use premium transportation."

Transportation costs, however, are just part of the total supply chain cost, which also includes inventory and productivity costs. Hyundai monitors the amount of inventory it carries at any given time, with the understanding that best in class for the automotive industry is never going to equate well with the high-tech industry's goals. "We tend to carry a lot of parts inventory because our automobiles last several years," Kurth says. "In contrast, Dell has virtually no parts inventory because a six-month-old computer is obsolete."

To stay on top of current automotive industry trends, Hyundai belongs to an independent automotive and heavy equipment group that collects performance and cost metrics from member companies and provides bench-marking services.[8]

Everybody's Talking about Benchmarking

Hyundai has recognized two crucial facts that many companies tend to gloss over when they try to evaluate their supply chain performance: (1) It's important to benchmark your supply chain against your peers to get a real-world evaluation of how good (or bad) you're doing, and (2) it's just as important that you recognize the limitations of a benchmark.

The biggest danger in benchmarking is assuming too much from any single study. Many benchmarking studies encompass companies and orga-nizations of all shapes and sizes. Typically, if a company is better than the average, it declares victory and moves on. And if it's worse than the aver-age, the usual rationalization is that it's being benchmarked against other industries, so it's not going to do as well in comparison. In short, the metrics end up being dismissed as irrelevant. This happens more often than you might think because while a lot of attention has been given to the idea of benchmarking, there's not much evidence that very many companies are actually doing it.

When Penn State's Center for Supply Chain Research, one of the nation's best-known supply chain programs, sent out a survey to more than 1,200 executives asking how satisfied (or unsatisfied) they were with their supply chain benchmarking efforts, they barely got a 10 percent response. "Nobody has the time to participate in benchmarking studies anymore," explains William "Skip" Grenoble, executive director of the center. Even members of the Supply Chain Council's SCOR board—a group that exists for no other reason than to promote the adoption of supply chain standards—initially ignored the survey, Grenoble notes, "because they thought we were asking them to fill out yet another benchmarking survey."[9]

Eventually, once Grenoble and fellow Penn State researcher Robert Novack reached the 10 percent response rate, they were able to identify exactly why companies don't undertake supply chain benchmarking. The number-one reason, surprisingly, isn't that they take a lot of time to conduct (that was the number-four reason); it's a lack of resources. Without enough people (and the right people) to participate in benchmarking activities, and without a sufficient budget, a company's efforts to benchmark its supply chain are doomed before the project even gets started.

The number-two reason is that internal measures and processes are difficult to define. If you don't know what you want to measure, then how can you discern if what you're doing is up to industry standards? As the saying goes, you can't manage what you can't measure. The third most prevalent deterrent to benchmarking is the difficulty in identifying proper benchmarking partners.

All told, 40 percent of the companies surveyed have never even conducted benchmarks. What makes that number even more surprising is that all of the companies in the Penn State study have revenues over $100 million, and in fact 72 percent of the respondents work at companies with $1 billion or more in annual sales. So while benchmarking may be seen as a proven pathway to improved performance, it hasn't yet achieved significant buy-in, even from those who know supply chains better than most.

Do the Right Things

So much for the doom and gloom, though. Looking again at the Penn State study, it turns out that more than 90 percent of the companies that do benchmark are using the results to encourage improved supply chain performance. Reduced operating costs, improved customer service, and improved productivity top the list of accomplishments tied to benchmarking.

"Benchmarking is the process of identifying, sharing, and using knowledge and best practices," observes Joe Walden, principal of the Supply Chain Research Institute, "which means you've got to admit that someone else does something better than you, and that you can learn something from them." According to Walden, the key to benchmarking is understanding what you're measuring as well as why you're measuring it. "If you're not measuring from the standpoint of the customer," he says, "then you're not measuring the right thing."[10]

The right things, Walden explains, include customer order cycle time, dock-to-stock time, fill rates, personnel turnover, training programs, and reverse logistics. "Benchmarking is not industrial tourism," he says, noting that if your sole motivation is to learn what your competitors are up to, you're missing the whole point. Benchmarking should be used to identify how your industry defines best in class and then to perform a gap analysis. Once you're able to determine the difference (i.e., gap) between where you are and where best in class is, then you can take the necessary steps to improve your performance.

Supply Chain Checkup

How do you know that you need help in the first place, though? Benchmark studies and process maps are both expensive and time-consuming. Many companies whose earnings put them well outside of the Fortune 1000 realize that their supply chains aren't all they ought to be, but they are still hesitant as to what to do about it. Consultant Mike Donovan of R. Michael Donovan & Company offers a relatively short but challenging checklist that provides a basic assessment of how healthy your supply chain might be. If you answer no to any of the following questions or, even worse, if you don't even *know* the answers to some of these questions, then the time to get serious about fixing your supply chain problems is right now:

1. Do your order fill rates meet management's specific and measured customer service strategy?
2. Are your delivery lead times competitive and predictable?
3. Do all of your supply chain departments agree on which products are make-to-stock and which are make-to-order?
4. Do sales and manufacturing share equally in determining the mix and investment in inventory?
5. Are the appropriate calculations being used rather than rules of thumb to establish the desired mix and levels?
6. Are management's inventory investment plan and customer service objectives being compared against the actual results that are achieved?
7. Are short-term forecast deviations being monitored and adjusted, and is long-term forecast accuracy continuously improving?
8. Is your inventory accuracy consistently above 98 percent?
9. Are you able to avoid carrying excess safety stock buffers?
10. Are your excess and obsolete inventories being measured, and are they less than 1 percent of total inventory?[11]

Time for a Turnaround

Automaker Nissan Motors is a good example of a company that recognized it was in trouble and used strategic benchmarking to launch a complete corporate turnaround. David Morgan, president and CEO of consulting firm D.W. Morgan Company, points out that Nissan was one of the relatively few companies that sat out the boom years of the 1990s, charting instead a decade-long course of failed products and poor financial results. In the year 2000, Nissan decided enough was enough as it began an initiative aimed at achieving an 8 percent profit on each vehicle sold.[12]

"Through data collected in its supplier benchmarking program, Nissan discovered that suppliers were consistently producing inferior products at higher than average prices. In effect, Nissan was giving away $2,000 on every car sold. Further, Nissan's distribution costs were the highest among automakers," Morgan explains.

Once it became aware of these problems, Nissan quickly responded by improving its supply base. "Today, Nissan employs sophisticated benchmarks for every partner doing business with them. Any partner that fails to meet established standards is notified of corrective action that needs to be taken," Morgan notes.

It took more than just benchmarking to effect these changes, of course. For one thing, Nissan expanded its closely held supply base to include global component suppliers. It also embraced many of the same lean manufacturing and quality philosophies that fellow Japanese automaker Toyota has pioneered. (The topic of lean supply chains is explored in depth in Chapter 17.) As a result of all these initiatives, Nissan has become a benchmark for the automotive industry. Not too bad for a company that had been written off as comatose at the turn of the millennium.

Learn the SCOR

By far the best-known and most detailed performance metrics are encompassed in the Supply Chain Operations Reference model (www.supply chain.org), which was created in 1995 and has been continuously refined ever since. The SCOR model provides an industry-standard approach to analyze, design, and implement changes to improve performance throughout five integrated supply chain processes—plan, source, make, deliver, and return—spanning the full gamut from a supplier's supplier to a customer's customer and every point in between. The SCOR model is aligned with a company's operational strategy, material, work flows, and information flows.

As explained by Peter Bolstorff and Robert Rosenbaum in *Supply Chain Excellence*, a handbook on using the SCOR model, the five SCOR processes encompass these measurable activities:

1. *Plan.* Assess supply resources; aggregate and prioritize demand requirements; plan inventory for distribution, production, and material requirements; and plan rough-cut capacity for all products and all channels.
2. *Source.* Obtain, receive, inspect, hold, issue, and authorize payment for raw materials and purchased finished goods.
3. *Make.* Request and receive material; manufacture and test product; package, hold, and/or release product.
4. *Deliver.* Execute order management processes; generate quotations; configure product; create and maintain a customer database; maintain a product/price database; manage accounts receivable, credits, collections, and invoicing; execute warehouse processes, including pick, pack, and configure; create customer-specific packaging/labeling; consolidate orders; ship products; manage transportation processes and import/export; and verify performance.

5. *Return.* Process defective, warranty, and excess returns, including authorization, scheduling, inspection, transfer, warranty administration, receiving and verifying defective products, disposition, and replacement.[13]

The SCOR model provides a supply chain scorecard (or SCORcard, if you will) that companies can use to set and manage supply chain performance targets across their organization. Given the increased attention and scrutiny Wall Street is applying to the supply chain's impact on a company's financial performance, being able to measure exactly how well each process is doing is one of the key steps on the road to developing a best-in-class supply chain. Therefore, one of the main roles of the SCOR model is to provide a consistent set of metrics a company can use to measure its performance over time as well as compare itself against competitors.

Supply chain metrics have three main objectives, according to Shoshanah Cohen and Joseph Roussel, authors of *Strategic Supply Chain Management*:

1. They must translate financial objectives and targets into effective measures of operational performance.
2. They must translate operational performance into more accurate predictions of future earnings or sales.
3. They must drive behavior within the supply chain organization that supports the overall business strategy.[14]

SCM for Dummies

SCOR is a multilevel process reference model, moving from Level 1 (operations strategy) to Level 4 (phased implementation). The SCOR model combines business process reengineering with benchmarking, best practices, and process measurement into an all-encompassing framework for executing a supply chain project. According to consultant Peter Bolstorff, principal of SCE Limited and one of the original developers of the SCOR model, SCOR is most successful when solid project management is combined with technology expertise for implementation in a series of six steps:

1. *Educate for support.* Find a project champion (Bolstorff describes this person as an "evangelist") within your company who has the passion to lead a supply chain project. At the same time, identify a key executive to actively sponsor the project. Both of these people must be willing to learn SCOR from top to bottom and be enthusiastic about sharing their knowledge throughout the organization.

2. *Discover the opportunity*. Form a business case that justifies investment in a supply chain project. A key outcome from this step is a project charter, Bolstorff notes, which sets up the supply chain project in terms of approach, budget, organization, communication plan, and establishing clear measures for success.

3. *Analyze*. In this step, you articulate the value proposition of the project in terms of cash-to-cash cycle time, inventory days, order fulfillment, and other performance factors. The intent here is to define the supply chain opportunity according to the company's profit-and-loss statement.

4. *Design*. The two key components in this step are material flow and work/information flow. According to Bolstorff, some of the questions you'll want to ask are: "What are my material flow problems and what's it worth to solve them?" and "How does work and information flow impact material flow?" Define the work first and then the information that moves the material.

5. *Develop*. The design team shifts to become an implementation team assigned to specific tasks. The goal, as Bolstorff explains it, is to create a master schedule for the projects that will take your supply chain from its present state ("as is") to its optimal state ("to be").

6. *Implement*. Based on the master schedule for each change, prepare and transition your company for the changes as you begin implementation of the supply chain transformation.[15]

Follow the Roadmap

Assuming your company has decided that it wants to pursue a SCOR project, what do you do next? For Imation, a company that provides data storage technology, adopting the SCOR model began by informing everybody in the company—from the president to the sales clerks and all positions in between—what impact the supply chain initiative was going to have on the business. The next step was to create a supply chain program office to coordinate the various activities as well as to keep costs in line with goals.[16]

At a Glance

SCOR

The Supply Chain Operations Reference (SCOR) model, developed by the Supply Chain Council, provides a standard methodology for managing supply chain projects centered on five measurable processes: plan, source, make, deliver, and return.

Ultimately, Imation determined that it could reach its goal by integrating its supply chain project roadmap with its annual business strategy and planning processes. This required strategic transformations in four key areas: customer behavior, product flow, system utilization, and collaboration. For customer behavior, for instance, Imation used the SCOR model to produce a set of invoices illustrating typical customer buying behavior as well as the policies driving that behavior. As Bolstorff describes it, for Imation, it was critical that the company was able to understand the invoice elements that were driving gross-to-net sales, such as deductions, terms, programs, and credits, as well as the impact of warehousing and transportation costs, order processing, purchasing, and planning.

Using the invoice exercise as a starting point, Bolstorff notes, Imation's supply chain team modeled a material flow strategy that would accommodate customer needs while supporting the company's competitive requirements. This type of exercise was also used to model (1) product flow, which focused on postponement—delaying final customization of a product until the last possible moment—as a key best practice; (2) system utilization, which overhauled Imation's overly complex pricing practices; and (3) a collaborative planning, forecasting, and replenishment initiative, which aimed at improving return on investment by working more closely with Imation's retail customers to effectively manage inventory.

"The SCOR project roadmap," Bolstorff explains, "can be effectively used at multiple performance levels: eliminating deficiencies, establishing a continuous improvement process, and defining strategic supply chain investments to support competitive advantage."

Make It All Meaningful

Whether your company adopts the SCOR model or chooses a less structured approach to tracking its supply chain, at some point you're going to have to put all that data you've been gathering into context, and that might prove to be even more difficult than setting up the metrics in the first place. "The toughest part of establishing measures is making them meaningful in the right way," admit consultants Mike Ledyard and Kate Vitasek with Supply Chain Visions. Even if you have an elaborate system of scorecards that measures every group within your company's supply chain, it'll just be an empty show of sound and fury if you can't link the performance measures to actionable plans linked to specific company goals. "Measures must be aligned to strategy," they note, "but it's important that the measurements be linked to logistics execution. Without that vital link and ample communication, the people performing the logistics tasks in your organization won't see the value or the connection between what they do and the larger corporate or division strategy."[17]

According to Ledyard and Vitasek, before getting too caught up in measurements and metrics, every supply chain professional needs to answer two key questions:

1. Will you change your behavior, or ask others to change their behavior, based on this measure?
2. Does the potential benefit gained from this information exceed the cost of obtaining it?

Citing advice from the late management guru Peter Drucker, Ledyard and Vitasek observe, "There is surely nothing quite so useless as doing with great efficiency what should not be done at all." And that, they say, sums up the wasted effort of the measurement trap—merely collecting measures for collection's sake, without a clear plan as to how you plan to meet your company's overall objectives and goals.

It's better by far to follow a path similar to that trod by high-tech giant IBM Corp.'s Integrated Supply Chain (ISC) group. To evaluate the performance of its suppliers, IBM uses a detailed scorecard that tracks how each supplier is performing and how well it delivers to Big Blue's requirements. "We routinely review scorecards with suppliers, including transportation providers, working as partners to improve the relationship," says Tim Carroll, vice president of operations with the ISC group. "If needed improvement doesn't occur, the scorecard is our basis for no longer considering that supplier a vendor of choice." No ambiguity there: IBM clearly states its expectations, both internally and externally.

The ISC's operating team meets every week to analyze how well the group is performing to various metrics. "We look for what we need to change or alter to meet our objectives," Carroll states. "We drill down to find out what's keeping us from meeting our objectives." Daily reports spell out exactly what each functional team ought to be doing to meet its goals, and the overall status of the ISC is reported twice monthly to IBM's CEO. "Every IBM executive has real-time visibility to these key metrics," Carroll notes, and what's more, they all are aware that the CEO pays close attention to the metrics because he'll send a memo whenever he sees something noteworthy.[18]

PART II

Traditional Core Processes of Supply Chain Management

CHAPTER 4

Planning and Forecasting
Headed for the Future

Flashpoints

Accurately forecasting product demand is the most important measure
of a company's supply chain operation.

Having too much inventory is not better than having too little.

A supply chain plan is only as good as the information that goes into it.

Consensus planning spreads the responsibility for accurate forecasting
throughout every department within a company's supply chain.

Every supply chain program, good or bad, launches from a plan. It's
the ability to forecast and analyze product demand, consumer buying
patterns, and economic trends that separates the winners from the losers. In
reality, any kind of a forecast is going to involve the black arts of predicting
the future, a process that inevitably will result in some errors even under
the best circumstances. It's not an issue of what happens *if* a forecast goes
wrong—it's more an issue of *by how much*.

Although the history of supply chain management is fairly recent, it
includes some notoriously bad plans—plans so far off the mark that they've
become legendary in the what-were-they-thinking-of? category. The bigger
the company is, the more spectacular are its supply chain glitches since the
ripple effects can extend well past the four walls of the company to include
suppliers and customers.

The main reason companies struggle with their forecasts is the fick-
leness of the marketplace. Try as hard as they might—and they've been
at it for centuries—manufacturers and retailers still haven't been able to

consistently figure out exactly how much of something consumers are going to buy. Accurately forecasting product demand is probably the single most important—and most challenging—measure of a company's supply chain proficiency. Improving forecast accuracy has gotten a lot of attention, but as meteorologists have always known, you can be right most of the time, but it's the one time you're wrong that gets a lot of people upset.

When analyst firm AMR Research Inc. studied forecast accuracy at several dozen manufacturers, it turned out—not surprisingly—that errors are very much a fact of life within the supply chain. Forecast errors at bulk chemical producers, for instance, range from 10 percent to 24 percent, for a median error rate of 11 percent. That's actually pretty good, though, since consumer goods companies get it wrong from 14 percent to 40 percent of the time, or an average 26 percent error rate. Consider that for a minute: One time out of every four the forecast is wrong. It's even worse in the high-tech arena. The error rate ranges from an outstanding 4 percent to a horrific 45 percent rate (with a median rate of 28 percent). That's right—at some high-tech companies, they're getting it wrong nearly half of the time.[1]

Case in point: A few years ago, Cisco Systems Inc. had a royal doozy of a glitch, centered squarely on the failure of its supply chain plan. As the leading manufacturer of networking routers and switches, Cisco was one of the most influential companies driving the dot-com boom of the late 1990s. In the spring of 2001, Cisco was riding as high as any high-tech company had ever ridden, having reported a profit for 40 quarters in a row. With a culture that literally knew nothing but growth, naturally enough Cisco's planning systems—which were considered state of the art—kept forecasting more of the same.

At a Glance

Supply Chain Planning

Supply chain planning coordinates assets to optimize the delivery of goods, services, and information from supplier to customer, balancing supply and demand. Supply chain planning solutions allow companies to create what-if scenarios that weigh real-time demand commitments when developing forecasts.

Unfortunately, the inevitable bursting of the dot-com bubble happened to coincide with a severe slump in the telecom industry, both of which had a direct impact on Cisco's business. The decade-long uptick had finally peaked, and demand for Cisco's products began to slow. Problem was, the company's supply chain didn't seem to recognize "make less this month than we did last month" as a viable plan. Instead, the planners kept following the system's advice to "make more."

You can imagine what kind of havoc that can play, not only on Cisco's system inventory but on that of its suppliers as well. Cisco had helped popularize the concept of *virtual manufacturing*, meaning that outsourced (or contract) suppliers were building the routers and switches and then shipping them direct to Cisco's customers. Now, all of a sudden, Cisco's customers didn't want or need any more networking equipment—in fact, they already had too much. But Cisco's supply chain plan kept steadily insisting "make more." The most important test of a supply chain plan is accuracy, and it became clear that Cisco was flunking that test.

A Bias against Good Plans

Cisco's supply chain planning suffered from a common malady that afflicts many companies: *bias*. It's a pattern of behavior within a company where different departments focus on their own individual priorities, often disregarding the overall health of the company in favor of propping up their own fiefdoms. A good supply chain plan will fail every time, for instance, if employees are incentivized to avoid stock-outs and as a result keep building up the safety stock. Because employees are not being penalized for making too much—in some companies, the only unpardonable sin is to be caught short—the importance of the overall supply chain plan ends up taking a backseat to the size of one's weekly paycheck. When it comes to protecting and keeping their jobs, employees learned long ago that management will rarely punish those who tell it what it wants to hear.[2]

In Cisco's case, forecasting growth had been the right answer for more than 10 years, so it seemed the most natural thing in the world to keep going forward, even when it started to look like the boom days were over.

"There's a growth bias built into the business of forecasting," explains Ajay Shah, a former director of Solectron Corp., one of Cisco's major suppliers and one of the companies that got caught up in the undertow when too many unwanted electronics products started to flood the marketplace. "People see a shortage and intuitively they forecast higher."[3] That kind of growth bias leads to the unwritten rule of forecasting demand that says "Err on the side of needing more, not less."

Forecasts need to make sense, adds Si Gutierrez, vice president of central planning and production control with chipmaker National Semiconductor Corp. A big part of forecasting at National involves an analysis of general economic conditions. Gutierrez uses the cell phone industry as an example: "If the forecast says we'll need 20 percent more chips, we ask, 'Does that make sense, given current market conditions?' Everyone can agree that's a reasonable expectation for total market growth. The challenge comes in meeting with major players in the industry. Everyone wants to win and everyone's planning for success, so they add 30 percent. But not everyone wins. If you add up all the players in the industry, you might double a realistic forecast," he explains.[4]

Ultimately, in the wake of the economic downturn in 2001, Cisco ended up with far more products than it could ever sell. How much more? The company wrote off $2.2 billion worth of unsalable, unusable inventory and reported a $2.6 billion quarterly loss. Although Cisco had gained the reputation of being the supply chain poster child for the New Economy, it reacted to the supply chain glitch in a typically Old Economy fashion: The company laid off 8,500 employees.[5]

From Soup to S&OP

How does a company overcome the inherent bias that seems to trip up even the best-laid plans? When Mike Mastroianni joined Campbell Soup Co., he saw many of the same cultural inhibitors to good forecasts that had stymied Cisco's planners. Brought in to oversee a sales and operations planning (S&OP) initiative at the world's leading soup maker, he found a supply chain that had become complacent, focused too much on managing internal costs and not enough on customer service.

"For Campbell's, like a lot of companies, manufacturing was king," explains Mastroianni, vice president of North American planning and operations support. Manufacturing was in a position to second-guess the forecasts, thanks largely to the fact that some people had worked in that department for 30 years and had a historical perspective on how the market fluctuated. Mastroianni's mission, however, was to realign the supply chain to facilitate the introduction of new products. "We had become complacent," he says, and to turn things around, forecast accuracy had to get a lot better.[6]

The average error rate of forecasts in the consumer packaged goods industry is about 26 percent, but Campbell's wasn't going to get too far if it merely maintained the status quo. "We decided to focus in on forecast accuracy, which meant we had to change the behavior of bias," Mastroianni explains. "People used to get their heads handed to them" for missing their numbers, so they tended to overforecast. As a result, they drove inventories up, as well as the costs of obsolescence, warehousing, expedited shipping, and everything else that was affected by overly optimistic forecasts."

How is a forecast created? No, they're not made up out of the thin air, as some wags have observed. Campbell's, like many other companies, uses a traditional S&OP consensus process, which triangulates among sales, marketing, and demand planning. These three groups get together to agree on a number. That forecast number ultimately ends up going to the general manager for endorsement.

"Instead of aiming for a single demand figure, progressive companies have turned to forecasting a range of potential outcomes," explains Yossi Sheffi, director of the MIT Center for Transportation & Logistics. "They estimate the likely range of future demand, and use the low end and high end to guide contracting terms and contingency plans." The goal of this range forecasting is to get companies to widen their planning horizons.[7]

Even after consensus planning, though, the odds are pretty good that a company is not going to hit that number, which makes it all the more important that a system of open and ongoing dialogue is in place.

No Time Like the Real Time

One element driving Campbell's need for better forecasts is its collaborative planning, forecasting, and replenishment (CPFR) efforts with key retail customers. "We were forecasting at a very high level, based on history," Mastroianni says, but to get to a truly collaborative relationship with its customers, the company had to be able to restate its history more frequently than once a month. Because CPFR requires manufacturers and retailers to share point-of-sale data over the Internet in real time, inaccurate forecasts only hasten the distillation of bad information. (See Chapter 13 for more on collaboration.)

"What fuels S&OP is facts," he observes. That meant Campbell's needed to put key performance indicators (KPIs) in place to hold people accountable as well as measure improvements in forecast accuracy. Mastroianni's team turned to a real-time forecasting tool capable of creating daily, short-term forecasts with 52 weeks of live data. Being able to forecast in real time allows Campbell's to track patterns that used to go undetected. The system might say, for instance, "Forget about the order today as it relates to your forecast. You need to be thinking about the next 7 to 14 days because, based on this current pattern, your next month is going to look like this," he explains. "Or it might say, 'You're holding on to a forecast that just isn't going to happen. So let it go, and produce to this lower number.'"

At National Semiconductor, the production group meets with the demand planning group weekly to review the forecast. "We gauge the effectiveness of forecasting at a high level rather than on each of our 15,000 chips," notes Si Gutierrez. "We also look at how we're scheduling orders compared to how customers requested them and fix any mismatches." Like

Campbell's, National Semiconductor looks at a number of KPIs (e.g., how close the company's production matches up with the forecast) and then analyzes the difference between forecast and performance.[8]

National's supply chain planning starts with an annual plan, and once that's in place, the staff looks at forecasting for each month, planning six months ahead, Gutierrez explains. "Sometimes we're surprised. Something we thought would do just okay goes like gangbusters. So we monitor the plan weekly and can revamp it weekly. Each day, we plan factory starts based on what happened the previous day. This allows us to maximize customer service and optimize inventory to maintain customer service levels."[9]

The Truth Plays Out

As Campbell's learned, no matter how capable and experienced its planners are, their plan is only as good as the information that feeds it. The big "aha!" moment at Campbell's came when the S&OP process illustrated exactly how broken many of the company's processes were throughout the organization—from finance to commercialization to label design, custom pack planning, and transportation. S&OP provides a heightened level of transparency to the extent that, over time, as Mastroianni puts it, "the truth plays out." By bringing all of Campbell's business plans into a single, integrated set of plans—the end game of an S&OP initiative—the company was ultimately able to fix a dozen or more major processes.

At a Glance

Sales and Operations Planning

Sales and operations planning (S&OP) aligns all of a company's business plans (customers, sales and marketing, research and development, production, sourcing, and financial) into a single, integrated set of plans. The end goal is a plan that more accurately forecasts supply and demand.

For instance, Campbell's has improved by as much as 50 percent the weekly accuracy of the item-level signals sent to its manufacturing plants, which resulted in an immediate benefit: The company can now better plan how many trucks it needs to replenish its distribution centers with product. That increased level of accuracy has also paid off by reducing how often

Campbell's has to use expedited shipping to make up for not having the right products at its customers at the right time.

Taking it a step further, Campbell's has leveraged its precision of accuracy to provide improved visibility to its warehouses and manufacturing plants. The company has used its long-range planning capabilities to pre-buy transportation with some of its carriers. It's also used those forecasts for labor management, specifically in determining when to add extra crews to its warehouses and when to cut back.

There's one last benefit to the best practices Campbell's uses for its supply chain planning: "It makes me sleep real good at night," Mastroianni says. "It's no fun getting your head handed to you."[10]

End-to-End Integration

The key to Campbell's S&OP program was being able to integrate all of those different departments and processes into one central plan, and that strategy can be applied in any company in any industry. At computer giant IBM Corp., for instance, integration is not only a key best practice for the company, it's included in the very name of its supply chain organization, the Integrated Supply Chain (ISC).

In 2003, IBM completed an end-to-end integration project that connects all of its business processes and supporting systems into the ISC, an organization employing 19,000 people at more than 50 locations worldwide. The ISC comprises manufacturing, procurement, logistics, distribution, customer ordering, and planning and scheduling—the whole nine yards of supply chain processes.

"There are many factors in supply chain planning," observes Rich Hume, vice president of operations and strategy with the ISC. "Every proposed idea or change at IBM must meet certain criteria. Initiatives must improve customer satisfaction, increase the flexibility of the supply chain, improve economics, and improve functional excellence. Proposals must be executable and include measurable economic results."[11]

Most of IBM's supply chain planning is done internally, involving such departments as logistics, fulfillment, manufacturing, and manufacturing engineering, as well as functional experts in the company's business consulting and business transformation groups.

"In other companies, these professionals are typically aligned with corporate functions like procurement or logistics," Hume notes. "Having them in one organization allows us to take advantage of their expertise within each function, while also benefiting from their integration across the supply chain."

The First Shall Be First

Not surprisingly, technology has a lot to do with defining best practices within IBM's supply chain planning processes. By integrating demand fulfillment capabilities with its enterprise resource planning (ERP) system, IBM can schedule an order throughout its supply chain within milliseconds, says Joe DiPrima, manager of supply chain planning and optimization with the ISC group. "That is a best practice because you can have the best planning tools in the world, but if you can't pull the data into the planning tools with integrity so that people trust the data and know that it's current, you're not going to use the planning tool," DiPrima observes. It took a while to convince people that the planning tools were accurate, he admits, but the sheer speed of the forecasts has won over those skeptics who were still relying on their trusty spreadsheets.[12]

At a Glance

Enterprise Resource Planning

Enterprise resource planning (ERP) software ties together manufacturing, sales, distribution, and finance by collecting data from each area and using it to plan a company's resource use—everything from employees to raw materials.

IBM used to schedule orders manually, which became a problem when the company began to dread the arrival of unexpected orders. In normal circumstances, getting new business is good news, but IBM's visibility into its supply lines was less than ideal. There was a fear within some quarters that a new order would divert supply from a high-priority customer that hadn't actually placed its order yet but was expected to. "We didn't want to schedule a lower-priority customer in the hopes that a high-priority order would come in," DiPrima remembers.

To get past that mind-set, IBM has done away with those manual processes and replaced them with new processes and new tools based on streamlining the order receipt to delivery time. In the past, order entry to delivery could take anywhere from 15 to 20 days; that process is now down to 5 to 10 days.

How did IBM pull that off? As DiPrima explains, the company instituted a business policy of first in, first out (FIFO). "Orders are now scheduled FIFO. If a customer wants supply, they need to get their orders in first. Very simple. We have exception processes that we invoke occasionally, but if a product is deemed to be FIFO—and over 95 percent of our products are FIFO—they're scheduled first in, first out."

Additionally, IBM has enabled direct shipment to customers from suppliers as they've gone global. "We've outsourced manufacturing to China, Eastern Europe, and Mexico," DiPrima observes, "and as a result, we've enabled these companies to direct ship on behalf of IBM. It looks like an identical order whether we ship it to the customer from our warehouse or whether the manufacturer ships it." This postponement strategy includes some subtle back-office processes, such as enabling the outsourcers to print invoices with the IBM logo. The goal, DiPrima says, is to postpone the building of the product until an order is received from a customer.

"From a demand planning standpoint," he continues, "we used to have to be able to forecast each end item a customer would buy." That was no small task since IBM had tens of thousands of end items. "If a customer wanted to buy a standard laptop computer, but with his corporate logo on the start-up screen, that was a new model number. So while we might only have 300 or 400 core models, it would turn into tens of thousands of models when we actually built them. We used to forecast demand that way, and it was extremely difficult to do. It was never accurate. We would always be chasing and remixing supply from what we had forecast to what actually got ordered."

IBM's solution was to move to a sales building block model, based on a best practice known as *attach rate planning*. "We have tens of thousands of components and tens of thousands of end items," DiPrima states, "but if you look at the sales building blocks, we only have several hundred to a couple thousand of those. So we find the pinchpoint in the development of a product by asking: Where can I have the fewest planning items in the plan, not only because it's easier, but also because I'll get all the advantages of risk pooling by doing it at that level? So we went to a forecast attach rate approach."

IBM's forecasting accuracy at the sales building block level is 80 to 90 percent, a marked improvement from the 50 to 60 percent accuracy it had when it was planning at the end item level. "We always knew how many units in aggregate we would sell, but where we would get it wrong was in trying to figure out the mix," he says. "Now that we know what the percentage mixes are, the planning process is a lot simpler."

Another best practice at IBM has been moving from a monthly planning cycle to a weekly S&OP process. "We also have an ad hoc process running daily to share our demands, including orders, with our suppliers via the Web, so they can respond back to us with their capabilities every day," DiPrima explains. "We used to only share that information with a supplier once a week. Now they see it every day, which is critical when you're trying to bring your order and delivery cycle times down below 10 days. We're a lot more collaborative today with our suppliers. Our supply chain is not limited to what happens within the four walls of manufacturing, or even inside of IBM. We extend it out to our suppliers, and even our suppliers' suppliers, so we can have Tier 2 visibility as well."

Analyze This

As software has become more sophisticated and computers more powerful, so too have performance tools evolved that allow companies to not only gain access to all of the supply chain-related data in their various systems, but to extract meaningful information that can provide them with an overall look at the current state of their operations. Business intelligence software (which used to be known as decision support software) shares a heritage with artificial intelligence software in that both are rules based, both focus on analytics, and both attempt to enhance human decision making. What business intelligence does, in a nutshell, is consolidate data from many operational areas of a company, analyze that data based on guidelines predefined by the company, and then present a dashboard-like overview of the company's performance. The latest generation of these tools offer a look not only within the four walls of a company but in fact within the entire supply chain of customers, suppliers, and third parties.

In other words, even though companies have gotten quite good at collecting transactional data, many are still beginners when it comes to making sense of that data. That's where business intelligence technology offers a helping hand. Here are some examples of companies that have gained new insights into their operations from business intelligence solutions:

- If you ever wondered what happens to the data retailers collect whenever you use a loyalty card, consider the situation with greeting card giant Hallmark Cards Inc., which runs 3,500 Hallmark Gold Crown stores and has point-of-sale purchase information from millions of card holders. So far, so good, but merely knowing who bought what, and when, doesn't always result in the right conclusions. Using business intelligence to create predictive models of consumer behavior, Hallmark discovered buying patterns that helped the company redirect its promotional efforts. For instance, instead of targeting once-a-year shoppers with Christmas offers, Hallmark found it was more effective to aim its online marketing efforts at customers who regularly visit its stores year-round. The company is now able to produce more customized direct marketing campaigns throughout the year, with better results.
- The U.S. military relies on Lockheed Martin Missiles and Fire Control Co. to develop and manufacture combat, missile, rocket, and space

systems. Compiling and producing monthly financial reports was a tedious process that took two weeks to complete, taxing the resources of Lockheed Martin's IT staff. Part of the problem was that everybody with input into the monthly reports, from corporate executives to administrative assistants, had to wait for the IT department to produce the specific information that each individual required. After Lockheed Martin adopted a business intelligence solution, employees no longer had to go running to IT for everything. Now individual users can get the data they need whenever they need it, and in a format customized to their needs. Instead of taking two weeks to close the books, Lockheed Martin can now do it in two to four days.

- As a growing industrial products manufacturer, The HallStar Company adopted an ERP system to collect and maintain all of its production and financial data, but the sheer quantity of information in the system proved daunting to HallStar's employees. A business intelligence application that offers a dashboard-level view of KPIs proved to be just what HallStar needed. The company, which maintains thousands of stock-keeping units worldwide, has been able to reduce inventory by 25 percent thanks to a tighter integration with its suppliers. This was made possible by the increased visibility the dashboard offers to employees throughout HallStar's supply chain.[13]

At a Glance

Business Intelligence

Business intelligence software collects all relevant performance data (manufacturing, sales, sourcing, labor, etc.) into one place where it can be analyzed based on predefined business rules. The information can then be presented in a visually meaningful way.

A Happy Ending

Improving its supply chain visibility has also proven to be the key to Cisco Systems' rebound from its forecasting nightmares, which were described at the beginning of the chapter. The company's turnaround began with a dramatic paring back of suppliers (from 1,300 down to 600) and the concurrent outsourcing of logistics, subassembly manufacturing, and materials management. All suppliers and distributors can now tap into the same supply chain network, dubbed eHub, and as a result everybody has access to the same forecasts and is working off the same demand assumptions.

Not only does eHub save Cisco millions of dollars by eliminating paper-based purchase orders and invoices, but it also has improved on-time shipment performance. And by applying "analytical rigor" to its supply chain plan, the company can make better decisions sooner in the process, such as what to do if a key supplier can't meet its commitments. By optimizing its supply chain plan, "we find you can remove emotions and bias from decision-making processes," explains Jim Miller, Cisco's vice president of manufacturing operations. "Supply chain has become a science now."[14]

CHAPTER 5

Procurement

Go Right to the Source

Flashpoints

The purchasing department should be managed as a strategic supply chain center rather than as merely a place to beat down costs.

An effective way to stay on the same page as your suppliers is to share transactional information with them.

Simplifying your product line can lead to a more efficient supply chain flow.

Purchasing materials through an online exchange can result in significant cost savings, if you do your due diligence first.

Although Motorola Inc. is credited for launching the now wildly popular Six Sigma initiative in the 1980s, nobody was using the word *quality* to describe the personal communications company's financial performance in 2001. (Six Sigma's origins at Motorola are discussed in Chapter 6.) *Dismal* was closer to the mark, as Motorola's sales were off by 20 percent, and over a two-year span the company laid off nearly 43,000 employees, more than one-fourth of the 150,000 people the company employed in 2000. In fact, the massive layoffs and poor performance of formerly high-flying blue-chip companies like Motorola helped draw the economy into a recession at the start of the twenty-first century.

And yet, while anything that sounded the least bit reminiscent of the dot-com craze was derided during the days of the dot-com bust, Motorola quietly tapped into Internet-based best practices like online reverse auctions and collaborative sourcing to drastically reduce its annual purchasing costs. Even during the dark days of 2001, the company was leveraging electronic sourcing to save 0.2 percent off its total annual spend. That percentage doesn't sound terribly impressive until you realize that at the time Motorola was spending $22 billion, which means that it managed to trim $50 million off that spend, thanks largely to its use of e-sourcing. For a profit-challenged company like Motorola, if you can save $10 million here and $10 million there, pretty soon you're talking about saving a lot of money.

Motorola ended up reorganizing its way back to prosperity, spinning off its semiconductor unit and leveling off its employee base to a workforce of 68,000. By championing next-generation procurement best practices in its darkest hour, the company ensured that it would be in position to recover quickly from its setbacks. Motorola's internal code name for its collaborative sourcing program, in fact, was "The Next Level."[1]

Giving Procurement Its Due

While not necessarily used interchangeably, the terms *procurement*, *purchasing*, and *sourcing* all describe one of the main supply chain management processes. As Larry Paquette, author of *The Sourcing Solution*, describes it, the role of sourcing is "to locate the one company out there that can provide needed product better than anyone else."[2] In *Essentials of Supply Chain Management*, author Michael Hugos gets right to the point when he notes that, by tradition, the main activities of a purchasing manager are "to beat up potential suppliers on price and then buy products from the lowest cost supplier that [can] be found."[3] Any mystery about the role of the purchasing manager is dispelled immediately in the title of Patricia E. Moody's book, *The Big Squeeze*.[4] At any rate, the notion that purchasing does the dirty work for accounting is well earned by the current supply chain literature.

Concurrently, there's also a long-standing perception that purchasing plays second (or third) fiddle to the star performers in a company, typically finance, sales, and marketing. However, warns Dave Nelson, vice president of global supply management at automotive supplier Delphi Corp., "The practice of allowing purchasing to be an underachiever is an expensive approach to global supply management because it underpowers a vital contributor to corporate profits and growth. Unfortunately, examples of low expectations (and low results) in procurement are common." When companies fail to recognize the positive impact good procurement practices can have on their bottom line, it makes it that much more difficult for significant and enduring supply chain improvements to take effect.[5]

Fortunately, word has gotten out that by collaborating with your key supply chain partners, rather than relying on the traditional supplier squeeze and taking a we-know-better-what-they-want-than-they-do attitude toward customers, the purchasing department can become a strategic corporate advantage rather than merely a necessary evil.

Managing the Changes

In its study of purchasing patterns, the Center for Advanced Purchasing Studies has found that a high percentage of procurement actually takes place outside of the purchasing department. Although generally a purchasing manager is assigned to the task of procuring products, whether they are components used in manufacturing a product or finished goods that are sold on retail shelves, it's usually the domain of the logistics manager to make other important supply chain buying decisions, such as the procurement of transportation.

That's not necessarily a best practice, according to Tom Mulherin, president of New England Cost Containment, particularly if transportation purchasing is being handled by somebody who lacks transportation expertise. From his perspective as a cost optimization expert, Mulherin believes that transportation purchases lack the rigorous process that companies typically apply to the purchase of materials. With transportation, he says, it's often just a matter of switching carriers on the basis of cost alone: "This carrier is going to give me a 5 percent discount, so let's switch over to them."[6]

A company needs to appreciate that changing a carrier or a supplier will result in a change in the company's organization as well, he points out. The nature of supply chains today means that carriers, as well as other suppliers, are integrated into a company's cost structure and operations, so any kind of significant change will have ripple effects. Any supply chain professional who is intent on making a sourcing change of any kind needs to ensure that the change will have a positive impact on at least one critical cost area of the company. Doing that will require that companies get better at managing change itself. "Change management," Mulherin observes, "is becoming a primary enabler of effective supply chain cost containment efforts."

To effect change management, he suggests companies stick to simple, easy-to-understand measurements that encourage appropriate behavior. Measure only key performance indicators, and determine that the benefits of reporting metrics are greater than the cost of gathering them. You'll need to involve the users in the process as well, which means having them be a part of the process of developing and rating supplier qualifications, going on site visits, and taking ownership of the final decision.

Keep Your Friends Close and Your Suppliers Closer

Keep in mind, however, that just as manufacturing companies are getting much more choosy about whom they want to do business with, so too are their suppliers becoming more particular about whom they want as customers. The philosophy in purchasing circles for several years, particularly in the automotive industry, has been to reduce the total number of suppliers to a manageable core of key partners. As Dave Nelson, Patricia E. Moody, and Jonathan Stegner describe in the book *The Purchasing Machine*, "Reductions in the supply base from thousands to hundreds of excellent suppliers will continue as intra-enterprise alliances focus on only the proven, strong performers, for whom finding new customers will be no problem, leaving marginal producers to scratch for a range of customers." The contrast, the authors continue, will grow even sharper in the coming years "as the best suppliers will pick the customers that bring them the most money, the best technology fit, and the most manageable schedules, all with the preferred lowest 'paperwork' or service costs."[7]

One of the most effective ways of ensuring that suppliers find your company worth their while is to do what supply chain leaders such as Wal-Mart Stores Inc. and Dell Inc. have done for years: Share transactional information with them. Ford Motor Co., for instance, has centralized its supply chain information and functionality into a single global material manufacturing system, which gives the automaker's suppliers direct access to real-time inventory and shipping data, updated on a daily basis. "We give customers and suppliers access to our proprietary systems," explains Joseph Hinrichs, executive director, material planning and logistics. "This ensures the decisions they are making are based upon real-time, accurate information."[8]

As a result, Ford has been able to reduce the number of days it takes to transport vehicles to dealerships. The average lead time required for material procurement has been cut, as has the number of people needed to contact suppliers. In addition, inventories at Ford's vehicle assembly facilities and the supply base are significantly smaller than in the past. Through the use of technology, Ford is able to provide more accurate and timely information to manage its internal and external business processes to a Six Sigma level of capability, according to Hinrichs. Furthermore, the company can provide its dealers with better information about their specific vehicle locations. These efforts include reducing inbound carrier discrepancies, such as parts deviations caused by shipment overages, and reducing how often it uses expedited shipments (the most expensive type of shipping). These efforts alone have saved Ford more than $1 million.

Looking Backward to See Forward

Hewlett-Packard Co. (HP) has one of the world's largest information technology (IT) supply chains, managing a spend of about $51 billion annually. The high-tech company is responsible for 32 manufacturing plants (though not all of them are owned by HP). For direct materials (i.e., core supplies and materials used to make HP products), the company has about 88 distribution hubs, about 700 key suppliers, and about 119 logistics partners, according to Greg Shoemaker, HP's vice president of central direct procurement. In all, the company has roughly 1 billion customers worldwide, in 178 different countries.

"With that amount of spend comes a significant amount of leverage," Shoemaker notes. "One of the things we discovered is that size alone isn't what gets you the best result. Obviously, size gives you a lot of leverage and a lot of ability to manage a very big spend base, but it's how you manage that. Even small companies can have an advantage if they are using the right approaches and the right techniques and stay on the cutting edge."[9]

As an example of a best practice any company can focus on, Shoemaker cites procurement risk management. "In our case, we look backward over time at such variables as price, supply, and demand, and we use analytical tools to predict going forward what those volatile numbers might be with some confidence levels. In a very volatile pricing area, for example, we would predict ranges of prices that we might expect. Or in a volatile demand portfolio, we would predict what our demand numbers—the highs and the lows—might be." What that does, he notes, is help to better educate and empower HP's procurement professionals to spread the risk between HP and its supply base.

"The typical mantra in IT in the past has been 'Mr. Supplier, you bear all the risk, and we'll buy from you.' That's not necessarily a long-term winning strategy for us or the supply base because there's so much consolidation that's occurred [in the high-tech industry]," Shoemaker says. "There are fewer suppliers and there are fewer companies like us, so it's not in our best interest to be so transactionally oriented."

Risk management is a tool HP uses that allows the company to manage risk from a statistical basis. DRAM (dynamic random access memory) chips used in PCs, for instance, are a very volatile commodity, where the prices can vary wildly from week to week. Using risk management, Shoemaker notes, "we might structure a deal with a supplier that allows us to say to them 'We're going to guarantee you a certain volume level, and in return for that, we'll ask you for a price cap.' Or we might agree to a price floor, and in return for that guaranteed amount of volume, they've got something they can depend on, and we can get some pricing conditions that we can depend on."

Working for Every Penny

E-sourcing—the use of online electronic marketplaces to purchase both basic commodities (indirect materials) and core production materials (direct materials)—is another best practice at HP that gets a lot of attention. "We are moving very rapidly to getting all of our strategic sourcing work in a Web-based environment," Shoemaker explains. "We believe that it provides us speed and efficiency, and our commodity managers and category specialists can be more efficient and effective."

Another thing e-sourcing provides, he adds, is greatly enhanced security in HP's data management. The company is able to confidently handle requests for quotes, requests for information, and similar sourcing relationships through the Web, where the information is encrypted and password protected. "Basically, we're trying to get off of e-mail and spreadsheets," he says.

Sharing sourcing information among other groups is vital to ensuring that HP's supply chain efforts are working in tandem. Shoemaker manages about 40 percent of HP's direct spend, and he also leads a procurement council that meets every month and involves the other 60 percent of the company's spend. "We focus on a few core items: best practices and processes—what's everybody doing, how are they achieving it, where are they spending their money, how can we better leverage it, and where do they need help? We focus on professional development as a function—how are we training, advancing, and preparing our best performers? We also focus on our IT toolset—what products will help us to better implement these practices in a more cohesive fashion?"

HP has saved a lot of money over the years thanks to its adherence to best procurement practices, but that doesn't mean it ever gets any easier. "The challenge that we have is that nobody just comes to us and says, 'Here's your price.' You've got to work for every penny of it," Shoemaker notes. For a high-tech manufacturer, a lot of the purchasing process is driven by market conditions and technology. "For instance, when a semiconductor fabricator goes to the next smaller die size, which reduces the price, it effectively does it for everyone. So what are you doing to manage that differently and get a better result?" That's what procurement is all about—not just getting the best price, but the best possible results.[10]

Ensuring a Healthy Supply Chain

How's this for a public relations nightmare: You're a major pharmaceutical wholesaler and you discover that, unbeknownst to you, you've been purchasing and distributing counterfeit drugs, which result in lawsuits against your company. That nightmare scenario is exactly what happened to McKesson in 2000, when it discovered it had purchased fake Serostim, a drug to treat AIDS patients. It's also what happened to AmeriSourceBergen in 2001 and 2002, when it bought more than $4 million worth of heavily diluted Epogen, a medication for patients with anemia who are on dialysis. The same thing happened to Cardinal Health in 2002, when it bought $2.4 million worth of tainted Procrit, another anemia drug.[11] And in 2007 Baxter International found itself at the center of the worst-possible scenario, when hundreds took ill and dozens of people died due to contaminated heparin, a blood-thinning drug.[12]

The discovery of fake Serostim served as a wake-up call for McKesson, explains Greg Yonko, senior vice president of purchasing. "At that point we immediately took very stringent steps to tighten up all of our purchasing processes," he says. Birth control pills and HIV drugs had long been favorite targets of counterfeiters, but according to Yonko, the Serostim incident was the first time a high-priced injectable growth hormone entered the marketplace as a counterfeit product.[13]

Although the U.S. Food and Drug Administration (FDA) heavily regulates and monitors the pharmaceutical food chain, counterfeiting worsens every year. As a result, the FDA has launched initiatives aimed at the adoption of radio frequency identification (RFID) technology to track and trace all pallets and cases of pharmaceuticals, and in certain situations the agency is requiring that this technology be applied to every package as well. (Pfizer, in fact, has been tagging every package of Viagra with RFID chips since 2006; see Chapter 2.) The ultimate goal is for every drug to have a unique serialized identifier that will allow all pharmaceuticals to be trackable throughout the healthcare supply chain.[14]

While technology can be used to identify and track authentic products, the larger issue threatening the pharmaceutical supply chain is what's known as the secondary market—small and loosely regulated wholesalers and suppliers whose products occasionally enter the mass market, sometimes to fill in the gaps during an inventory shortage and sometimes because their products are priced significantly lower. Most of the counterfeit drugs have come through these small distributors, which are typically state-licensed entities that are supposed to be inspected by the pharmacy board, notes Dr. Thomas McGinnis, director of pharmacy affairs at the FDA. However, "a lot of them are very small businesses that are approached by somebody with product to sell. They don't have a business relationship with them.

They've probably never done business with them before. And yet they buy the product without making a phone call to the manufacturer or to the FDA to ask if this guy who has a great deal is legitimate."[15]

Since 2001, McKesson only buys drugs directly from pharmaceutical manufacturers, and of the hundreds of millions of products that go through its system every day, less than 1 percent are from the secondary market. According to Yonko, McKesson has an active business relationship with 10 alternative-source vendors and initiates a rigorous due diligence process, including background and security checks as well as site visits, before it will purchase products from these vendors. The large drug makers, meanwhile, have proactively taken their own steps to reduce the likelihood of counterfeit drugs entering the market. Many drug companies, including Pfizer, Johnson & Johnson, and Eli Lilly, now require that their distributors only purchase drugs directly from them or from authorized resellers.

The War on Complexity

Returning to the Motorola story, the company's overhaul eventually resulted in a $1.4 billion reduction in inventory, with an overall $2.6 billion in costs driven out of the supply chain. Theresa Metty, the company's chief procurement officer, cites those figures as evidence that what Motorola is doing is working—namely, that it is winning "the war on complexity."[16]

As Metty explains, "We started out identifying 39 separate but related and integrated projects that would reposition the supply chain to not only be incredibly lean, efficient, flexible, and responsive for Motorola, but also would put us in a position to offer supply chain services to our most preferred customers. It's turning out that the vision we had was right. Our most important customers don't want to be in the hardware management business. They want us to provide supply chain services for them."

One of those services (which is addressed in greater detail in Chapter 13) is collaborative planning, forecasting, and replenishment. "We partner with customers on what they're going to promote in their stores, and how long they want to carry the product," she describes. "We do the forecasting and replenishment based on the collaborative plan that we develop with them— in some cases on a weekly basis, and others less often."

In describing Motorola's war on complexity, Metty notes that simplifying the company's product line is a key to achieving a best-in-class supply chain. "The war on complexity is all about promoting things that make products flow through our supply chain in an efficient and effective way." *Design for postponement*, for instance, is a process whereby Motorola uses industry-standard components as often as possible. Not only does this reduce how much inventory it has to carry, but also, at the end of a product's life cycle,

Motorola can resell those industry-standard parts back into the market rather than having to absorb the costs of excess and obsolete material.

Whenever possible, Metty adds, the company also reuses components and design elements that are common in various cell phone models, which helps shorten time to market. "The real magic is, you're carrying a lot less inventory. If you're using many of the same industry-standard components in your products, you don't need to carry very much inventory."

As we saw in our look at metrics (Chapter 3), just having a supply chain program in place won't get you very far if you're not able to accurately measure your progress. In setting its goal of winning the war on complexity, Motorola created a complexity index, Metty explains, "which measures every one of our products relative to our competitors' products and relative to a theoretical best- in-class product. We've identified 10 complexity factors, and we measure every one of those factors on our products and our competitors' products." For example, a complexity index score of 1.0 means a product is at parity with the industry average. A best-in-class score would be 0.5, meaning the product is much less complex, and hence easier to source and manufacture. A score of 1.5, on the other hand, would indicate a product that is significantly more complex than one of Motorola's competitors, and thus a product that should be reconfigured to be less complex.

For Motorola, complexity is a leading indicator of how efficiently a product is going to behave in its supply chain. It's also proven itself as a way the company can strengthen its supply base as its suppliers become better at producing fewer and cheaper components.[17]

It Seemed like a Good Idea at the Time

Back in the days of the late 1990s dot-com boom, virtually every discussion of supply chain management began with an evaluation of the importance of electronic marketplaces. The premise was both seductive and simple: Manufacturers would be able to purchase parts, supplies, and components directly off the Internet, thanks to the emergence of procurement software and sufficient security protocols that would safeguard any online transactions. These e-marketplaces (also known as online trading exchanges or net markets), which seemingly sprouted out of nowhere about the same time that user-friendly Web browser software (i.e., Netscape) became widely available, enabled companies to buy and sell raw materials and other products in real time via the Internet.

The hook that tantalized so many businesses—and business writers— was that companies would be able to save tremendously on their regular purchases of both direct materials (the core supplies and materials manufacturers require to make their products) and indirect materials (commodities that companies need to run their business, but that aren't necessarily part of their production process, such as office supplies) through *reverse auctions*. Let's say you were a glue manufacturer and you needed 10,000 tubes by the end of the month. You would post your specifications on a public exchange, where all of the tube suppliers that had been properly vetted could bid on your business. After a predetermined period of time, the auction would conclude and you could decide whether to accept the lowest bid or a slightly higher bid if you harbored doubts about the low bidder's ability to actually deliver the products.

Thanks to a little bit of revisionist history, many analysts today laughingly deride online exchanges as a bad idea from Day One. The same market watchers who once championed these exchanges—at their heyday in the year 2000, there were supposedly a thousand or more—are now pooh-poohing them as fatally flawed. But the *idea* of online marketplaces always was a good one; it was the lack of *execution* that led to their quick fadeout from the public eye. That, and the hubris that convinced venture-funded start-ups they could "insert themselves between established trading partners and take a piece of the action," as author David Taylor puts it. "As soon as the potential of exchanges became apparent, the major buyers and sellers set up their own captive exchanges, bypassed the start-ups, and took their markets back."[18]

An Online Car Wreck

There are three basic types of online marketplaces: private, public, and consortium. The private exchanges actually predate the Internet era, with one of the best known being Wal-Mart's Retail Link, which in the pre–World Wide Web days used a proprietary electronic data interchange pipeline to communicate transactional data between the retail giant and its suppliers. Aerospace manufacturer Boeing Co. was another early adopter of the private exchange model with its Part Analysis and Requirements Tracking (PART) Page, a Web site that provides airlines and their maintenance contractors with a direct link to half a million airplane components. Because these types of exchanges were by definition private, they didn't really make headlines (at least not until reporters began taking a much closer look at what made Wal-Mart so successful).

Thanks largely to eBay, public exchanges captured the imagination of American consumers, who were alternately fascinated and amused by the idea of being able to sell virtually anything to anybody (even though only eBay seemed to be able to make any real money from it).

But the consortium-based exchanges threatened for a time to turn all the old assumptions of purchasing on their head. And the biggest exchange of them all, at least in terms of potential and mindshare, was Covisint, an attempt by General Motors, Ford Motor, and Chrysler to link up their supply chains through one common online procurement platform. This effort, they hoped, would allow them to get much better prices on components from their suppliers, many of which sold to all three of the Detroit Big Three.

Problem was, the automakers failed to ask their suppliers what they thought about the idea of having their products commoditized on an exchange where price presumably would be king. So Covisint never got buy-in from the suppliers, and the same lack of supplier interest also doomed many of the other big industry-wide exchanges. Their proponents claimed that members would save millions on their procurement costs, but they never took into consideration that the suppliers had so much to lose from the concept that they'd just refuse to play ball.

As Thomas Stallkamp, former president of Chrysler, observes, "Covisint was a horrible idea. Nobody thought it through. [Trading] exchanges are fine, but Covisint and the way it was done was an absolute failure—it never got off the ground."[19] Adds economist Stan Liebowitz, "The laws of supply and demand are not so fragile as to be overcome by anything so small as a new method of communicating with each other."[20]

A Rating Service for Buyers and Sellers

What ultimately derailed the consortium model and relegated the public exchange model to the back burners was the simple reality that spot-buying direct materials from companies you have no relationship with is a bad idea. However, using the Web as a medium to conduct transactions and to communicate with suppliers is, in fact, a very good idea so, not surprisingly, online marketplaces targeted to specific industries are still flourishing. For instance, Tesla Motors, a manufacturer of electric sports cars, uses online marketplaces that specialize in bulk parts, such as metal castings, plastic molds, and small subassemblies.

These exchanges offer quick access to a wide range of quotes and pricing options, explains Stephen Davies, materials program manager for Tesla. "You save a lot of time on the front end because you're being introduced to a much larger number of potential suppliers in a very short period of time. Instead of cold calling, you're getting 50 responses that can easily be vetted down to five suppliers that you never would have known about otherwise."

According to Mitch Free, chief executive of online exchange MFG.com, buyers like Tesla can access MFG.com for free, whereas suppliers pay a subscription fee to be listed on the exchange. One key element to the popularity of these types of sites plays into the same community spirit that Web sites like eBay and Amazon have fostered: Suppliers are rated by buyers for such things as timely delivery, customer service, and product quality. Buyers, similarly, are rated on such factors as timely payment, quality of technical data, and how easy they are to do business with. "The community can be an extremely powerful force in policing and evaluating the participants of an online marketplace," Free says.

Regardless of how good a potential supplier's online ratings look, Tesla still follows the best practice of performing an on-site evaluation before completing a transaction. "We don't just send a check to whoever won the bid and hope they send the parts," Davies says. "We're trying to develop a relationship and a partnership with that supplier."[21]

CHAPTER 6

Manufacturing
Supply Chain on the Make

Flashpoints

Supply chain management begins with breaking down the silo mentality.

Best-in-class manufacturers have cycle times shorter than their order lead times.

Having visibility into your supply chain will help you make smarter decisions for your company and your customers.

Top supply chains consistently design and develop products their customers want to buy.

One of the major objectives of supply chain management is to break down the silos that operate within any company. The term *silo* refers to the silhouetted portrait of a typical manufacturer: smoke-belching chimneys towering over several-stories-tall factories situated near tall office buildings. Every school kid recognizes that picture, and it's become the default icon for every PowerPoint presentation that needs an instantly recognizable image of a production facility. Unfortunately, it's not just the silo image that lingers in the public consciousness—it's the entire silo mentality that supply chain proponents keep trying to break down, with varying degrees of success.

Let's face it: Taking control of the supply chain and aligning a company's processes so that improvements are regular and long-lasting are very difficult tasks to accomplish. For some companies, though, an even harder task is deciding whether to start the process at all, particularly given the long tradition of "throwing it over the wall" between various production departments. When it comes to aligning manufacturing within a supply chain context, it's a lot easier to talk about it than to actually accomplish it.

Today, thanks largely to the historic success of Japanese automaker Toyota and the more recent but equally storied success of American computer maker Dell, textbooks outlining the principles of lean manufacturing sit on the bookshelves of countless executive suites. Yet for all the talk about lean, there's still a pervasive wait-and-see attitude at most of those companies, especially outside of the automotive and high-tech industries. While manufacturers and distributors of all types of products recognize that lean offers a more or less direct route to eliminating waste, reducing inventory, and becoming more profitable, wanting those benefits and actually having a plan in place for going after them are two very different things.

Improving efficiencies within a lean environment takes a concerted and coordinated effort to align all facets of the supply chain toward achieving the same goals. And the job is far from done once a company has all its internal oars moving in the same direction; that same process must be replicated throughout the main supply base. Any breakdown in communication with a key supplier will result in those lean inventories getting bloated again in very short order. (Best practices in lean and continuous improvement are discussed in Chapter 17.)

The patience that is required for a successful supply chain transformation can evaporate after one bad fiscal quarter, and any kind of company-transforming initiative by definition requires significant expenditures of time, money, labor, and other vital resources. Confronted with put-up-or-shut-up ultimatums from top management, many supply chain managers are stymied in their attempts to streamline manufacturing operations, even in the face of evidence that such efforts have been successful at other companies. There's also the business-as-usual mind-set that looks on supply chain initiatives as mostly one-time opportunities to reduce costs in a single area, with little or no thought given to a sustained effort throughout all corporate operations.[1]

Nevertheless, companies continue to seek ways to break down the silo mentality for one basic reason: That's what the best manufacturing companies in the world have done. Best-in-class manufacturers have at least this one thing in common: Their cycle times are shorter than their order lead times. What's more, they've figured out how to reduce waste in numerous areas, which allows them to control their costs as they increase capacity and inventory turns. And in supply chain circles, nobody does that better than Dell.

A Direct Line to Supply Chain Success

The secret to Dell's success is really no secret at all—the company's *direct-to-consumer model* works because of a single-minded dedication to its customers, focusing on one customer at a time. Since its founding in 1984, the company has pioneered a make-to-order philosophy within an industry that was traditionally make-to-stock. Rather than sell its personal computers through retailers, Dell decided to customize every PC to the unique specifications of the individual end user. So customers get exactly what they want, while Dell builds PCs that have already been sold. In 2007, Dell started selling in some retail stores, including Wal-Mart and Best Buy, but as of mid-year 2009, the strategy had not yet caught on.[2]

Dell's direct model has become legendary not just in the computer industry but throughout all of manufacturing. (See the "Consumer Packaged Goods" section of Chapter 2.) The company manufactures more than 50,000 computers every day but carries only three to four days' worth of inventory, when many of its competitors carry between 20 to 30 days of inventory. However, Dell isn't content to pat itself on the back for a job well done.

"We're on the tip of the iceberg," says Dick Hunter, vice president, Americas Manufacturing Operation. "Most people think we've reached the ultimate goal in supply chain management—an inventory of three days. We disagree; every day we work to bring that number down. Our current goal is to get down to two days. Long term, I think we can get it even lower."

The key to that is transition management. "We sell what we have and we don't sell what we don't have," explains Hunter. "We don't tolerate excess inventory. We do whatever it takes to move inventory, even if it means creating demand. Working through our direct model and having such tight control of the supply chain allows us this significant competitive advantage."

The company keeps a report card on every supplier, and tracks each supplier's performance against a set of metrics maintained by Dell. It's long been whispered that Dell's remarkably low inventory levels come at the expense of its suppliers, but Hunter points out, "About 30 suppliers provide 75 percent of our direct material purchase spend, and most of them maintain eight to ten days of inventory in nearby, multi-vendor hubs." If those levels exceed ten days, Dell will work with its suppliers to lower them. Dell's culture will not accept excess and obsolete components, Hunter notes.

The company adheres to chairman Michael Dell's philosophy: "Keep your friends close, and your suppliers closer," and to that end it works with its suppliers to prevent their inventory levels from becoming too low. "For Dell and our suppliers, information is increasingly replacing inventory, and we are regularly identifying, gathering, and sharing new types and levels of data," Hunter says.

Half of Dell's more than 50,000 orders each day come through the Internet and are processed through the company's order management system, which records all of the orders and releases them to manufacturing. "We schedule production lines in every factory globally every two hours," Hunter explains. "We have no inventory and no warehouses in any of our factories. Instead, we pull material into our factories based on actual orders. We literally push a button and two things happen. We lock in the schedule by actual order and order number into the factory. At the same time we send a message over the Internet to our third-party logistics providers, supplier logistics centers, or hubs." Those hubs then have 90 minutes to pull material out of the racks and deliver it to Dell.[3]

Better Decisions for the Customer

Dell's strategy hinges on having visibility into the latest supply and demand trends. The company posts its hub-level inventory on the Web, enabling suppliers to check their inventory levels at the hubs, since materials suppliers aren't necessarily the same set of companies as those at the hub. Dell issues forecasts through its supplier extranet, and suppliers commit back to Dell based on those forecasts. Dell then works from that information, covering any deviations from what it asks for against what a supplier or a set of suppliers can promise.

Suppliers maintain inventory in their hub facilities located near Dell's assembly plants. Dell sends orders to the suppliers on a rolling basis, and factory-scheduling software generates material requirements every two hours per facility. Those requirements get posted to Dell's supplier Web site, and the hubs then pick, pack, and ship the materials to Dell for the next two hours of production. The result is a built-to-order computer.[4]

"The more we know about the capabilities of the supply chain and our suppliers, the better decisions we're going to make for our customers," Hunter observes. In practice, that sometimes means that Dell makes a better choice for a customer than it does for itself, at least for the short term. Lean manufacturing experts James P. Womack and Daniel T. Jones have observed that there is "a logical disconnect" between what Dell does for its customers and what it ought to be doing for them based on cost effectiveness.[5]

"Because the short-term spikes in demand can be several times long-term demand and extra capacity is very costly, it is not practical for Dell to maintain enough capacity to respond instantly to every swing in the market," Womack and Jones explain. To be able to respond to individual consumers who want their own customized computer at a good price, then, Dell tries to create customer demand by changing the prices on optional features or even entire systems based on how many or few of any given item the company has.

What sometimes happens, though, is a consumer will request a system that includes components Dell doesn't have readily on hand. Rather than requisitioning a part that might have to be shipped via air freight (by far the most expensive transportation mode), the computer maker will instead substitute an upgraded component it has in stock. The consumer gets a better computer, though the wait for the system will be longer than originally expected. In effect, Dell will take a loss on the cost of the components if it can save on transportation costs and in the process keep a customer happy. And it's been Dell's ability to "cost-effectively supply exactly what its customers want" that has made its supply chain best in class.

Tying It All Together

IBM Corp., another computer industry leader, spends roughly 50 cents of every dollar of revenue on its supply chain, which, based on 2008 sales of $103.6 billion, represents a supply chain spend of $51.8 billion. Big Blue describes it as an *on-demand supply chain*, which Nick Donofrio, executive vice president of innovation and technology, explains is one that can sense and respond to customers' demands and to changes in the marketplace—no matter how frequent and sudden.[6]

"In the past, manufacturing was a rather isolated activity," Donofrio says. "It was located at or near the end of the supply chain. The manufacturing team didn't get involved in anything until after the product had been designed and developed, the planning and forecasting had been done, and the customer had placed the order. That model is history. It will never suffice for today's customers who demand instantaneous response to their inquiries. What's required now is the complete integration of manufacturing into the overall supply chain, as well as the integration of the overall supply chain itself."

IBM's transformation to an on-demand model didn't happen overnight. A key factor in its integration was a razor-close examination of how an order moves throughout its system. "We looked at how we could integrate logistics and inventory, and what we needed to purchase from suppliers," Donofrio explains. "By embracing the e-business model, we were able to deploy capabilities that would increase efficiency of our supply chain, and strengthen our relationships with our suppliers and customers. We were able to link customer-facing systems, such as order entry, order scheduling, and confirmation, to the supply-facing systems that drive procurement, warehousing, manufacturing, distribution, and invoicing." In short, IBM now ties together all of the relevant "plan, source, make, deliver, and return" elements of its supply chain.

Digital Supply Chains

Yet another computer giant, Apple Inc., has won accolades for its ability to sell products with no physical supply chain at all. While the company, like any other manufacturer, earns the bulk of its revenues from physical products such as its lines of Mac computers and iPod devices, Apple also makes more than $1 billion every year from its iTunes virtual store. Welcome to the world of the digital supply chain, where a company like Apple can sell more than 1 billion MP3 files that require no material sourcing, no production, no transportation, and no warehousing. The company is experiencing similar success by selling applications for its popular iPhone mobile device, again circumventing the traditional supply chain.

The digital supply chain is a new media term, according to the Web-based encyclopedia Wikipedia, that refers to "the process of the delivery of digital media, be it music or video, by electronic means, from the point of origin (content provider) to destination (consumer). In much the same manner a physical medium must go through a supply chain process in order to mature into a consumable product, digital media must pass through various stages in processing to get to a point in which the consumer can enjoy the music or video on a computer or television set."[7]

As C. J. Wehlage, high-tech research director with analyst firm AMR Research Inc., points out, with digital supply chains, "warehouses are being replaced with data centers, boxes replaced by bits, and trucks replaced by bandwidth."[8] At first glance, he observes, it may seem that these supply chains are a lot easier to manage, since there are no apparent inventory carrying costs, supplier scorecards, product obsolescence, or quality issues to deal with. However, the real challenge of the digital supply chain comes in the integration of the digital content with constantly evolving hardware capabilities.

Apple's supply chain, Wehlage says, has transformed an industry. In fact, as noted in Chapter 3, AMR Research named Apple the top supply chain of 2008 and again in 2009, largely on the strength of its digital offerings. "iTunes, while shifting supply chain investments to technology and infrastructure, provides a platform for higher margin hardware sales, increased agility through higher cash flows, accelerated turnaround times with on-demand content, and speed to market through a recognized Web-based storefront," Wehlage notes.

Not surprisingly, the two manufacturers ranked 1 and 2 on AMR's list of top supply chains—Apple and Dell—are also the only two manufacturers on *Internet Retailer*'s list of top 10 online retailers (ranked by sales). And not coincidentally, those same two companies also had by far the most inventory turns of all the supply chains ranked by AMR. That kind of success inevitably breeds competition; Hewlett-Packard Co., for instance, has made an initial foray into offering digital products via its Digital Home Entertainment Center.

Collaborating on Product Designs

Of course, Apple's recent string of successes is due not so much to the digital supply chain as it is to product innovation, which is one of the great equalizers among companies. One of the most obvious characteristics of a best-in-class supply chain is an ability to consistently design and develop products that customers want to buy. And thanks to a relatively new software-based technology—product life cycle management (PLM)—manufacturers are now able to automate the collaborative design of products from anywhere in the world. Using PLM, developers can tap into a central workspace and get access to part designs, bills of material, product specifications, production schedules, and other data. PLM includes elements of earlier computer-based technologies, such as computer-aided design, engineering, and manufacturing (CAD/CAE/CAM), as well as product data management, but PLM is much more of a supply chain solution because it allows the sharing of product information not only throughout a company's many offices but throughout the offices of supply chain partners and suppliers as well.

The Joint Strike Fighter program, for instance, is a prime example of supply chain collaboration. (The topic of collaboration is discussed in greater detail in Chapter 13.) This multibillion-dollar initiative to build a next-generation aircraft for both the American and British militaries includes Lockheed Martin as the lead contractor and fellow aerospace and defense manufacturers Northrop Grumman (U.S.), BAE Systems (U.K.), and Fokker (Netherlands) as major subcontractors. Product experts from these companies can tap into Lockheed's virtual workspace platform to work on their own piece of this massive international project. As many as 1,500 engineers can access the virtual workspace as heavy users, and another 3,000 can tap into it on a more limited basis.[9]

At a Glance

Product Life Cycle Management

Product life cycle management (PLM) technology enables manufacturers to manage and share complex design and production information across an extended enterprise, with the goal of streamlining the product development process.

Like aerospace companies, automotive and high-tech manufacturers have also been early adopters of PLM software because of the complex

nature of their production process. However, given the increasing importance of developing new products and getting them to market as quickly as
possible, consumer packaged goods and pharmaceutical companies have
also turned to PLM as a supply chain best practice because, when properly
deployed and managed, it can help reduce costs while increasing efficiency.
Here are some examples:

- Playtex Products, a manufacturer of personal care consumer products,
  outsources 70 percent of its manufacturing to seven facilities throughout North America. Tracking document routing and product record data
  was increasingly difficult because this information was maintained on
  any number of electronic systems or, in some cases, on paper. By stan-
  dardizing on a common PLM platform, Playtex enjoyed a 98 percent
  improvement in its document routing time. Time to market improved
  significantly as well, contributing in part to added revenues in the neigh-
  borhood of $20 million annually.
- Regulatory requirements from the U.S. Food and Drug Administration
  as well as legal bodies in Europe have become more demanding for
  pharmaceutical manufacturers such as Roche Diagnostics. Roche was
  having difficulty stepping up its quality management processes because
  its quality data were scattered among a dozen nonintegrated systems,
  with much of that information being shared via fax machines rather than
  over a computer network. By implementing a PLM solution throughout the company, Roche has been able to automate its documentation
  process, which helps the company manage its growing product lines as
  well as satisfy the government audits.
- At Eaton's Hydraulics Division, a maker of hydraulic products for farm
  and construction machinery, it frequently took up to 10 days to distribute CAD files throughout the company. The process began with the
  transfer of completed drawings to microfilm, which were then sent to
  the main library and duplicated so they could be sent to other sites'
  libraries. Not only did it take too long, but the error rate was as high
  as 6 percent at some of the libraries. A PLM solution capable of storing
  and retrieving more than 70,000 imaged documents has not only made
  the microfilming system obsolete, but it has also shaved the wait time
  from 10 days down to a mere three hours.[10]

The latest trend in product development technology involves the merger
of PLM capabilities with manufacturing execution system (MES) software,
with the goal being to integrate product design with shop-floor production.
"In the next generation of PLM, we expect to see that PLM is as much
about effective product life cycle decision-making as it is about product

engineering," explains Joe Barkai, an analyst with Manufacturing Insights. "PLM tools must be used not only to support engineering tasks, but, more importantly, to create and manage a comprehensive product management strategy, culture and processes."[11]

At a Glance

Manufacturing Execution System

Manufacturing execution systems (MES) deliver production instructions to the shop floor and then track everything that happens to a product as it progresses through the manufacturing process.

Nearly Perfect

Supply chain manufacturing concepts often seem to emerge fully formed out of nowhere, and while there have been numerous short-lived trends *du jour*, in reality the legitimate best practices have gestated for many years, sometimes for decades. There's nothing new about lean manufacturing or the Toyota Production System (TPS), for example, even though they're currently popular buzzwords. (See Chapter 17.) The TPS, after all, emerged in Japan shortly after World War II ended and in fact was based on concepts popularized even earlier in the twentieth century by Henry Ford. So even though lean is at the top of many people's minds these days, the only thing truly new about lean is the acceptance it's finally gained in the United States.

Another manufacturing concept that is frequently associated with lean is Six Sigma, a structured, quality-centric approach to manufacturing. Seen as the successor to the earlier Total Quality Management movement, Six Sigma began at Motorola in the 1980s as a way of improving the quality and reliability of its products, which would enable the company to deliver a consistently high level of customer service. (See Chapter 5.) Based on quality initiatives developed by the Japanese, Motorola's Six Sigma program involved every employee in the company.

Motorola learned from the Japanese that "simpler designs result in higher levels of quality and reliability," explains consultant Alan Larson, a divisional quality director at Motorola when Six Sigma was launched. The company also learned that it needed to improve manufacturing techniques "to ensure that products were built right the first time."[12]

At a Glance

Six Sigma

Six Sigma is a measure of quality that strives for near perfection, which is defined as no more than 3.4 defects per million opportunities.

The term *Six Sigma* refers to the idea of near perfection, defined as six standard deviations between the mean and the nearest specification limit. In practice, this means a product or process can have no more than 3.4 defects per million opportunities. Six Sigma, like the Supply Chain Operations Reference (SCOR) model (see Chapter 3), focuses on five areas: define, measure, analyze, improve, and control. Six Sigma programs typically use statistical process control tools to monitor, control, and improve a product or process through statistical analysis.

To achieve the desired result of enabling continuous improvement, rather than merely putting a temporary bandage on a problem, Larson recommends that every department, group, and unit within a company complete these six steps:

1. Identify the product you create or the service you provide.
2. Identify your customers, and determine the customers' needs.
3. Identify your suppliers and what you need from them.
4. Define your process for doing the work.
5. Establish metrics for measuring the goodness of your process and feedback mechanisms to determine customer satisfaction.
6. Ensure continuous improvement by establishing a team that measures, analyzes, and completes focused action items.[13]

Proponents of the Six Sigma approach typically cite its lack of ambiguity as a major plus. The Six Sigma methodology applies a mathematical precision to what might otherwise be highly imprecise supply chain processes. A corollary benefit comes when a company insists on getting commitment from every employee and requiring everybody to focus on the better good of the entire supply chain.

"Getting our business units to accept change has been accelerated because we're talking a common language and common methodology through Six Sigma," observes Lori Schock, site supply manager with Dow Corning, a manufacturer of silicone-based products. "It removes the 'doubting Thomas' attitude because it is a common process based on facts."[14]

To date, Motorola credits Six Sigma as providing financial benefits worth $17 billion; General Electric Co., another major proponent of the methodology, estimates the total value of its thousands of Six Sigma projects at $5 billion. It's not just Fortune 500 companies that are benefiting from Six Sigma, either. Machine tool manufacturer MAG Giddings & Lewis, for instance, says it's saved at least $9 million from its projects since 2002. One of those projects led to the reduction of the number of parts required to build products, along with a standardization of parts, according to Ellie Kemp, a Master Black Belt (yes, trained Six Sigma experts are awarded designations highly reminiscent of Japanese martial arts practitioners). As a result of these various efforts, lead times on building some milling machines, for instance, have dropped from 12 to 18 months down to five months. Kemp says that Six Sigma projects are the most important way a company can improve its competitive position.[15]

The Future of Manufacturing

As we saw earlier in the section on digital supply chains, the definition of *manufacturing* itself is in transition, no longer limited to the making of physical goods. Similarly, many companies today call themselves "manufacturers" even though none of their employees is actually involved in any stage of the traditional labor production process. "Leading manufacturers are evolving from being manufacturing companies to being manufacturing management companies," notes a study produced by the University of Edinburgh and Capgemini. This means that the production process—the "make" from the "plan-source-make-deliver-return" SCOR model—is done by other companies, often in other parts of the world. "While many [manufacturers] hold on to core activities such as R&D [research and development], marketing, and finance, increasingly even intellectual property, such as design and engineering, is outsourced."

For instance, GPS developer TomTom International saw early on that it was better at product innovation than it was at making things, so it focused on best practices within outsourcing rather than manufacturing capabilities. Automation and power products company ABB, meanwhile, engages in strategic outsourcing on a case-by-case basis. The company outsources robotics for the automotive industry; the manufacture of its core power distribution products, however, is kept in-house.[16]

As production work increasingly moves to low-cost-labor countries, especially China, it's become an open question in the United States and other industrialized nations as to whether it's a best practice or in fact a *worst* practice to offshore jobs to other countries. Working with the Council on Competitiveness, Harvard professor Michael Porter, one of the pioneer thinkers in modern supply chain management (see Chapter 1), has suggested that it's in the best interests of U.S. manufacturers to shift low-value production jobs overseas while focusing instead on high-value services. "Competitiveness is not a zero-sum game," Porter points out. "The success of other economies is not a failure of U.S. competitiveness—a job created there does not mean a job lost here, a new R&D lab built there does not mean one lost here, a rise in another country's exports does not necessarily mean a decline in ours."[17]

Porter's argument is bolstered by the overall rise in productivity in the U.S. manufacturing industry, largely due to the adoption of automation technologies. According to the National Association of Manufacturers, manufacturing productivity has risen by 94 percent since the 1980s, a pace markedly quicker than that experienced by other U.S. businesses over the same period.[18] The dark side to this productivity gain, however, is the fact that the U.S. economy has lost millions of manufacturing jobs over the past decade. Much of that job loss has been due to a worldwide recession, and indeed, other countries—even China—have experienced similar significant job losses in the manufacturing sector. In any event, as globalization forces are influencing the relocation of production facilities, companies are rethinking their supply chains to maximize productivity while minimizing costs. (The topic of globalization is covered in Chapter 10.)

CHAPTER 7

Transportation

Logistics à la Mode

Flashpoints

The faster your goods travel, the more you'll spend on transportation.

Transportation is a relationship business, so take the time to get to know your carriers.

Price volatility is a bigger problem than rising fuel costs because of the unpredictability.

When it comes to transportation, rule number one is: Get it there on time.

Transportation is the lifeblood of any supply chain, but a company's logistics department tends to be an invisible link in that chain. If senior management thinks about freight transportation at all, their thoughts tend to focus on questions like "Why are we spending so much on trucks?" or "Why are our products always shipping so late?" Those are fair questions to ask, especially when you consider that U.S. companies spend more than $800 billion each year on transportation. And yet the supply chain professionals who manage that spend are rarely given credit for keeping costs as low as possible.

Freight transportation—the physical distribution of goods—involves four major modes: highway, rail, air, and water carriers.[1] Many shipments move on two or more modes, such as from a railcar to a truck, and these shipments are classified broadly as intermodal. Because more than 70 percent of all goods in the United States at some point are transported on a truck (and 80 percent of all transportation costs are for motor carriage), this chapter will by design concentrate largely on best practices when dealing with motor carriers.[2]

The reasons why transportation costs are so high are almost as numerous as the types of goods being transported, which is another way of saying there is no single set of best practices that will work for every company, every time. The basic rule of thumb is: The higher the level of service (including speed of delivery), the higher the cost. The cost per pound for shipping goods by rail, for instance, is proportionately less than if they're shipped overnight by an expedited courier. And not coincidentally, the value of the goods generally determines what mode is chosen: High-value electronic components are frequently shipped by air, while steel moves by water and grain by rail. There are numerous exceptions to every typical scenario, but historically those are the mode basics that transportation managers work from.

Reducing transportation down to its core elements, there are three entities involved in any movement of goods: the *shipper*, which owns the goods (e.g., a sporting goods manufacturer), the *consignee*, which is the one receiving the goods (e.g., a discount retailer), and the *carrier*, which physically transports the goods (e.g., a trucking company). In this example, the manufacturer (shipper) sends a full truckload of its basketballs on a 53-foot truck (carrier) to the retailer's (consignee) distribution center.

Out of this basic structure are countless possible configurations. Companies both ship and receive goods every day, so at any given time, the only way to determine whether a company is a shipper or a consignee is to look at the bill of lading. For simplicity's sake, this chapter will look at best practices from the shipper's point of view.[3]

Riding the Roads

The most economical motor carrier mode is to ship by *truckload*, which is exactly what it sounds like: A shipper fills the entire capacity of a truck with its products, whether the truck is part of the shipper's own private fleet or a contract carrier. However, most shipments by truck are *less than truckload (LTL)*, where any number of shippers occupy a portion of the same truck's capacity to carry their goods. Because the carrier has to handle many shipments and make many more stops, LTL rates tend to be much higher than truckload rates. For that reason, shippers are always looking for ways to shift as much freight as possible from LTL to truckload. The challenge for a shipper is to configure its supply chain so that it's usually shipping out full truckloads, which takes a lot of planning and is a relatively rare event for most small and medium-size manufacturers.

An alternative strategy for domestic transportation—particularly during periods when capacity is tight (meaning there aren't enough trucks or drivers available to transport all the goods at any given time in certain areas of the country)—is to bypass the motor carriers entirely for most of the transportation period in favor of an intermodal strategy. Certainly the use of river barges and the railroads to move goods throughout the country has a much longer history than the use of trucks, but as previously noted, there's a reason why three-quarters of all freight transported in the United States is on a truck: It's faster and more reliable than rail or water, and it's cheaper than shipping by air.

The least economical method involving a motor carrier is *expedited* or *express* service. Although the public tends to think same-day, next-day, and overnight deliveries are always accomplished via air transportation, an expedited shipment often travels most of the distance on a truck and the last mile in a courier van and actually may never be put on a plane at all.

Most of the tractors on the nation's highways are pulling *dry van* trailers, which means they are completely enclosed but accessible by one or two doors. Other standard types of vehicles include *flatbeds*; *tankers*, which carry liquids; and *refrigerated vehicles* (or *reefers*), which carry food and other goods that need controlled environments.

Regulations and Deregulation

Coincidence or not, the idea of supply chain management started becoming popular just as a spirit of deregulation was sweeping through Washington, DC, in the late 1970s and early 1980s. In quick succession, the Airline Deregulation Act (1978), the Motor Carrier Act (1980), and the Staggers Rail Act (1980) effectively deregulated three core transportation industries, which opened up the whole nature of shipper/carrier relationships.

Since deregulation took effect, the rate structure of the motor carrier industry has been largely influenced by supply, demand, and cost of service— the major forces of the marketplace, explains Gerhardt Muller, a professor with the U.S. Merchant Marine Academy. Before deregulation, he notes, interstate and intrastate rates were set by government regulations and agencies, such as the Interstate Commerce Commission (ICC).[4] The ICC was terminated in the mid-1990s and was replaced by the Surface Transportation Board, which operates within the U.S. Department of Transportation.

Despite operating under an aura of deregulation for nearly three decades, transportation is still a heavily regulated industry, almost to the point that it's astonishing that anything actually can move from point A to point B according to schedule. Consider just a brief list of transportation activities and areas that come under the jurisdiction of a government agency:

- The number of hours in a day and in a week that a driver can be behind the wheel of a truck
- The carriage and movement of hazardous goods, including routes, parking, surveillance, packaging, and placarding
- The type of fuel used in motor vehicles as well as the engines themselves
- The tracking and tracing of pharmaceutical and food products throughout their life cycle
- The filing of electronic manifests before crossing international borders
- Compliance with homeland security requirements, such as the Customs-Trade Partnership Against Terrorism and the Container Security Initiative. (The topic of supply chain security will be covered in detail in Chapter 14.)

Fuel for Thought

The one question transportation managers get asked by their bosses more often than any other is: "Why are transportation costs going up?" The regulatory issues noted previously are just a small component of the factors that make transportation so expensive. While fuel price increases are never good news for anybody except the oil companies, price volatility is more damaging to a transportation budget because predictable increases can at least be budgeted for, as opposed to random price spikes and valleys that can wreak havoc on even the best-managed transportation plan.

One shipper that's taking a proactive approach to managing its costs is fiberglass manufacturer Owens Corning Corp. The company has developed a fuel reimbursement program for its carriers that provides better and more predictable transportation budgets and forecasts, explains John Gentle, the company's global leader of transportation affairs. Owens Corning spends $350 million on freight per year, spread among 400 carriers, mostly for truckload freight, and the program was set up to help the company recover a portion of the fuel supplement paid to carriers.[5]

Owens Corning changed the formula it uses for its current base fuel program, converting from the standard weekly retail survey of pump prices generated by the U.S. Department of Energy to a New York Mercantile Exchange (NYMEX) base. The advantage of the new program is that carriers can monitor their fuel reimbursement throughout the month. "This program helps carriers learn how fuel prices are established and how the system works," Gentle points out.

The formula doesn't change how much Owens Corning pays the carriers; the change comes in how the information is accounted for and is largely a result of the increased scrutiny on all business processes resulting from Sarbanes-Oxley compliance measures, Gentle notes. Owens Corning offers side-by-side comparisons of the two fuel programs on its Web-based supplier portal.

A Capacity for Change

As global supply chains become increasingly complex, so too do the factors that affect the cost of moving freight from door to door. The greatest challenge in transportation in recent years has been managing the fluctuation in available capacity, particularly when it comes to motor carriers. It's a twofold problem, directly impacted by the state of the economy: When the economy is robust, there are not always enough trucks or truck drivers to deliver the amount of freight that needs to be moved. Conversely, when the economy is in decline, it becomes much easier—and cheaper— to find a trucking company willing to move your freight, but the challenge becomes finding customers who want to buy your goods in the first place.

Prior to the economic recession that started near the end of 2007, the American Trucking Associations (ATA) was predicting that the United States was on the verge of a severe shortage of long-haul, over-the-road truck drivers. The ATA estimated that the industry would need at least 20,000 additional drivers per year to handle the amount of freight moving on U.S. highways prerecession and forecast that the number could exceed 100,000 by 2014.[6] As of 2009, the shortage had ended, according to Bob Costello, chief economist of the ATA, but he predicted that the situation was temporary and that a driver shortage would return once the economy recovers.[7]

According to Bill Sanderson, president of food company Golden State Service Industries, part of the reason for the recurring driver shortage is the image of the job itself. The average age of a truck driver today is 57 years old, and the lifestyle of a long-haul driver—who often spends a week or more away from home and frequently has to sleep in the cab of the truck—tends to turn away many eligible young men and women. After all, there are plenty of other jobs, such as construction and service industry occupations, that pay comparably well and let their employees go home every night. Until the trucking industry directly addresses these quality-of-life issues for drivers, Sanderson notes, carriers will have to keep paying more to attract them, and as a result, transportation costs for shippers will continue to increase.[8]

Also contributing to a shortage of available capacity has been the consolidation of many major trucking companies and the bankruptcy of many smaller companies. According to analyst Donald Broughton with Avondale Partners, at least 2,700 U.S. trucking companies went out of business in 2008, idling 127,000 trucks and reducing trucking capacity by 6.5 percent. As if that's not bad enough, many of those idled trucks were sold and exported to Russia and eastern Europe, so even when the economy recovers, those vehicles will no longer be available to haul U.S. freight.[9] There is every reason to expect that these volatile capacity swings will continue into the foreseeable future, and given that transportation best practices are very much characterized by collaborative relationships, shippers will have to stay adept at establishing and reestablishing relationships with those carriers most likely to stay in business.

Know Thyself, and Thy Carrier Too

As Steve Huntley, director of logistics operations at Tyco Healthcare/ Mallinckrodt, sees it, "Transportation is not a commodity—it's a service. Without transportation there is no supply chain." At Tyco, a manufacturer of medical products, best practices in transportation start at the grassroots level—developing a partnership with the carriers. "There's a difference between a relationship and a partnership," Huntley points out. "A relationship simply means you know somebody. With a partnership, however, you understand what their needs are, and you know what you can do to help them." That takes not only knowing your operations inside and out, but understanding the carrier's operations as well.[10]

Carriers are always going to ask for rate increases; that's just the way the supply chain cycle works. However, Huntley suggests that you find out *why* the carriers are asking for more, because there's a good chance you might avoid the increase if you can change your operations to make the rate hike unnecessary (e.g., by making your loading dock more efficient, you might be able to avoid unloading charges).

You should empower everybody on your team to ask what they can do to make the partnership work better, Huntley urges, and that openness should extend to the carriers as well. Good communication can lead to opportunities to share ideas and discuss operational challenges.

On the distribution side, you need to look closely at whom you're shipping products to and how often. "When is the last time you looked at your transportation and distribution patterns?" Huntley asks. What mode of transportation do you use most frequently, and can you shift to a less expensive mode while still maintaining service levels? What are your inventory levels compared to your customers' inventory levels? "Do not let your customers use your facilities as a warehouse," he urges. And make sure you measure your costs on a month-to-month as well as a year-to-year basis so you can consistently track how well you're doing.

How to Achieve Sustainable Savings

One popular transportation best practice for shippers is to establish a *core carrier* program, where shippers commit a specified number of loads to a carrier to gain a preferred rate. In some cases, a carrier will also agree to dedicate a certain number of its trucks to one customer. This type of relationship is called a *dedicated carrier* program. While the advantages of these programs seem obvious—shippers have access to what amounts to a private fleet without having to maintain the equipment—the results of these programs have been uneven.

According to consultants Michael DuVall and Mark Beischel with Charter Consulting, "Many shippers watch the savings from these programs deteriorate over time, while others fail to realize any financial benefit at all. Further, few companies see improvement in service levels." There are substantial savings to be had from these programs, the consultants point out, but it requires "a fundamental shift in the way shippers do business with their carriers."[11]

They offer six ways a shipper can gain sustainable savings:

1. *Optimize, don't minimize.* Traditionally, shippers bid out their freight to obtain the lowest possible rate per lane. However, by focusing solely on rates, a shipper is at risk of undervaluing the importance of service and availability as well as precluding any kind of long-term relationship with the carrier. Hidden or unexpected costs, such as service failures, can erase any potential savings gained by going with the lowest rate.
2. *Provide full disclosure to the carrier.* When describing its freight situation, the shipper should include details about inbound freight, backhaul opportunities, long-term growth rates, any anticipated changes to the mix of products, freight density, lane-by-lane volume, and any additional services that may require accessorial charges.
3. *Let the carriers help.* To put it another way, shippers need to recognize that the carrier is going to know best which routes or lanes it can most affordably service and especially which lanes are the most profitable. Shippers should let the carriers identify which lanes they can serve rather than trying to squeeze carriers into taking on business they might be better off not accepting. The goal should be for shippers and carriers

alike to know both the benefits and the associated costs involved at the start of the relationship.

4. *Do the math.* A shipper's goal is to get the lowest cost and the highest quality of service using the fewest number of carriers. That type of complex optimization problem is beyond the capability of spreadsheets and is best accomplished with analytical software capable of running what-if scenarios.

5. *Drive from the top down.* Senior management is in the best position to see the value of a core carrier program, and only the chief executive or chief operating officer can properly balance the needs of the transportation department with the needs of sales, customer service, production, and other key corporate departments. For that reason, the success or failure of freight programs hinges on getting executive-level sponsorship.

6. *Measure everything.* Use a weekly compliance scorecard to keep everyone on the same page. Track whatever cost reductions you achieve. Track new rates against old rates at the new volumes. Track service levels to ensure you're achieving sustainable progress. In short, keep track of everything.

Collaboration Is a Two-Way Street

When analyst firm Aberdeen Group asked 286 companies which transportation best practices had been the most important in driving supply chain improvement, by far the top answer was *collaboration*.[12] Here's a look at the results of Aberdeen's study, indicating how prevalent each best practice is among respondent companies. (Respondents could answer yes to more than one choice.)

- Collaborate with carriers, suppliers, and customers to create more economical transportation processes (88 percent)
- Centralize transportation planning across the company via a load control center (77 percent)
- Reconfigure transportation network to optimize total delivered cost (76 percent)
- Create a more customer-centric transportation process (73 percent)
- Take greater control of inbound freight (69 percent)
- Synchronize activities across corporate functions (66 percent)

Now, collaboration happens to be one of those buzzwords that suggests a high level of *something* is going on, but it's often unclear exactly what that something involves. Let's look at how a couple of companies have demonstrably improved their transportation by working together in a spirit of cooperation—rather than confrontation—with their key supply chain partners. (Collaboration is covered in more depth in Chapter 13.)

PolyOne Corp., a supplier of polymer products, uses a dedicated carrier to ensure that it has sufficient capacity to meet the needs of its customers. With 30 plants and 30 regional warehouses located near its major customers throughout North America, the company used to operate its own private fleet but shifted to a dedicated carrier to better service its regional network. To ensure that it has sufficient capacity to satisfy its customers, PolyOne has not only increased the size of its dedicated fleet but has also significantly increased its use of rail and intermodal transportation. The company also uses transportation brokers for those specific lanes where capacity isn't readily available from its dedicated carrier.

An additional strategy to circumvent capacity challenges is to provide more lead time to the carriers. "We used to give them 24-hour advance notice on pickups," notes Steve Feliccia, PolyOne's director of corporate logistics. "Now we try to provide a minimum of two days' advance notice on all pickups, particularly in those areas where we've historically had trouble."

Until recently, transportation for Cargill Meat Solutions Corp. (CMS), one of the largest beef suppliers in the United States, was provided mainly by the larger-size motor carriers. To improve its availability to capacity whenever it's needed, CMS has supplemented its carrier base with some smaller carriers. Roughly 10 percent of all transportation activity is accomplished by its own in-house carrier, Cargill Meat Logistics Solutions.

"We basically use the carrier for perspective," explains Jon Meier, vice president of transportation and logistics for CMS. "We run it not only to have available and flexible capacity when needed, but also to be able to relate to and occasionally challenge our contract carriers." CMS also has its own in-house brokerage business, which has allowed it to offer backhauls to some of the smaller carriers that might otherwise be stuck with empty trailers on the return trip. "Our goal is to be a preferred shipper for carriers," Meier states. "We are open to collaboration with our customers and carriers and other shippers."[13]

A Carrier by Any Other Name

Choosing the motor carrier that best serves your company's shipping needs is a decision that involves weighing numerous variables. However, you can simplify the process by answering these three questions:

1. Does the carrier have the equipment your company needs?
2. Can the carrier meet your service requirements?
3. How much will it cost?

According to Edward Marien, longtime director of transportation and logistics management programs at the University of Wisconsin–Madison (now retired), it's gotten more difficult for companies to make the right transportation choice because carriers have begun to offer overlapping services. He cites four areas of supplier services:

1. At the most basic level, a motor carrier furnishes its own equipment (i.e., tractors and trailers).
2. Going beyond just providing transportation, many carriers now also offer consulting services, such as shifting the balance of distribution to capitalize on the most efficient routes. (This trend is largely responsible for the terminology shift away from "transportation" providers to "logistics" providers.)
3. Some carriers also function as third-party logistics providers, where they assume many of the traditional management roles companies are outsourcing, such as warehousing. (See Chapter 12.)
4. As technology has increased in importance, some carriers offer their own software solutions, such as transportation management systems.[14]

Automate to Consolidate

Consider how many decisions a supply chain manager has to make regarding the transportation of goods: What modes should we use? What carriers should we hire? What rates should we pay? What paperwork do we have to file? What route should the driver take? Those sorts of questions, and dozens more, have to be answered for every single shipment that leaves a company's loading dock.

For instance, Pella Corp., a manufacturer of windows and doors, faces a constant stream of shipment consolidation challenges. The company utilizes a number of production facilities throughout the United States, and it's not unusual for a customer to request, say, vinyl windows made in one area of the country and a mahogany door made in another. Pella's customers, however, expect the full order to arrive at the same time on a single truck. Since most of Pella's freight is shipped via LTL carriers, delivering the complete shipment to the customer requires a considerable amount of consolidation and deconsolidation planning.

At a Glance

Transportation Management Systems

A transportation management system (TMS) is a software program that automates a company's shipping process, from carrier selection to routing and scheduling.

Pella, like numerous other companies, opted to automate its logistics planning by implementing a transportation management system (TMS). A TMS is a software program that automates many key transportation functions, using analytical capabilities within the software to optimize the best shipping choices, whether they are carrier selection, load building, fleet management, routing and scheduling, or freight audit payment. Although these programs can be expensive—from $50,000 for a stripped-down module to more than $1 million for a best-of-breed implementation—they have become a popular solution for a simple reason: They're designed to help companies cut costs, and the return on investment for a TMS is generally less than a year.

For Pella, adopting a TMS has helped to eliminate inefficiencies that were the result of manual plans, such as the scheduling of LTL carriers arriving at cross-dock facilities, where shipments are moved and consolidated onto other trucks without having to be warehoused. (See Chapter 8.) The TMS automated a process that formerly relied on Pella having to print and fax reports to the individual carriers. "We were able to design an automated solution that keeps our trucks filled and running on schedule, while reducing manual processes in our outbound planning operations," explains Peter Genheimer, Pella's IT supply chain manager. As a lean manufacturer, Pella is particularly resourceful in identifying and then eliminating wasteful processes, and thanks to the TMS, the company is better able to plan out trailer loads, carrier schedules, and network routing.[15]

Consumer products manufacturer Unilever uses a TMS to manage the 50,000 inbound and outbound shipments the company handles every month in the United States. The company is largely driven by promotional activities at retailers, and as Mary Lane, director of transportation for Unilever U.S., explains, "The TMS allows us to more proactively plan for those promotional activities so we can maintain and manage spikes in our business, as opposed to just struggling to gain capacity when all of a sudden something has to ship tomorrow."

Unilever had a six-months-out promotional schedule, but that information wasn't factoring into transportation plans. Using the TMS, the company was able to translate its promotional schedule into a volume-by-lane schedule for its carriers. This allows Unilever to accommodate significant volume increases due to promotions with no decrease in delivery performance because the company is now able to provide advance notice to the carriers. As Lane explains, not only is Unilever able to measure its on-time availability for its customers, but it's also been able to shift freight from LTL to the less expensive truckload mode.[16]

Get It There on Time

In the final analysis, what matters most to your customers is not what technology you use, what kind of vehicle the products are being transported in, or what route a driver took to reach the final destination. For your customers, transportation rule number one is: Get it there on time. Based on analysis conducted by Aberdeen Group, best-in-class companies have an on-time delivery rate of 96.6 percent or greater. Average companies, by contrast, are on time 90.8 percent of the time, while those Aberdeen describes as laggards have only an 83 percent rate. In terms of dollars and cents, laggard companies are continually compensating for their delivery inefficiencies by resorting to costly expedited service. There's something wrong with that picture when a company spends more but consistently delivers less. Best-in-class companies, however, use expedited service only 2.9 percent of the time.

"The automation of processes and visibility has enabled transportation managers to better plan for and adjust their shipping decisions on a daily basis, helping them find the most cost-effective options for them and their customers," points out Brad Wyland, senior research analyst with Aberdeen Group. By focusing on collaboration and visibility across internal and external departments, he notes, companies can overcome the rising costs in fuel and other shipping costs.[17]

CHAPTER 8

Distribution and Warehousing
Going with the Flow

Flashpoints

Cross-docking offers a replenishment strategy aimed at moving products as quickly as possible.

Knowing how much inventory you need is important, but equally important is knowing where that inventory is.

Warehouse management isn't so much about space as it is about how to use that space effectively.

Know your warehousing situation and know your capabilities.

Warehousing is one of the core functions of logistics, and yet more often than not, it tends to be the forgotten stepchild in a company's supply chain. In the Supply Chain Operations Reference (SCOR) model of plan, source, make, deliver, and return, warehousing is implicit in sourcing (after you've purchased the products, you have to store them somewhere), delivering (products loaded onto a truck had to have been stored somewhere first), and returns, which encompasses the reverse logistics process (see Chapter 11). And yet 70 percent of North American companies outsource at least some of their warehousing to a third party,[1] a clear indication that they do not consider warehouse management to be one of their core competencies.

Conversely, the biggest company in the world—retail giant Wal-Mart Stores Inc.—built its discount empire largely on the efficiency of its distribution network. By strategically locating regional distribution centers (DCs) in close proximity to its stores, Wal-Mart broke with the long-standing retail tradition of maintaining just one or two DCs to serve the entire United States. As a retailer that got its start by opening stores in small, rural towns and offering a tremendous assortment of products for the lowest possible price, Wal-Mart found that transportation and replenishment were too expensive and too time consuming under the traditional retail plan. Thus necessity begot the concept of strategically locating warehouses to provide more timely and economical inventory replenishment. As a result, Wal-Mart could keep its shelves stocked more often, because each of its stores was being serviced more frequently than its competitors. More products on the shelves translates to happier customers, and the rest is retail history.

Just ask Sears, Roebuck & Co. Having watched Wal-Mart come out of nowhere to overtake Sears as the nation's dominant retailer, Sears borrowed a page from Wal-Mart's book and began focusing on replenishing its inventory as quickly as possible. "If you can't manage transit moves predictably, you will tend to buy more inventory than you need," observes Bill Kenney, Sears's vice president of logistics planning and productivity.[2]

Sears stocks three basic types of products, Kenney explains: seasonal products, such as snowblowers and lawn mowers; fast-moving, perennial best sellers that have to be replenished rapidly, like home improvement products; and slower-moving products that need to be moved to stores as economically as possible. Sears also makes 6 million deliveries directly to customers' homes every year, particularly for big-ticket items like washing machines, refrigerators, and treadmills. The retailer ships full truckloads from its suppliers to direct delivery centers, and wherever it can Sears utilizes a strategy that has changed the entire nature of distribution—*cross-docking*.[3]

Virtual Inventory

In cross-docking, inbound products are unloaded at a distribution center, sorted by destination, and then reloaded onto trucks. The goods are never actually warehoused at all—they're just moved across the dock (hence the name). This strategy allows a retailer like Sears to unload, say, a truckload of high-definition TVs at a regional DC and then load a single TV onto different trucks headed for different retail stores. Cross-docking has lately developed into a best practice for manufacturers, too, thanks to the needs of companies to consolidate and reduce their inventory as much as possible.

Over the past two decades, 66 percent of the cash-to-cash improvements throughout all industry sectors have come from reductions in days of inventory, notes Ted Farris, a professor with the University of North Texas, and he credits cross-docking for some of those reductions. According to Farris, the cash-to-cash formula adds accounts receivable to inventory and then subtracts accounts payable:

accounts receivable + inventory − accounts payable = cash to cash

So if companies are using cross-docking to reduce how much inventory they're holding, that's good. However, if they're only shifting inventories within the company and holding them elsewhere, that's not so good because there's no change in the cash-to-cash cycle, Farris points out. Since the inventory hasn't been sold, it's still considered accounts payable.[4]

"Most people define cross-docking as the process of rehandling freight from inbound trucks and loading it into outbound vehicles," notes Ken Ackerman, principal of warehouse consulting firm Kenneth B. Ackerman Company, but there can be more to it than that. For instance, some of the merchandise for the outbound loads may already be stored in the DC, he points out. "In other cases, merchandise from a truck that arrived a few days ago is held in a staging area until the complete mix is available to fill an outbound order." Some cross-docking facilities are designed with a large storage area and a cross-dock staging area because their requirements involve withdrawing product from storage as well as rehandling inbound freight.[5]

So the key is to use cross-docking strategically. Sears, for example, positions its inventory in four regional warehouses so it can cross-dock and provide next-day service to customers. Geographic postponement coupled with cross-docking can eliminate the need to have product inventory at all locations, Farris notes.[6]

Here's how cross-docking works, as described by warehousing expert James Tompkins, president of Tompkins Associates:

- The supplier is notified of the shipping time, date, carrier, stock-keeping units (SKUs), and quantity for each order.
- The supplier is notified by the carrier of the arrival date and time for each shipment.
- The supplier receives the order details from the customer.
- The outbound carrier is notified of the pickup time, load description, destination, and delivery date and time.
- The customer is notified of shipment detail, carrier, and arrival date and time.
- A dock location is selected for trucks involved in receiving and shipping.
- Labor and handling equipment are scheduled.
- Receipts are recorded and reconciled, and any receiving variances are noted.
- Labels are created, and cases and pallets are routed and tracked from receiving to dispatch.

Given all these steps, it's very important that a company collects performance measures on carriers and warehouse operations.[7]

Cross-Docking, Compliance, and Collaboration

At semiconductor manufacturer National Semiconductor, cross-docking has taken an entire day of cycle time out of the logistics process, which has improved the company's flexibility. If product is ready to ship much earlier than the customer needs it, National can opt for slower (i.e., less expensive) transportation, explains Larry Stroud, the company's manager of global logistics. If the product needs to arrive sooner, Stroud will spend a little more for faster transportation.[8]

National produces 5 billion chips every year from two plants in Singapore and Malaysia and ships them direct to 4,000 customer locations worldwide from a single DC in Singapore, managed by a third-party logistics provider (3PL). Having its inventory in one facility gives National a tremendous advantage from an inventory standpoint, Stroud says, because it allows the company to systematically look at orders worldwide.

When chips destined for a specific customer leave the manufacturing floor, National sends the DC an electronic advance ship notice with multiple orders to multiple customers. The DC then combines cross-dock orders with orders filled from inventory, which allows it to consolidate shipments to a region. This not only lowers shipping costs but also reduces the amount of time it takes to clear Customs, which is largely how National achieved a one-day reduction in its transit time.

Cross-docking tends to work most effectively with companies that have strong compliance programs with their suppliers and ship to their own DCs or retail stores, says Dave Gealy, a consultant with Forte Industries. "Retailers do it best," he observes, "because their vendor compliance programs give more control and visibility into what's coming into their systems, and they control their own stores." Unless your company is a Fortune 100 giant, it can be difficult to set up compliance programs with all of your suppliers. That calls for a close spirit of collaboration so that when information is exchanged, the suppliers will understand what the client wants to order and the receiver will be able to see what's being sent.

At a Glance

Cross-Docking

Cross-docking is the distribution process of rehandling freight from inbound trucks and loading it onto outbound trucks, without first storing the freight.

Cross-docking is directly related to timing, Gealy explains. You need to be able to receive and ship products with just a few touches in a limited time. It's also important to be able to quickly inspect inbound goods, which means a strong quality control program is essential. "If you experience a high level of rejects and don't detect them, you could end up with inferior product downstream," notes Jerry Vink, Gealy's colleague at Forte Industries. "Strong vendors who consistently produce quality product are good candidates for cross-docking."

On the issue of product quality, coffee and baked goods restaurant chain Dunkin Donuts uses a cross-dock facility to minimize incidents of product damage. At 300,000 square feet, the facility is more than twice the size of the previous building (125,000 square feet), and features dedicated picking and receiving areas to separate the functions, explains Warren Engard, director of distribution operations. The product flows keep lift truck traffic away from pick traffic, reducing congestion. "There is no forklift traffic by the pickers and no pickers in the forklift traffic aisles," he says. Coupled with the implementation of voice recognition technology (see the section titled "Can You Hear Me Now?"), moving to a cross-dock facility has led to a decrease in goods damage of 80 percent.[9]

How do you know if cross-docking is a good strategy for your distribution operations? According to a study conducted by Saddle Creek Corp., 48 percent of respondents are cross-docking durable goods, followed by high-value products (25 percent), nondurable goods (19 percent), and perishable goods (17 percent). Tom Patterson, senior vice president at Saddle Creek, says that cross-docking is worth considering if:

- Your traditional distribution methods and current order cycles are not sufficient to handle customer needs.
- Your distribution network is outdated and inefficient, leading to extended cycle times and compromised shelf-life guarantees.
- Your transportation networks are overextended, negatively affecting your on-time delivery performance and requiring excessive reliance on expedited service.
- Your distribution costs are increasing faster than your sales growth.[10]

Handle with Care

Warehouse management isn't exactly a recent phenomenon. Some say the practice dates back at least to the fifteenth century B.C. when Hebrew patriarch Joseph (the one with the many-colored coat) pioneered the use of grain warehouses to stave off famine in Egypt. Commercial warehousing can be traced back at least to fourteenth-century Venice, and cross-docking has its roots in nineteenth-century transit sheds. So while the idea of warehousing may not be quite as old as Methuselah, it's pretty close.[11]

Nevertheless, in today's world, thanks to the insistence by customers on perfect orders, just-in-time delivery, quick response, and fully integrated supply chain processes, "the role and mission of warehouse operations are changing and will continue to change dramatically," observes warehousing expert Ed Frazelle, founding director of the Supply Chain & Logistics Institute at Georgia Tech. Companies are being pushed to minimize their inventories, which severely reduces the margin for error in their supply chains. As a result, Frazelle notes, "the accuracy and cycle time performance pressures in warehousing are immense."[12]

Companies are being pushed in opposite directions simultaneously, as market pressures demand they increase warehouse productivity while employing fewer workers. More often than not, the solution to that operational tug-of-war involves the use of material handling technology (increasingly, a combination of hardware and software) within a company's warehouse operations. Material handling, as defined by the Material Handling Industry of America trade association (www.mhia.org), encompasses "the movement, storage, control, and protection of materials, goods, and products throughout the process of manufacturing, distribution, consumption, and disposal. The focus is on the methods, mechanical equipment, systems, and related controls used to achieve these functions."

Material handling equipment includes powered vehicles, such as lift trucks and automated guided vehicles; conveyors and sortation systems; automatic identification (including radio frequency identification, or RFID) and data collection systems; lifting, positioning, and overhead handling equipment (including robots); automated storage and retrieval systems; order picking equipment; and packaging and shipping materials. This equipment is used in support of the eight main warehousing functions, as described by Frazelle:

1. *Receiving* happens when materials enter the warehouse, are verified as to the quantity and quality of these materials, and are disbursed.
2. *Prepackaging* occurs when products are received in bulk and are subsequently packaged in specific quantities.
3. *Putaway* involves the placing of materials in storage.
4. *Storage* refers to the physical containment of materials.
5. *Order picking* is the act of removing items from storage to meet a specific demand, whether for production or to satisfy customer requests.
6. *Packaging* is the step where individual items or assortments are containerized for more convenient use.

7. *Sortation* refers to the process of collecting picks into individual orders.

8. *Unitizing* and *shipping* encompass the preparation and packaging of orders into shipping containers, preparing shipping documents, weighing shipments, and loading outbound trucks.[13]

Where the Rubber Meets the Load

The focus of any distribution operation is inventory, but that's about the only thing that all companies will agree on. When it comes to inventory, how much a company should carry changes according to the time of year, the industry a company is in, the corporate philosophy of senior management, the flexibility of its suppliers, and, most especially, the demands of its customers. No company wants to be caught short, but sometimes having too much inventory can be just as bad as not having enough. The short answer, then, to the question of how much inventory a company should carry is: It depends.

Knowing how much inventory your company needs is important, but equally important is knowing where that inventory is at any given time. The role of tracking product location within a warehouse is typically assigned to a warehouse management system (WMS), a software application that interfaces with supply chain planning, order management, enterprise resource planning (ERP), and transportation management systems, and can track the whereabouts of a company's products by purchase order, bar code, lot number, pallet location, or other identification system. Thanks to the rapid adoption rate of RFID tags, urged on manufacturers by Wal-Mart, other large retailers, and the U.S. Department of Defense, companies can already track at least some products in real time. (RFID is described in detail in Chapter 15.) The end goal is being able to know exactly when and where those products were manufactured, packaged, and shipped.

At a Glance

Warehouse Management System

A warehouse management system (WMS) controls, manages, and regulates the movement of goods within a warehouse or distribution center. Typical features of a WMS include inventory management, picking and putaway, order visibility, and fulfillment.

Del-Nat Tire Corp., a distributor of private-brand tires, maintains a daily inventory of nearly 700,000 tires in its DC, and although the company is an expert at selling and marketing tires, keeping track of its inventory had been a constant challenge. Although Del-Nat handles roughly 2,000 SKUs, every one of those tires looks pretty much the same, explains Glen Tosco, the company's manager of information technology. "Finding lost tires in a warehouse that encompasses 500,000 square feet is not easy. If five tires go missing, they're gone."[14]

The problem for Del-Nat was that, even though each tire had its own unique bar code, the company's processes made it possible for a tire to be put on the wrong stack after it had been bar-coded. It became something of a logistical nightmare to try to identify which black tire in a 30-foot-high rack of black tires didn't belong there. For Del-Nat, like many other companies with large distribution operations, part of the answer was to phase out its paper-based inventory system in favor of a WMS solution integrated with handheld bar code scanners.

Del-Nat can now enter an order directly into its ERP system, which will send that order to the warehouse floor for picking and shipping, Tosco explains. "When the order is picked, shipping is acknowledged, and the order is automatically invoiced to the customer." Order pickers on the warehouse floor use the bar code scanners to check each rack location and to verify each tire they pick. The scanner tells the order picker exactly which dock door to use for that order. (Del-Nat has 68 dock doors.) The tires are dropped in a loading queue at the dock door and are scanned again as they are loaded into a trailer.

Automating its DC has helped Del-Nat improve its order fulfillment speed by 35 percent. What that means is, a warehouse worker can now do in 6 hours what used to take 10 hours using the old paper-based system. "We've reduced overall expenses and reduced one whole shift, plus six people from two other shifts," Tosco explains.

That kind of labor savings is typical of companies that have adopted a WMS, observes warehousing expert Ken Ackerman, as the typical range of savings is between 20 and 40 percent. Space utilization should typically be 10 to 20 percent more efficient when using a WMS, inventory should drop by 50 percent after about three years, and the costs of conducting a physical inventory check should be reduced by 75 percent.[15]

Can You Hear Me Now?

When it comes to having the right products in front of customers at the right time, food distributors have almost no margin of error. Delivering the right orders 95 percent of the time is nowhere near good enough anymore.

"We have restaurant customers who are ordering in the morning for products on their menu in the evening," observes Steve Fasulka, a warehouse manager with U.S. Foodservice, a wholesale distributor to such restaurant chains as Chili's, Damon's, and Pizzeria Uno, "so there's a sense of urgency to make sure the orders are picked, delivered, and received properly." The company operates more than 82 DCs throughout the United States and offers 43,000 products. With such an extensive product line, picking the wrong products or coming up short was a problem U.S. Foodservice could not afford to have.[16]

The distributor adopted an increasingly popular distribution best practice: *voice recognition technology.* "The simplest way to describe a voice recognition device is to compare it to a traditional handheld computer," explains consultant Patti Satterfield. "Rather than reading a display, the operator hears the instructions. Rather than keying or scanning in a response, the worker speaks back." A radio frequency network handles the voice device as it would any other radio frequency-equipped portable computer. A company's WMS software takes in the data from the voice terminal as if it were entered via a handheld scanner or keyboard.[17]

For U.S. Foodservice, voice recognition is a strategy that paid off quickly with a 75 percent reduction in mispicks. Warehouse workers now wear wireless voice-powered computers that let them hear their directions instead of having to read them off a pick list. "The voice system directs you to the location," Fasulka explains. "When you arrive at the location, you're required to voice input the proper check code. If you don't, you can't proceed from there. You have to be at the correct physical location to move on with the system."

Previously, selectors occasionally might pick from a top level instead of a bottom level, or would pick to the left or to the right of the correct location, and sometimes even pick the same bay number in a different aisle, Fasulka remembers. "Because the voice system is focusing the selectors on one specific location which has a random three-digit check code, they're being directed exactly to the slot."

The order selectors initially resisted using the voice systems, Fasulka admits, but after training them on the technology and exposing them to the benefits of improved accuracy, the selectors discovered that using voice recognition helped improve their productivity. From the vantage point of the selectors, voice systems have become a best practice for a very practical reason: 30 percent of their pay is incentive based, so the technology is putting more money into their pockets. "Today, they would not pick orders without the voice systems," Fasulka says.

Wireless in the Warehouse

Warehouses are increasingly going the wireless route, which in addition to voice systems includes RFID, handheld devices, global positioning systems, geofencing, wireless networking, and other solutions that facilitate real-time access to inventory data. According to analyst firm Aberdeen Group, 75 percent of the companies identified as best-in-class use real-time mobile devices to process transactions.[18]

For instance, Ace Beverage Co., a major beer distributor for Anheuser-Busch, has a wireless data system that communicates real-time delivery data throughout the day. This system has greatly improved delivery efficiency, helping the distributor to eliminate 15 to 20 hours per week that it used to spend on driver and loading dock worker overtime. Thanks to the wireless system, when retail orders are in-house by 2 P.M., Ace Beverage starts loading the trucks according to scheduled stops, gaining a big jump on the loading process, explains Mike Krohn, the company's vice president of finance and administration. "We can start preparing loads early by picking the products from the warehouse inventory and staging them without loading them onto the trucks."[19]

Twinlab Corp., a manufacturer of nutritional supplements, uses a wireless data collection system as a complement to its ERP system and in the process has gained greater visibility across its entire enterprise. Warehouse workers can send product data, such as lot numbers, quantities, and item weights, to the ERP system via a handheld scanning device. The wireless technology has contributed to a 25 percent gain in resource management throughout the warehouse.[20]

Turn, Turn, Turn

Accuracy is extremely important within a DC, but for retailers it's just as important to move products out to the individual stores. Grocery store chains, for instance, measure lead time from a DC to individual stores in hours rather than days. "Some stores receive goods in 12 hours or less," explains Bill Parry, vice president of logistics with grocery retailer Giant Eagle. "All stores receive deliveries in a day or less." That's possible, Parry notes, because the retailer is able to provide its suppliers with better and more timely information through use of an electronic data interchange (EDI) system as well as a Web-based transportation management system (TMS).

Giant Eagle uses the TMS to automate and improve its processes for inbound transportation by providing the retailer, as well as its suppliers, with increased visibility to where its suppliers' trucks are and how soon they'll arrive. "Our goal was to see how reducing lead time affects inventory," Parry explains. "Once we have lead time where we want it, we can attack safety stock in the DCs. We've had success in frozen foods, with a substantial increase in turns, and we were able to reduce use of outside storage," he notes.

Working with a group of key suppliers, Giant Eagle has reduced the supplier-to-DC process from more than a week down to two or three days, but the retailer isn't sitting on its laurels; it hopes to get the lead time down to one day. Where it pays off is in *turns*, which is the average number of times a product is sold and replenished in a year. The retailer's turns with a large dogfood vendor's products, for example, have increased from 19.8 to 31.7 at 99 percent service level, according to Parry, while lead time has been reduced from eight days to four. And in retail, product turns is what the business is all about.[21]

Half Full or Half Empty?

When the Logistics Institute at Georgia Tech asked 200 warehouse managers what they would change about their facilities, 58 percent said they would add more dock doors, 31 percent said they would raise the ceiling height, 30 percent said they would make the building deeper, and 25 percent said they would make the building longer. Two-thirds of the managers in the study are in charge of warehouses smaller than 100,000 square feet, and according to Georgia Tech, the overall average size of a DC is 150,000 square feet. So clearly, if money was no object, most warehouse managers would opt to be in charge of a bigger facility. But bigger isn't necessarily better, especially if your problem isn't space but how to effectively use that space.[22]

"Few people know when their warehouse is full," Ken Ackerman observes. "In most operations, you can create a formula to reveal the percentage of space used in the warehouse." For instance, Lenox, a fast-growing, direct-to-consumer supplier of fine china and kitchenware, found that it could improve its distribution productivity without having to build another warehouse. Lenox didn't want to be undone by expanding too quickly to accommodate a higher volume of business, but on first glance, it didn't seem like it had any other choice.[23]

"We were growing at such a great rate we knew we could not continue to handle our holiday season requirements," admits Greg Petro, Lenox's director of distribution and facilities. The company seemingly had used up every square inch of available storage space and could accommodate no more than 2,100 SKUs in its pick areas, many of which served separate and disconnected channels. That's when Lenox decided it was time to look closely at its entire operation.

"We had to manually combine orders that crossed channels," Petro says. It used to take two shifts to ship 28,000 packages per day during the peak holiday season. By investing in a new WMS and an automated conveyor that could move orders automatically throughout the DC, Lenox was able to handle 17 percent more volume with 5 percent less labor. The company can now accommodate 4,500 SKUs throughout all of its channels and can process 35,000 packages per day with just one shift, Petro notes.

What is Lenox doing differently? "We scan bar codes that signal the conveyor system to send orders to the appropriate pick zones, including specialized areas such as gift wrapping," Petro explains. Fully 50 percent of its active warehouse is dedicated to pick, pack, and ship activities. The fastest-moving products are now replenished from a high-bay, narrow-aisle storage facility located six miles down the road, where the operation costs are much lower than at the active facility.

What it took to get the transformation under way was Lenox's acknowledgment that it had to improve its distribution processes if it wanted to support its business growth. "We knew we would not be successful if we didn't improve," says Petro. "We were shipping 75 percent of orders next day. Now, even in peak season, we ship 95 to 99 percent of orders the same day."

How to Better Manage Your Warehouse

Lenox's experiences illustrate the main principle that drives distribution best practices: Know your situation and know your capabilities. You don't necessarily need a new warehouse to handle increased business, and while Lenox took a technological route to increasing productivity, it's quite possible that better processes are the answer, not newer systems. "Look at your entire business as you search for solutions," suggests Terry Harris, managing partner with supply chain consulting firm Chicago Consulting. If you make changes in one area, it will affect other areas.[24]

Following are several best practices that companies have taken to maximize the productivity of their distribution facilities that go well beyond a throw-money-at-it-and-pray strategy:

- *Reduce your inventory*. Run as lean an operation as possible. In particular, eliminate all the obsolete products in your warehouse, the so-called dead inventory that your finance department has resisted writing off because it assumes storage is free. Work more closely with your suppliers to time the receipt of goods as closely as possible to the time of use.
- *Be selective in what you stock and where you stock it*. Examine your order pattern to determine which are your fastest-moving products, and then keep them at the front of the warehouse. If you use both regional and central DCs, keep the most expensive items upstream to avoid having to move that expensive inventory.
- *Add hours or shifts*. Sometimes even the best technology and processes aren't enough to satisfy customer demand, particularly during peak

season. In these situations, many companies opt to increase throughput by increasing hours of operation. While your labor costs will increase, you'll gain in the short term by not having to invest in capital equipment. As a long-term strategy, however, you'll have to determine if running an extra shift year-round is more cost-effective than investing in technology.

■ *Clear the dock area.* Sometimes the best solution is also the easiest: Insist that every incoming truck have an appointment, so that every dock door is run off a firm schedule. The more predictable your operation, the more efficient will be the flow-through. Consider *drop-and-hook* for truckload deliveries, where an inbound trailer is unhooked and dropped off in the yard, brought via a jockey truck to the dock for unloading, and then returned to the yard. In any event, ask yourself how much staging you really have to do. You'll hear all sorts of reasons and excuses why somebody can't take a load off the truck and put it straight into a stack without ever putting it down, notes Ken Ackerman, but those reasons are no longer valid.[25]

■ *Bypass the DC entirely.* This strategy, known as *predistribution management* or more colloquially as the *DC bypass*, aims at delivering products directly to retail stores or the point of consumption rather than to a warehouse. The greatest benefit here is timeliness.

■ *Outsource your warehousing to a third-party logistics provider.* Before you consider hiring a 3PL to take over the bulk of your distribution processes, it's vital that you first analyze your specific needs and determine if your company will be better served by letting a specialist run your warehouse. (See Chapter 12.)

CHAPTER 9

Site Selection

Location, Location, Location

Flashpoints

A best-in-class distribution network delivers on customer demands while keeping costs in line.

It takes collaboration across the entire supply chain to design the optimum distribution network to bring a product to market.

All logistics is local.

The ultimate goal of a distribution network plan is a supply chain properly balanced between inventory, transportation, and manufacturing.

On-time delivery is a fundamental premise behind supply chain management, and it's a key benchmark on the road to achieving the perfect order. Although same-day delivery is available from many logistics providers, any company relying on the fastest and most expensive transportation options to fulfill its delivery obligations isn't going to be in business very long. The old adage "Build a better mousetrap and the world will beat a path to your door" is now hopelessly out of date. It's no longer good enough to build that better mousetrap—you also have to build a better distribution network from which you can optimally service your customers. According to a study undertaken by consulting firm ProLogis Global Solutions, the number-one challenge for supply chain professionals is to create a distribution network that can deliver on customer demands while still keeping costs in line.[1]

High-tech manufacturer Hewlett-Packard Co. (HP) operates one of the largest supply chains in the world as well as one of the most sophisticated distribution networks. Its 88 distribution hubs serve more than 1 billion customers worldwide, in 178 countries. HP's supply chain also includes 32 manufacturing plants, 700 suppliers, and 119 logistics partners, and all told the supply chain group manages $51 billion—or 64 percent—of the company's total spend.

The company credits much of its success to its adaptive supply chain—a product-agnostic supply chain portfolio that allows multiple supply chains. After direct materials, logistics is the company's main cost driver, according to Robert Gifford, HP's vice president of worldwide logistics and program management. It is "an absolute necessity to consider logistics activity" when deciding where to source products and where to build factories, he emphasizes.

"We don't just say 'We're going to put up a factory here,' and then figure out how we'll move product," Gifford notes. Instead, HP relies on collaboration across its entire supply chain to design the optimum distribution network to bring a given product to a specific marketplace.[2]

Where once upon a time HP, like other high-tech companies, relied on design for manufacturability strategies to build products as efficiently and inexpensively as possible, the company recently has adopted a best practice known as *design for supply chain*. This relatively new concept looks at all of the costs throughout a product's life cycle, even past the point of its functional use. By its very nature, design for supply chain requires the involvement of multiple departments when a product is being designed.

"Design for supply chain includes not only research and development type people but also people involved with logistics and packaging, and people who are focused on the environment," explains Greg Shoemaker, HP's vice president of central direct procurement. "When we design for logistics enhancements, for instance, we make sure we've got the right size box that'll fit on the right size pallet to optimize our shipping costs. When we design for tax and duty reduction, we may manufacture in certain places in the world in order to reduce our taxes or duty."[3]

The applications of design for supply chain are seemingly limited only by a company's imagination as well as its ability to pull together disparate functions effectively. Design for postponement, which is popular with the apparel industry as well as high-tech companies, allows a company to wait until the last minute to finish making a product, pushing off configuration or a value-added feature until the product is as close as possible to the end customer.[4] HP also engages in design for commonality and reuse, which involves using similar or identical components in different products. HP's designs for take-back and recycling efforts are supplemented by its own recycling operation plant, which has recycled more than 4 million pounds of computer hardware.

"What we're really working on and making a lot of progress in is making sure that the development teams get a good view and understanding of all the supply chain variables that can be affected by their design, depending on what the particular sourcing strategy is," Shoemaker explains. "So we try to identify all those needs up front, even where the product is going to be manufactured, so that the designers can spend a good amount of quality time creating the best package."

Striking the Proper Balance

A well-run supply chain depends on having a streamlined distribution network to receive raw materials and deliver product to the end user, and that network needs to use the least number of intermediate steps possible. Developing such a network where total system-wide costs are minimized while system-wide service levels are maintained involves studying and weighing numerous factors. The ultimate goal of this network planning is a supply chain that is properly balanced among the competing considerations of inventory, transportation, and manufacturing.[5]

"The objective of strategic distribution network planning," according to Dale Harmelink, a partner with supply chain consulting firm Tompkins Associates, "is to come up with the most economical way to ship and receive products while maintaining or increasing customer satisfaction requirements; simply put, a plan to maximize profits and optimize service."[6]

At a Glance

Distribution Network Planning

Distribution network planning determines how many warehouses or distribution centers a company requires to satisfy its customer base, as well as where those warehouses should be located.

A distribution network plan, Harmelink suggests, should answer these nine questions:

1. How many distribution centers (DCs) do you need?
2. Where should the DCs be located?
3. How much inventory should be stocked at each DC?

4. Which customers should be serviced by each DC?
5. How should customers order from the DC?
6. How should the DCs order from suppliers?
7. How often should shipments be made to each customer?
8. What should the service levels be?
9. Which transportation methods should be used?

Depending on the market needs of a company and its overall supply chain mission, the answer to question 1 may necessitate adding one or more DCs to the network, or conversely, it may require consolidating several DCs into a single regional distribution hub.

A Site for Sore Eyes

When you get right down to it, all logistics (like all politics) is local. HP, as noted earlier, maintains 88 distribution hubs throughout the world. IBM Corp. has at least one major logistics site on every continent in the world except for Africa, and 28 in all. The Gillette Co. has four distribution centers in the United States and 60 total worldwide. In the United States alone, retail behemoth Wal-Mart has 128 distribution centers strategically located in 38 states.

And yet there's a feeling that the site selection process is more art than science, more luck than strategy. Determining exactly where in the United States a company should locate its logistics and distribution centers requires a study of many factors beyond just transportation costs (although transportation is a major factor in the decision).

To provide a consistent set of metrics, *Expansion Management*, a magazine that specializes in site selection, teamed up with *Logistics Today* (one of the author's publications) to produce the Logistics Quotient—a tool that offers an objective ranking of the 362 major U.S. cities (i.e., metropolitan statistical areas, as defined by the U.S. Office of Management and Budget). Based on research conducted by various government agencies, such as the Bureau of Transportation Statistics, the Logistics Quotient offers a look at each city's proficiency in 10 categories that, taken as a whole, illustrate a city's overall logistics friendliness:

1. The *transportation and warehousing industry* ranking is based on the number of businesses and the employment base within a city that provide transportation, distribution, warehousing, and related services.
2. The *workforce and labor* ranking is geared to existing and available logistics-related workers in the area as well as their average salary.

3. *Road infrastructure* measures factors like available lane miles per capita, interstate highway access, miles of paved roads, and average daily traffic per freeway lane.
4. *Road congestion* ranks a city on traffic volume and delays as well as accident statistics and other factors affecting the smooth flow of traffic.
5. *Road and bridge condition* looks at the percentage of bridges that are functionally obsolete or structurally deficient.
6. The *interstate highways* metric rates a city's access to interstate highways as well as the number of auxiliary interstate routes.
7. The *taxes and fees* ranking provides a measure of logistics-related costs, including truck user fees and motor fuel excise taxes.
8. *Railroad service* is determined by the number of rail carriers serving a metro area.
9. *Waterborne cargo service* includes ocean port capacity as well as inland waterways.
10. *Air cargo service* includes the number of air courier companies and the total air cargo tonnage for a metro area.

The 10 most logistics-friendly cities in the United States, based on the Logistics Quotient's 2007 rankings, are:

1. Atlanta, Georgia
2. Kansas City, Missouri/Kansas City, Kansas
3. St. Louis, Missouri
4. Dallas-Fort Worth, Texas
5. Houston, Texas
6. Cincinnati, Ohio
7. Louisville, Kentucky
8. Cleveland, Ohio
9. Chicago, Illinois
10. New Orleans, Louisiana[7]

Finding the Right Place

The Logistics Quotient was designed to help companies find the right city or region for their distribution needs. Because virtually every company uses motor carriers at some point in its distribution network, access to good roads is an important factor, but it's not the *only* factor. The city of Memphis, Tennessee, for instance, was ranked at number one (the highest rating) for air cargo service in the 2007 study, which is not too surprising given the city is the headquarters and main hub for FedEx. Similarly, Chicago, the traditional hub of the nation's rail system, ranks at the top of the Logistics Quotient's ranking for railroad service.

Memphis scores poorly in road infrastructure, however, while it's strictly middle of the pack in such categories as workforce and taxes and fees. Chicago, meanwhile, is near the very bottom of the rankings for road infrastructure.

In a study from 2005, the city of Trenton, New Jersey, was ranked at number one for road infrastructure, which is a reflection of the city's proximity to major highways and turnpikes. Trenton is also strategically sandwiched between two major metropolises—Philadelphia, Pennsylvania, and New York, New York. However, the condition of its roads is not very good at all, and in fact Trenton ranked almost dead last in that category. Taking a look at some of the other categories, we find that Trenton had a good score for taxes and fees and a fair-to-middling ranking for rail access and transportation and warehousing industry (number 154). All things considered, Trenton finished just inside the top 20 percent nationally.[8]

But because most site selection decisions focus on a region of the United States rather than the entire country, it's also helpful to identify how well a city does compared to other cities within the same region. In that same 2005 study, Trenton ranked as the fifteenth most logistics-friendly city within the U.S. Northeast. The condition of its roads is far less of a factor for companies with supply chains in the Northeast because, frankly, none of the roads in that part of the country are in very good shape, relatively speaking. The one-two punch of congestion and Mother Nature accounts for the perpetual epidemic of orange cones on highways in the Northeast. As a result, road condition is almost a nonfactor for companies making site selection decisions centered on the Northeast.

Chicago Consulting undertook a study to determine the best warehouse networks in the United States, with best indicating the lowest possible transit lead times to customers, based on population patterns. Using that criterion, the best place for a company managing one distribution center would be Bloomington, Indiana. The average distance to a customer would be 803 miles, with an average transit time of 2.28 days. For a company operating two DCs, the optimum locations would be Ashland, Kentucky, and Palmdale, California.[9]

According to Terry Harris, managing partner of Chicago Consulting, cost and service are the most important criteria when it comes to designing a warehouse network. Other relevant issues include highway infrastructure, real estate issues, labor climate, and carbon footprint concerns. (The topic of green supply chains is examined in Chapter 16.)

A Look at Gillette's Distribution Network

When The Gillette Co., a manufacturer of personal care products, batteries, and other consumer packaged goods, launched its North American Network

Study, the goal was straightforward: Identify the best distribution network that would allow the company to deliver excellent customer service at the least cost. As solutions manager for the company, Louise Knabe's job was to figure out how many DCs Gillette should have and where they should be. Least cost was an important consideration, Knabe points out, because if Gillette's goal had been simply to provide the best possible customer service, the network study could well have suggested putting a distribution center in every state.

"From a logistics and distribution perspective, Gillette measures customer service by order cycle time (time from when the customer places the order until they receive the order) and on-time delivery performance (percentage of shipments that arrive on time)," Knabe explains. "The strategic DC network design affects the order cycle time because the location of the DCs affects the transit time to the customer."[10]

At the time of the network study (2002), Gillette had two DCs located on the East Coast, one near Boston, Massachusetts, and the other near Chattanooga, Tennessee. The Tennessee warehouse stocked only Duracell batteries, while the Massachusetts warehouse stocked everything else. Neither warehouse carried all of Gillette's products. Why was this a problem? "Our project analysis revealed that this situation made it difficult to deliver top-quality customer service," Knabe points out. "Let's say I was a customer based in Virginia. That meant I was getting a shipment from Tennessee of batteries and shipments from Massachusetts of everything else. So I've got two trucks showing up with Gillette products on it, which was a bit of a nuisance."

The bigger issue for Gillette, though, was that because neither warehouse had all of the company's products, many customer shipments had to be delivered by less-than-truckload (LTL) carriers, a more expensive transportation mode than truckload. The transit times were longer and the reliability was lower than it would have been if Gillette had been able to get all products loaded onto the same truck. Gillette concluded that in order to deliver top-quality service, it needed to find a way to convert as many of those LTL shipments into full truckload as possible.

That's when Gillette got to work on its site selection best practices, with the goal of developing a network that would locate the DCs close to the customer and make it possible to regularly ship by truckload.

Cost versus Service

To answer the questions of how many warehouses it needed and where they should be, Gillette conducted a complete theoretical analysis to identify the best locations. The company factored in such considerations as the location of its manufacturing plants and its sourcing points. Equally important, Gillette looked at where its customers were located, and specifically at who ordered what, and in what volume. "You take those two things and then ask: How do I marry them up and how do I figure out where my warehouses should be?" Knabe says.

"In terms of distribution cost, we looked at the freight cost of going from the plant to the warehouse, and then we also looked at the freight cost of going from the warehouse to the customer," she explains. Using an optimization software tool to evaluate every possible scenario, Gillette asked questions such as: If we had three warehouses, where would we locate them to minimize our freight costs? The company looked at other distribution costs, including real estate, labor, and taxes, and utility costs, such as electricity ("That ruled out Manhattan pretty fast," Knabe notes). Inventory carrying costs were also factored into the plan.

On the service side, the big question Gillette asked was: How can we impact customer service when we're designing our distribution network? According to Knabe, there were two ways. As noted earlier, the first way was to set up the distribution network so that Gillette could maximize its use of truckload, which meant stocking all products in all warehouses.

The second part of the answer involves *order cycle time*. "The location of our warehouses affects transit time to the customer," Knabe says, "so we looked at how many warehouses we needed if we had to be able to get to every customer within 48 hours. And then we asked: How many warehouses would we need if we only had to get to 85 percent of our customers within 48 hours, and so on? We looked at our network from both of those angles—cost and service—and figured out what made the most sense."

Match Your Network to Your Business Strategy

However, Gillette's theoretical analysis ended up taking a backseat to a practical consideration: The company was locked into significant lease commitments with its current warehouses, which made it prohibitively expensive just to pack up and leave. So the question became: How can Gillette deliver much better customer service without changing its physical infrastructure?

"The goal was, at a minimum, to have a warehouse on the East Coast that carries all of our products," Knabe says. Ultimately, Gillette ended up keeping both its Massachusetts and Tennessee DCs, but what changed was how they functioned in terms of what products they carried and whom they shipped to. Both warehouses now stock all Gillette products.

So far, so good. Gillette discovered it could improve its customer service without having to invest in new infrastructure. However, as Knabe discovered, carrying all products in both warehouses would have significantly increased inventory levels, which was a no-no. To get past this potential sticking point, the company conducted a *statistical safety stock analysis* to optimize its distribution network. Gillette made some process changes to set its safety stock targets, which made it possible to hold inventory constant while improving customer service.

"Your distribution network should be a function of what your business strategy is," Knabe emphasizes. "If your business strategy is to be the low-cost provider, you set up one kind of a network. Wal-Mart, for example, sets up its distribution network to be as cost efficient as possible. If your business strategy is to be as responsive as possible, you set up a different network. For Boston Scientific, a maker of surgical equipment, it's not about the cost of its distribution network, it's about having the right product at the right place instantly."

In the end, by adhering to best practices in configuring its distribution network, Gillette was able to maximize its use of truckload shipments while improving its on-time deliveries to its customers. As a result, its goal of "excellent customer service at least cost" became a reality.

How Much Is Too Much?

How do you know if you're spending too much on your distribution network? Using the Logistics Quotient index of the most logistics-friendly cities, location consulting firm The Boyd Company developed a comparative cost model that identifies how much it costs, on average, to operate a warehouse in the top 50 markets.[11]

Boyd's comparative model focuses on a hypothetical 350,000-square-foot warehouse employing 150 nonexempt workers. This hypothetical warehouse serves a national distribution network that delivers products to 10 destination cities. Not surprisingly, New York City is the most expensive city in which to own a warehouse, in terms of annual operating costs, which Boyd estimates to be $15.8 million. Of the cities studied, the least expensive is Mobile, Alabama, at $10.4 million.

The most expensive city in which to lease a warehouse is San Francisco ($14.5 million), while Mobile again ranks as the least expensive ($9 million). Overall trends play out pretty much as you'd expect: Cities in the Southeast tend to be the least expensive, those in the Northeast and on the West Coast are the most expensive, and the Midwest places in the middle.

Boyd also looks at a hypothetical outbound shipment model that assumes a volume of freight in 30,000-pound truckload shipments costing $1.46 per mile to move. This model indicates that it costs the most to serve a national market from Portland, Oregon ($4.1 million), while the most economical city for outbound shipments is St. Louis, Missouri ($2.4 million).

According to Jack Boyd, principal of The Boyd Company, companies now prefer to build their own warehouses rather than lease them. The trend today is also toward building fewer but larger facilities, often including non-warehousing corporate functions within the buildings to save on costs. In effect, this involves moving white-collar workers into blue-collar locations. You're locating to a warehouse where real estate costs $5 per square foot versus the $20 or more per square foot you would pay in an office building, Boyd points out. "Staffing requirements for warehouses have been elevated over the years as companies become more information technology intensive," he explains. "There are greater labor and skill set demands, and it does require more labor cost analysis as part of the mix in terms of where these warehouses should be located."[12]

Weighing the Intangibles

When retail giant Wal-Mart decided it needed a food distribution center to serve the U.S. Northwest, several site selection criteria had to be weighed before it eventually chose Grandview, Washington, as the location for its 800,000-square-foot facility. For instance, it was advantageous that the land had been zoned for light industrial use and environmental reviews had already been completed. Although the land had to be annexed into the city of Grandview, relatively few people lived in the area, so the vote went in Wal-Mart's favor.

Grandview is situated near an interstate highway, I-82, and the land chosen was flat, which were important considerations for the retailer. The city is centrally located within 200 miles of three major cities: Seattle, Spokane, and Portland. More than 60 local trucking companies serve the outlying area as well as two railroads and nine air freight operators. Nearby, the Port of Pasco, located at the convergence of the Yakima and Snake rivers, offers barge service on the Columbia River to the Port of Portland for containerized cargo.

In Grandview, Wal-Mart (not exactly known for paying top wages) found a populace with the lowest median wage in the area for warehouse workers—$8.11 per hour, more than $2.00 lower than the $10.58 Seattle pays. What's more, the average hourly wage for truck drivers in Grandview is $14.02, considerably lower than the $17.62 they earn in Seattle.

And then there were the intangibles that no index or study can accurately categorize but that played a huge part in Wal-Mart ultimately opting to go with Grandview. One of those intangibles is that the community was eager to attract Wal-Mart's business and the jobs that went with the new DC. Other companies that had chosen Grandview as a distribution site—notably retailer Ace Hardware, which operates a 500,000-square-foot DC there—spoke positively of the area's capabilities. Even the mayors of surrounding communities came forward to support Grandview as the best site for the DC.

Yakima County, where Grandview is located, offered hiring and training support, and hooked Wal-Mart up with the state employment services agency, WorkSource Washington. The agency screened more than 6,000 applicants for the 400 jobs at the DC and then sent the best candidates to Wal-Mart for final interviews. Overall, while labor costs and logistics capabilities made Grandview an attractive site for a DC, Wal-Mart's site selection best practices demonstrated a willingness to explore the qualities of a community that aren't necessarily published in a government report.[13]

Quality over Quantity

Sometimes having just one DC is plenty, even when a company has gotten too big for its current facility. That describes the situation of The Container Store, a retailer of storage and organization products. Thanks to a 20 percent annual growth rate, the Dallas-based company outgrew its 300,000-square-foot DC, so it added a 155,000-square-foot satellite facility nearby. That still wasn't quite sufficient, though, so it also arranged for space for 5,000 pallets under a third-party contract.

Even when the retailer reached the point where it had more than 30 stores throughout the United States, it still determined that one centrally located DC would be enough. "We looked into our whole network and asked whether it was time to do store replenishment out of our DC and direct customer fulfillment out of a different site," explains Amy Carobillano, The Container Store's vice president of logistics and distribution.[14] The retailer decided that keeping to a single site worked to its advantage. For instance, all of the inventory is in one place, with corporate headquarters directly attached to the DC. That central location works well for the company's logistics network, which imports from Asia through the U.S. West Coast and from Europe through the Gulf of Mexico at the Port of Houston.

So the retailer opted to remain in Dallas but to expand into a new 1.1-million-square-foot DC in another part of town. Not all of that square footage is currently being used, since The Container Store's master distribution plan calls for taking over the entire facility in stages. "Once you know what the vision is, you can buy part of it now and develop the solution in phases," Carobillano says.

Even though The Container Store was staying in the Dallas area, it recognized that a move of any distance could affect some of its workers, so it sought their input throughout the site selection process. "We took out a map of the Dallas–Fort Worth metroplex and put a pin where every single employee lived," Carobillano explains. Then the retailer looked for a site that would allow it to retain its employee base. "We talked to the employees who lived furthest away and would have the longest commutes," she notes, and offered to help them find a different way to get to work or to hook up in carpools. As a result, the company didn't lose a single warehouse or office worker after it relocated. "Nobody knows your business or cares about your business like you do," she points out.

When moving day arrived, The Container Store shut down its old DC over a four-day weekend and opened the new facility, and then began moving the merchandise from the old DC to the new one. The entire process took about eight weeks, at which point the retailer began receiving inbound merchandise at the new DC.

Focusing on its employees is definitely a best practice for The Container Store, where the corporate philosophy of "One great employee is worth three good ones" has fostered an environment conducive to developing great people. That kind of thinking pays off, as the company is consistently listed on *Fortune* magazine's list of "Best Places to Work."

A Quick Guide to Site Selection

What sorts of decisions do supply chain managers have to make when choosing sites and considering new locations? Kate McEnroe, who runs site selection firm Kate McEnroe Consulting, insists that the decision process need not be overly complicated. She offers this to-do list of issues to focus on:

- Define required and preferred criteria, and set a realistic timeline.
- Create a format for organizing and analyzing site selection data.
- Gather objective data.
- Eliminate areas that fail to satisfy required criteria.
- Rank the remaining areas on their ability to satisfy preferred criteria.
- Visit communities on your short list to assess sites, workforce, and business operating conditions.
- Consider property and incentive negotiations.

Too often, she notes, companies allow themselves to go overboard on gathering every piece of data on prospective sites, with the assumption that site selection can be reduced to a mathematical formula. "Too much information can make it difficult to maintain focus on the project's purpose," McEnroe says. It's just as important, if not more so, to develop a list of criteria that force a company to identify what is required versus what is merely convenient or familiar.

Questions that need to be asked include:

- What local workforce skills are required, and how many potential employees live in the community under consideration?
- What are the geographic constraints of your distribution network, both for inbound and outbound logistics?
- What are your financial objectives?
- What is the optimal physical environment for your facility, in terms of size, utilities, and support services?
- What are the risks involved, and how can you avoid them?[15]

CHAPTER 10

Globalization

It's a Not-So-Small World

Flashpoints

The main attraction of offshoring is lower labor costs, but those savings tend to be short term rather than long term.

Companies too often fail to calculate the total supply chain cost of offshoring, which includes total landed cost, inventory holding cost, and the cost of product obsolescence.

When it comes to setting up your global supply chain, the ultimate best practice is to go the countries and look for yourself.

Nearshoring—bringing the key supply chain tasks back closer to home—is the fastest-growing globalization trend.

Technology has increased the speed and pace of commerce to such an extent that companies of all sizes now think in terms of global supply chains. While globalization expert Thomas Friedman credits recent technologies such as personal computers, workflow software, and Internet search engines for "flattening" the world, in fact the process started at the midpoint of the twentieth century, when container shipping was introduced.

In the 1950s, trucking executive Malcom McLean had one of those epiphanies that seem blindingly obvious in hindsight but took a while to catch on at the time: Instead of having stevedores at a port physically unload a truck and then store and secure the freight onboard a ship, McLean thought it made a lot more sense to leave everything in the trailer and load the entire container onto a cargo ship specially fitted to accommodate these containers. It took quite a few years of retrofitting ships, trucks, and containers to streamline the loading and offloading process; it took even longer to convince labor unions and port operators that container shipping was a good idea and not just a threat to their way of life. But eventually the idea took hold.

Today, a half century later, McLean's vision has resulted in enormous cargo ships capable of carrying 6,000 or more 20-foot-long containers (known as twenty-foot equivalent units, or TEUs), dropping anchor at so many international ports that many U.S. companies now find it more cost effective to have their products made in low-cost factories in Asia and Latin America than in their own country. As we saw in Chapter 7, shipping containerloads by oceangoing cargo vessels is the least expensive (albeit slowest) transportation mode, so thanks to dramatically lower labor costs and generally lower logistics costs, outsourcing work to other countries—better known as *offshoring*—has become a veritable no-brainer for entire industry sectors, such as apparel and electronics manufacturers.[1]

In Chapter 9 we looked at best practices that companies are following when designing their domestic U.S. distribution networks; in this chapter we'll look at what companies are doing when their supply chains extend far beyond the boundaries of North America. In recent years, China has become a focal point for offshoring initiatives, but U.S. companies have been sourcing from numerous countries for many years, with varying degrees of success.

There's no single set of best practices for globalization since every country has its own cultural and supply chain requirements. As Louise Knabe, solutions manager for personal care products manufacturer The Gillette Co., points out, "In the U.S. market, our customers expect shipments within a few days of placing the order. In Hong Kong, customers expect shipments within a few hours. Space is so precious there that our customers do not hold inventory—period. They expect you to show up with the products when they need it." For that reason, Gillette maintains a distribution center in Hong Kong.

Knabe continues, however: "In Africa, with a few exceptions, such as Egypt and South Africa, Gillette sells directly to distributors, who have completely different expectations—they expect shipments each month. And in Russia, the distributors come to our warehouse to pick up the product." The differences between regions around the world are so extreme, she notes, that it's hard to generalize on what the best distribution methods are to meet customer demand. The short answer is: It depends.[2]

Playing by Somebody Else's Rules

In Chapter 9 we looked at the objectives of a distribution network plan for a domestic operation (see section titled "Striking the Proper Balance"). When setting up a distribution network in another country, all of those objectives still have to be met and those questions answered, but additional considerations come into play when managing a global supply chain, especially when deciding exactly where to locate a production or warehousing facility. Here are some key points to focus on when making site selection decisions overseas:

- Is it part of your company's business strategy to own foreign real estate? Will your ability to serve certain global markets be enhanced by owning your own facilities overseas?
- How flexible is your market strategy? If the market develops more quickly or more slowly than anticipated, how easily can you add to or scale back from your distribution resources?
- How quickly can you enter and serve the market? That question can also be restated as: Can you *afford* to quickly enter and serve the market? The most effective way to serve a foreign market is to gain access to existing facilities near key distribution areas—airports, seaports, major highways, and railroad hubs. However, securing these facilities can be prohibitively expensive since demand for them is quite high. In any event, the larger your budget, the better your chances of establishing your facility in a strategically located area.
- Location is extremely important, but remember that you're operating by another country's rules now, so you need to identify if logistics services are available and reliable in the area. If not, you may find yourself centrally located in the middle of nowhere.
- Have you established a relationship with the local Customs department and other officials? Have you obtained the proper bonds and licenses to move goods into and out of the country? No matter how well you designed your distribution network, it can be dismantled easily by a cranky official who doesn't know you, doesn't know your company, and doesn't see any reason to meet you halfway on compliance matters.
- Have you established a local supply base? The more familiar you become with local labor laws, as well as the culture of the region, the more effectively you'll be able to tap into the supply of logistics workers in the area. It's particularly helpful if you can hire a manager with both logistics experience and knowledge of the key end markets.[3]

Develop a Global Vision

Companies that succeed in developing global supply networks have several best practice characteristics in common, explain Robert B. Handfield and

Ernest L. Nichols, Jr., authors of *Supply Chain Redesign*. For instance:

- These companies create an effective corporate global vision "as a primary driver for investing resources and effort in seeking global suppliers and customers," Handfield and Nichols report. This vision becomes the primary focus for developing and deploying a global supply base.
- They invest in enabling management structures and systems to deploy their global vision. Best practices include global commodity councils and reporting systems; international procurement offices and sales offices that share expertise about regional sourcing and sales opportunities; improved total cost models for decision making; and global information systems with sourcing and demand planning capabilities.
- They configure their supply base to optimize the mix of local suppliers and global suppliers. This mix is prone to change as companies gain more experience with local suppliers.
- They deploy resources to ensure that suppliers' capabilities are aligned with their competitive and manufacturing strategies. Process specialists are assigned to correct isolated technical problems. When systemic problems are prevalent within a supplier's organization, best-in-class companies apply a full-scale intervention process to effect positive changes.

"By understanding the cost drivers that underlie total cost, managers can implement strategies designed to reduce these costs," Handfield and Nichols observe.[4]

Friendly Nations

In Chapter 9 we looked at the various transportation and infrastructure factors that go into determining a city or region's logistics friendliness, based on site selection criteria that take into account the similarities and differences between major U.S. cities. While a similar study of international cities and countries would be equally valuable to supply chain professionals, unfortunately no such study currently exists, for a simple reason: lack of data. The kind of site selection criteria the United States makes publicly available is sometimes next to impossible to acquire from other countries, especially those just beginning to emerge from third-world status.

However, the World Bank and the Finland-based Turku School of Economics have developed the next best thing: They've compiled an index that weighs the logistics performance of 150 different countries in seven areas:

1. Efficiency of the Customs clearance process
2. Quality of transportation and information technology infrastructure for logistics

3. Ease and affordability of arranging international shipments
4. Competence of local logistics providers
5. Capability to track and trace international shipments
6. Cost of domestic logistics
7. On-time delivery performance[5]

This logistics performance index is particularly useful because it provides a counterargument to the prevailing wisdom current in many circles that there is very little downside to offshoring production and sourcing to other countries simply on the basis of cost. Many of the low-cost alternatives—China among them—are in fact totalitarian regimes whose idea of "free trade" is very much different from what is practiced in the United States, Canada, Australia, and the European Union. In many countries, the concept of collaboration—fostering a mutually beneficial relationship with key supply chain partners—is largely unknown. As noted in the World Bank study, "traditional measures of performance such as direct freight costs and average delays, while important, may not capture the overall logistics performance [of a country] and thus the ability of countries to use trade for growth. The predictability and reliability of shipments, while more difficult to measure, are more important for firms and may have a much greater impact on their ability to compete."

According to the World Bank study, the 10 most logistics-friendly countries are:

1. Singapore
2. Netherlands
3. Germany
4. Sweden
5. Austria
6. Japan
7. Switzerland
8. Hong Kong
9. United Kingdom
10. Canada

The United States ranks at 14. Three popular offshoring destinations—China, India, and Mexico—rank 30, 39, and 56, respectively.

Pulling up the rear in the bottom 5 are:

146. Tajikistan
147. Myanmar
148. Rwanda
149. Timor-Leste
150. Afghanistan[6]

"Low Cost" Sometimes Means "Poor Service"

The main reason why companies opt to source their manufacturing offshore is because the labor costs are much cheaper, sometimes extraordinarily so. A typical American, for instance, earns in one hour what the average Chinese citizen earns in one year, according to futurist James Canton.[7] For many U.S. companies, the opportunity to save 50 percent or more on labor and associated costs is all the justification necessary to move production overseas. Admittedly, transportation costs generally will increase, but when compared to the savings on labor, spending more to move products from one side of the globe to another seems like a worthwhile trade-off. Since most U.S.-bound goods sourced overseas cross the ocean on maritime vessels, one of the least expensive transportation modes, logistics—at least at first—typically ranks quite low as a consideration when a company weighs the pros and cons of offshoring.

However, within a year or two, after the advantages gained on the labor front have leveled off, many companies typically—and belatedly—wake up to the reality that they've relocated their manufacturing operations to a country whose government is totalitarian and exploitative, whose roads are substandard, whose logistics infrastructure is still in the planning stages, whose ports are alarmingly congested, and whose citizens have been known to appropriate American intellectual capital as their own. That's certainly the case in China, the offshoring capital of the world, where labor costs are rising as the country leverages U.S. investment to rapidly expand its own manufacturing base. However, while China is growing at an unprecedented rate along its East Coast, much of its interior regions remain remote and logistically challenging.

What's more, the costs of Chinese labor are rising as the country's agricultural workers leave the farms in search of production work. "It's absolutely not the Chinese game plan that they're going to work for peanuts wages forever for you and me," points out James Womack, chairman of the Lean Enterprise Institute. "If you're going to develop a country, you have to move from a lower- to a higher-wage situation. The central government wants to employ the best production methods and they want to be the best in their industry rather than just the cheapest." Even so, Ming Zeng and Peter J. Williamson, authors of *Dragons at Your Door*, predict that Chinese manufacturers will enjoy "a hefty cost advantage" for at least another 20 to 30 years.[8]

A study conducted by analyst firm Aberdeen Group indicates that 91 percent of U.S. companies aren't sure that the cost savings they hoped to gain from going global are being achieved. Unexpected supply chain costs can quickly erode the potential savings on labor. Every time a company has to rely on expedited shipping to compensate for inadequate in-country transportation, or has to pay Customs fines because of documentation errors, going offshore becomes less of a no-brainer and more of a "What were we thinking?"

Nevertheless, American companies will continue to look overseas for whatever savings they can garner, and the companies obtaining the best results from their offshoring efforts are doing so by building more flexibility into their logistics networks. "Rather than creating the absolute lowest cost fixed network, these companies are looking to trade some of the cost aspects for more agility and more points of flexibility," explains Beth Enslow, vice president of enterprise research with Aberdeen Group. "This is enabling them to manage in-process and in-transit inventory much more aggressively."[9]

"Companies are chasing savings through overseas sourcing, but their internal structures are likely to prevent the full benefits of these savings from occurring," adds John Blascovich, a vice president with consulting firm A.T. Kearney. "They need a sharper understanding of these new markets. Waiting too long to develop the right strategy or skill set could mean losing access to scarce, capable resources and the competitive edge they provide."[10]

What Blascovich finds alarming, however, is how unprepared companies are at managing their offshore sourcing. Only 53 percent have strategies that indicate a clear understanding of the supply chain and logistics costs associated with emerging market alternatives. For instance, just 41 percent have made improving their market skills and language capabilities high priorities for their sourcing organization. Only 39 percent have formal plans in place to increase their supplier base from global sources.

According to a study of North American, European, and Asian manufacturing companies conducted by PRTM Management Consultants, 42 percent of all manufacturing and 38 percent of final assembly had already been globalized by 2008. The study also predicts that by 2010, 51 percent of all manufacturing activities and 47 percent of final assembly will be offshored. China, not surprisingly, is by far the predominant choice as a manufacturing or sourcing destination, as 34 percent of the PRTM survey respondents chose China, with India the next closest choice at 13 percent, Eastern Europe at 12 percent, and the rest of Asia at 11 percent. (The United States, incidentally, was the choice of 9 percent of respondents.)[11]

Living in a Somewhat Flat World

The biggest mistake a company can make regarding China, observes globalization expert Thomas Friedman, is to assume that China is winning strictly due to cheap labor, and not by improving quality and productivity. Citing a study by the U.S. Conference Board, Friedman points out that China lost

15 million manufacturing jobs (presumably to even lower-cost countries) between 1995 and 2002, a period when the United States lost 2 million jobs.[12]

"Most companies build offshore factories not simply to obtain cheaper labor for products they want to sell in America or Europe," Friedman observes in *The World Is Flat*. "Another motivation is to serve that foreign market without having to worry about trade barriers and to gain a dominant foothold there—particularly a giant market like China's. According to the U.S. Commerce Department, nearly 90 percent of the output from U.S.-owned offshore factories is sold to foreign consumers. But this actually stimulates American exports."

Every dollar a company invests in an offshore factory yields additional exports for its home country, Friedman notes. "If General Motor builds a factory offshore in Shanghai, it also ends up creating jobs in America by exporting a lot of goods and services to its own factory in China and benefiting from lower parts costs in China for its factories in America."

Friedman probably should have chosen a better example than GM, which has not only laid off tens of thousands of its own workers in recent years but which has also been blamed for the loss of potentially hundreds of thousands more should the economic meltdown of the U.S. automakers extend to the suppliers reliant on the Detroit-based auto industry for their jobs. Friedman also only tells half the story about the loss of Chinese jobs. Between the years 2002 and 2006, the United States lost another 1.4 million manufacturing jobs while China added nearly 12 million manufacturing jobs, according to the U.S. Bureau of Labor Statistics (www.bls.gov).

In part due to suspicions that China has unfairly manipulated its currency to gain an edge on its western competitors, the country is frequently cited as causing the loss of manufacturing jobs in other economies. Nevertheless, as noted earlier, it still leads every other nation by a wide margin as the offshoring country of choice. However, according to a survey conducted by Deloitte Touche Tohmatsu, most manufacturing executives believe North American will not lose any competitive ground to China—or any other country—in such key areas as sourcing, sales and marketing, research and development, customer service, and information technology. "While globalization will continue and some manufacturing jobs will follow, North America is showing significant resiliency," observes Craig Giffi, vice chairman of Deloitte.[13]

Keeping an Eye on China

Companies doing business in China not only need to keep a close watch on the state of China's logistics network and infrastructure, but they must also recognize the very different nature of doing business there. "China is moving fast and changing faster, an environment in which few Western companies are structured to compete," observes James McGregor, author of *One Billion Customers* and one-time China bureau chief for the *Wall Street Journal*. "Your China business model must be configured for constant changes in every aspect of business and politics." Although China appears to be a bottomless pool of opportunities and cheap labor, McGregor cautions, "Never use the Chinese market as a last resort to save your business. The Chinese can smell desperation and will take advantage of your weakness."[14]

According to EFT Research Service, the Chinese logistics market is "fragmented, underdeveloped, and poorly serviced in respect of physical and communications infrastructure. It imposes logistics costs on businesses that can account for up to 21 percent of the product costs, which is more than twice the average for developed markets." Although China's logistics infrastructure is growing rapidly, most of the investment in the transportation system has been along the East Coast. While highways and railroad lines are being built at a phenomenal pace—EFT reports that China plans to invest $250 billion in building 15,500 miles (25,000 km) of new rail lines by 2020—the country's railroads can only handle 30 percent of the current demand.[15]

Most multinational companies with sourcing or manufacturing operations in China prefer to use established global logistics providers for imports to and exports from the country, primarily because they can keep costs down by leveraging global contracts and service-level commitments, according to EFT. A study by Harris Interactive observes that when senior corporate leaders in the United States and Europe were asked to evaluate the effectiveness of their global supply chains, 66 percent rated their North American infrastructures as high and 47 percent gave the same rating to their Western European infrastructures. However, only 16 percent rated their supply chains in China as highly effective. And yet 80 percent of those surveyed said that China plays an important role in their company's growth objectives.[16]

There's a follow-the-leader mentality within otherwise rational-thinking executives, according to J. Michael Kilgore and Jeff Metersky of supply chain consulting firm Chainalytics. They're too prone to knee-jerk reactions whenever sales are in decline and are too easily tempted to seek out the lure of low costs. However, when calculating the potential savings of offshoring production to China, or any other country with a still-evolving infrastructure, companies too often fail to take into account the *total supply chain cost*, which includes total landed cost plus the inventory holding cost and cost of product obsolescence. As Simon Ellis, a supply chain practice director with analyst firm Manufacturing Insights, explains, a company should continue to source from low-cost countries "as long as the cost of additional inventory/obsolescence buffer required to compensate for longer lead time remains within acceptable limits."[17]

Kilgore and Metersky add that a logistics analysis should focus not just on how much it costs to transport goods to a port but to the end customer, as cross-country transit times, as well as interfacility costs to reposition product from ports to regional manufacturing and distribution points, can add millions of dollars in unplanned-for logistics costs. Companies need to evaluate the changes in inbound, outbound, and interfacility logistics costs that will occur as sourcing points are changed. Kilgore and Metersky also recommend that companies continuously analyze their outsourcing strategies, as significant changes in exchange rates, capital costs, and transportation costs can make last year's decision to go the offshoring route look downright foolish today.[18]

Take a Look for Yourself

When it comes to setting up your global supply chain, the ultimate best practice is also the most obvious: Go to the countries and look for yourself. There's nothing better than an on-site evaluation, recommends Laird Carmichael, executive vice president of International Outsourcing Services, especially in potentially volatile situations. "If it seems like chaos and instability, it probably is. Sure, it might be the cheapest deal in terms of labor costs, but if the news yields stories of political unrest over time, it's best to look elsewhere. Too little or too much police and military personnel, lack of traffic control, and illegal behaviors occurring in broad daylight without consequences are all bad indicators. None of these things can be determined without a trip to the country to view it firsthand."[19]

What you need is a *regional logistics assessment* that evaluates a country's or region's logistics assets and abilities. Both geography and physical infrastructure are key differentiators. While the global site selection process looks at the same basic things a domestic U.S. process would examine, there are some not-so-subtle differences in practice. For instance, instead of asking about how congested the highways are, you might have to ask if any highways have been built yet.

Many historically important cities got that way thanks to good geography, points out author Douglas Long, especially if they are centered on natural ports. "Having good geographic features does not help if there is not infrastructure, such as roads, ocean ports, or airports," he notes. "Public infrastructure makes an enormous difference to a company's ability to operate. No business can avoid the consequences, good or bad, of where they are located." That public infrastructure includes not just major projects like bridges and roads but also things like road signs.[20]

As noted earlier, the downside to locating a manufacturing or distribution facility near an established port is that procuring these properties may be prohibitively expensive because the area is already built up. What's more, many ports and airports restrict, or even prohibit, land ownership by foreign companies. The only way to secure property in some ports is to rent it from the port directly, notes Edgar Kasteel, vice president of Holland International Distribution Council. The trade-off to the difficulty and expense of getting a portside property is that you gain proximity to transportation infrastructure.[21]

Global site selection decisions don't end with the physical infrastructure. "Modern businesses require a legal system with rules of trade and commerce, Customs officials, and legal enforcement of business contracts," Long points out. "There is also a need for banks to provide financing. Trade and logistics require a wide variety of services provided by other businesses and the government. Without these services it would not be profitable to do business, regardless of how good the infrastructure or ports may be."[22]

Pay especially close attention to duties and tariffs, Carmichael adds. These fees can have a profound effect on the bottom line. "It basically comes down to the country of origination of the raw materials, where they enter the country (via U.S. or Mexico, etc.), and in what form. Because of a free trade agreement, the materials could be duty-free if handled within legal guidelines for a specific country." Every country has different duties, he points out, and there are legal loopholes based on their Customs' classification of materials. "Raw materials versus cut or partially assembled materials play a factor in many cases."[23]

Finding the Next Global Hot Spot

If "look for yourself" is the first best practice of globalization, the second would be "get there before everyone else does." Timing is everything when it comes to being one of the first companies to enter an emerging market, particularly because labor is widely available and eager to demonstrate their capabilities. The so-called BRIC countries—Brazil, Russia, India, and China—have gotten most of the attention, representing as they do the fastest-growing economies after the United States and the European Union, but it's actually the less-developed nations that offer the greatest potential for cost savings. As both the political structure and logistics infrastructure of these emerging countries are likely to pose some risks, perhaps the third best practice of globalization should be "know what you're getting into before you go there."

Among the best-kept secrets that are drawing attention from multinational companies are Southeast Asian countries (Vietnam, Malaysia,

Thailand, Indonesia), Eastern European countries (Poland, Romania, Serbia, Czech Republic, Bulgaria), Africa (Kenya, Egypt, Morocco, South Africa), Peru, Chile, and Turkey. Take Vietnam, for instance, which globalization expert Mark Minevich refers to as "the new tiger on the horizon. It has the ability to spread across all sectors—from pure manufacturing to performing R&D [research and development] for some of the largest companies in the world." Calling Vietnam "the Asian alternative to China," consultant Alex Bryant points out that the country has an aggressive program of corporate tax incentives to attract foreign companies and has invested 10 percent of its gross domestic product into basic infrastructure services, such as electricity, water supply, ports, and telecommunications.[24]

On the African continent, Egypt boasts good ports and air services as well as a large and relatively low-cost labor supply, Minevich notes. The government is investing in high-growth areas and is providing tax incentives. While Egypt ranks high on PricewaterhouseCoopers' emerging markets index for manufacturing, the country's overall transportation infrastructure is still lacking in some areas, and there are doubts about the government's policy implementations.[25]

Ultimately, the decision process for choosing an offshore manufacturing or sourcing site is the same no matter which country you're looking at, says David Hoover, vice president of strategic procurement with office furniture maker HNI Corp. "In the end, human beings are always the ones doing the business, and everyone has an interest," he says. The challenge in any global supply chain relationship, Hoover explains, "is to understand what the other party's interests are, so that you can help satisfy them." When you do that, they will be compelled to help satisfy yours. And when it comes to expectations, Hoover suggests that you take every possible measure to ensure that your quality requirements are clearly and explicitly spelled out.[26]

The Need for Supply Chain Visibility

Although apparel company Limited Brands, along with the rest of the American apparel industry, offshores its manufacturing, that doesn't mean the company has outsourced the responsibility for monitoring its supply chain. Limited Logistics Services, the company's logistics subsidiary, assigns its own people to oversee operations in its Asian factories as well as the flow of goods into the United States.

According to Nick LaHowchic, president and chief executive of Limited Logistics Services, the company works with key logistics suppliers to make sure it has the capacity it needs, especially during peak season. "We get continuous feedback from the factory and the Asian consolidator, and daily reports from our ocean carrier," he explains. "To maintain speed and reliability, we assess supply chain events before goods leave the factory." For instance, if a rush order needs to be put on certain goods that are scheduled to move by an ocean carrier, Limited's visibility into its supply chain is extensive enough that it can identify exactly which shipment needs to be expedited.

"Stuff doesn't stay within our four walls very long," LaHowchic comments. It takes 72 hours for goods to travel from Hong Kong to Limited's Ohio distribution center. The products are finished there within 36 hours and then, within two-and-a-half days, those products are shipped and delivered to all 5,000 of the company's retail stores in the United States. "We spend a lot of time thinking about where product should be, a fair amount of time getting system information on where it is, and a small amount of time dealing with exceptions," he notes.

Mike Duciewicz, vice president of supply chain with office products supplier Ricoh Corp., agrees that visibility into the entire supply chain is absolutely essential when it comes to managing a global operation. The company uses an integrated global system that provides timely, online status reports from its transportation providers.

"Once a purchase order is placed in the system, we know the production schedule, the estimated time of arrival (ETA) at the port of departure and the receiving port, offloading of the container, and the ETA at our distribution center," Duciewicz says. Ricoh employs an internal non-vessel operating common carrier, which is responsible for coordinating the company's international shipments as well as providing online information from the carriers. "The key point is that most product is manufactured by our own family group."[27]

Closer to Home

Record high fuel prices. A worldwide economic recession. Rising costs of raw materials. Piracy on the high seas. Fluctuations in the value of the U.S. dollar. All of these factors have contributed to a recent phenomenon known variously as *nearshoring*, *rightshoring*, *inshoring*, and *reverse globalization*. The concept is simple: Rather than establishing manufacturing facilities at a low-cost country halfway across the world, a company will choose a relatively low-cost country within its own hemisphere to save on logistics costs. In some cases, the choice will be the country of record where the company is headquartered.

According to a supply chain risk survey conducted by AMR Research, U.S. manufacturers believe that nearshoring is the fastest growing globalization trend. "Mexico is the preferred nearshoring destination [for U.S. companies], with 84 percent of the respondents choosing it as a place for sourcing or manufacturing," reports analyst Noha Tohamy, "followed by Canada at 55 percent and Brazil at 49 percent. Respondents also indicated an increase in sourcing and manufacturing in Eastern and Central Europe." Tohamy attributes this trend to "the increased cost competitiveness of nearshore locations, as well as company desires to build a more balanced geographic portfolio to avoid some of the risks associated with low-cost country sourcing."[28]

"Mexico is a good alternative where you have a blend of low-cost labor in addition to a reliable and relatively cost-effective transportation system," observes Tom Jones, general manager of supply chain solutions for logistics provider Ryder System Inc. "For some other products it makes sense to source back in the United States, where the cost of offshoring outweighs the higher cost of labor."

For example, Desa, a Bowling Green, Kentucky-based heating products manufacturer, followed the offshoring trend to China at the turn of the century, thanks in large part to a sizable 15 percent value-added tax rebate the company received from the Chinese government on its exports. In 2007, however, China reduced that rebate to 5 percent, which cut significantly into Desa's cost savings. When fuel and raw material prices jumped dramatically as well, Desa found that its shipping price per container had increased by 50 percent over a one-year period. After factoring in the additional costs of moving inbound freight from the Port of Long Beach to Kentucky, during a period when gas was over $4.00 a gallon, having production in China no longer was cost effective, explains Claude Hayes, Desa's president. Facing a combination of higher energy costs, an exchange rate more favorable to the United States, the reduction in the value-added tax, and the increased costs of materials and commodities, bringing the work back home to Kentucky made good business sense for Desa.

Although Desa has to pay more for labor now, the company is breaking even thanks to its savings on transportation and commodities. "Being located in the central part of the United States, almost 60 percent to 70 percent of the U.S. population is within 12 hours of us," Hayes points out. "If you want to get to [your customers], it's a good place to be."[29]

CHAPTER 11

Customer Service

Keeping the Customer Satisfied

Flashpoints

Customers prefer to deal with companies that can deliver perfect orders and shipments every time.

Accurately identify the top 20 percent of your best customers because that's where your profits are coming from.

Companies that excel at service parts management can eliminate inefficiency while improving inventory turns and delivery times.

Insist that every employee in your organization focus on the customer, and then empower them to do so.

To most American children—and to most American grocery and drug-store retailers—Halloween is synonymous with one thing: candy. The costumes, the pumpkins, and the spooky decorations are all secondary trappings of the season, but if there isn't any candy, there just isn't any Halloween.

So what happens if you're one of the world's biggest candy makers, and you don't have enough candy to satisfy your retail customers' orders for the Halloween season? And what do you do if the reason your Halloween is turning into a total nightmare is because of a breakdown within your supply chain?

That's exactly what happened to The Hershey Company in 1999. That whole experience has become part of the supply chain legend, a kind of worst-practice horror story used to frighten young supply chain professionals who are tempted to take shortcuts when developing their time-to-market strategies. "If it can happen to Hershey's," the warnings sound—a $4 billion industry leader with a reputation for quality people and processes—"then it can happen here, too."[1]

What made Halloween '99 such a sour experience for Hershey's? In a nutshell, the candy maker experienced a failure to integrate—it couldn't get its order fulfillment system to talk to its enterprise resource planning system. While Hershey's continued to receive orders from its customers, the company couldn't fill those orders in a timely fashion because it wasn't exactly sure who had placed those orders. And that spelled disaster, to the tune of $150 million—the amount that snafu cost Hershey's in lost sales.[2]

Hershey's technology problems were certainly not intentional, but to the retailers that had to scramble to fill their shelves with other companies' chocolate bars, and to the consumers who ended up filling the neighbor kids' sacks with Nestlé Crunch bars instead of Hershey bars, it didn't really matter *why* Hershey's came up short. It only mattered that there were a lot of unsatisfied customers. And when it comes to supply chain management, that's not just a worst practice—it's the one unforgivable sin.

The Perfect Order

As the pace of commerce has dramatically increased, the patience of customers has similarly decreased. "Better, faster, and cheaper" just isn't good enough any more; customers today are demanding perfect orders, shipped on time to the minute, at a cost that barely leaves any margin for error—or profit. Every manufacturer faces the same crucial challenge: Your customer expects perfect orders and shipments every time—can your supply chain deliver them, every time? If it can't, then your company faces the consequences of invoice deductions, lost sales, and even lost customers if your customer's expectations are not met.

Edward Marien, longtime director of supply chain management programs at the University of Wisconsin, describes exactly what a perfect order should look like when he refers to a "customer bill of rights." According to Marien, the customer has the right to expect:

1. The Right Product in the
2. Right Quantity from the
3. Right Source to the
4. Right Destination in the
5. Right Condition at the

6. Right Time with the
7. Right Documentation for the
8. Right Cost[3]

Failure to deliver on any of these rights can be costly, and the farther up in the rights hierarchy that a problem occurs, the more devastating the ripple effect of the failures will become. By failing to provide the right product in the right quantity—Rights 1 and 2—Hershey's deprived many of its customers of Rights 3 through 8 as well. Since Hershey's simply didn't have enough of its candy bars to meet all of its retail customers' orders, none of the other rights—like the condition of the products or the accuracy of the documentation—even came into play.

Hershey's did eventually fix its inventory problems, but the $150 million the company lost was an extremely expensive lesson to learn, and that's not even taking into account the pain Hershey's customers felt. Let's face it: If you're planning to hand out Hershey's Kit Kat bars on Halloween and the local drugstore doesn't have any, you might just hop back in the car and try the Wal-Mart down the street, especially if Junior starts pitching a fit about his candy preferences. Hershey's may end up with a sale after all, but that drugstore didn't get your business, or the business of countless other customers looking for other Hershey's products, like Mr. Goodbars and Twizzlers and Reese's Peanut Butter Cups.

The point is: Business customers are just like consumers—they prefer to do business with companies that can deliver perfect orders and shipments every single time. Anything less is simply unacceptable.

The High Cost of Imperfection

Companies today are measuring their supply chain performance by analyzing how often they can deliver perfect orders as well as how much it costs to be perfect. Consumer packaged goods giant Procter & Gamble Co. (P&G), for instance, defines a perfect order as a product that arrives on time, complete (as ordered), and billed correctly. When P&G set out in the 1990s to measure how close it was coming to this high water mark, it discovered that every imperfect order was costing it $200. P&G found it had too many areas of imperfection that added unnecessary costs: the cost of redelivery when orders were late; replacement costs if shipments were damaged; processing costs for quantity adjustments as well as price and allowance deductions.[4] Since that time, the company has committed to a customer focus by forming its Consumer-Driven Supply Network (see Chapter 2).

In the book *Supply Chain Redesign*, authors Robert B. Handfield and Ernest L. Nichols, Jr. offer an equation that companies can use to calculate the total cost of moving a product through their supply chain and then determine how best to reduce costs without reducing service:

Price per unit
+   Containerization cost
+   Transportation freight costs
+   Duties and premiums
=   Landed cost
+   Incoming quality control
+   Warehouse costs
=   Dock-to-stock cost
+   Inventory carrying costs
+   Defective materials
+   Factory yield
+   Field failures
+   Warranties
+   Service
+   General and administrative costs
+   Lost sales and customer goodwill
=   Total cost[5]

One Good Return Deserves Another

Our consumer culture has become so fickle that the cost of product returns has reached $100 billion. That's how much it costs U.S. manufacturers and retailers in lost sales, transportation, handling, processing, and disposing of goods that were purchased but ultimately returned. It's estimated that customer returns can reduce a retailer's profitability by 4.3 percent and a manufacturer's by 3.8 percent.

According to the Supply Chain Consortium, a benchmarking organization, the top six reasons customers return products are:

1. Customer ordered incorrect product or size.
2. Customer decided product was not needed or wanted.
3. Customer returned the product without giving a reason.
4. Product did not fit description on Web site or in catalog.
5. Product did not fit customer's expectations.
6. Company shipped incorrect product or size.

These six reasons account for nearly 75 percent of all reasons for returns, according to the Consortium, and yet only the sixth reason is attributable to company error. "From the customer's viewpoint, it really doesn't matter who caused the product return," observes Bruce Tompkins, executive director of the Supply Chain Consortium (www.supplychainconsortium.com). "The customer wants to return the product with as few difficulties as possible, and the company wants to retain its customer and keep costs down. Returns are inevitable, so why not use metrics to monitor and improve reverse logistics activities?"

That's precisely what high-tech manufacturer Logitech has done. Product obsolescence is a constant irritant to the high-tech industry, where the value of a consumer device seems to start dropping as soon as the product leaves the design stages. "Price erosion is the silent killer," says Gray Williams, vice president worldwide of supply chain for Logitech, which manufactures such computer devices as mice, joysticks, and keyboards. Because returns can amount to as much as 10 percent of all outbound shipments, Williams is constantly striving to synchronize supply and demand to keep inventory moving.[6]

That synchronization involves a process called *progressive dispositioning*, where the goal, Williams explains, "is to continuously identify and disposition excess as early in the cycle as possible." Dispositioning includes repairing, refurbishing, liquidating, and recycling/scrapping. The returns process includes auctioning off excess inventory via online Web sites. "You need to keep your inventory moving," he says, "so disposition your excess and obsolete inventory wherever it is located, whether that's in the factory, a distribution center, or the channel."

Reverse logistics is often misinterpreted as simply a way of making pennies on the dollar off products that you didn't think you could even give away any more. Logitech, however, is methodical in the way it measures its return processes. It uses an excess inventory index that calculates the cost of doing nothing (i.e., how much money the company stands to lose by not properly dispositioning its returned/excess products):

period costs + [price erosion factor × (excess in warehouse + excess in channel)]

Period costs include warehousing, standard revision costs, maintaining excess and obsolete reserve, and the cost of capital. The price erosion factor depends on the company and its products, but by way of example, let's assume it's 1 percent. If a company is carrying $40 million in current excess inventory and has $30 million excess in the channel, when you add those together you get $70 million; when you multiply that amount by 1 percent, it equals $700,000. Then add in the total period costs—let's say it's $1.3 million per month. For that hypothetical company, the cost of inaction for one month is $2 million.

To benefit from a reverse logistics effort, a company first has to know what its actual return rate is and then determine what return rate is acceptable. James Stock, a professor with the University of South Florida, studied product returns and found that many companies don't know what's coming back, how much is coming back, or what recovery rate to expect. "In our study, companies doing really well are seeing 80 percent to 90 percent recovery rates. Average companies realize rates around 60 percent. For companies doing poorly, 40 percent is the norm," Stock observes.[7]

Supply Chain in Reverse

Although historically many companies have more or less accepted returns as a necessary cost of doing business, that's no longer the case. In addition to allowing companies like Logitech the opportunity to reclaim revenues that would otherwise be lost, a reverse logistics program can also help companies improve their products. "Product failure and returns information can be fed back to sales or research departments to identify root causes such as packaging or product design errors," note consultants Jonathan Wright and Michael Joyce, with Accenture's Supply Chain Management practice. Focusing on reverse logistics can also help companies reduce or eliminate the product defects that led to the returns in the first place.[8]

Because most companies do not view handling product returns as a core competency, reverse logistics tasks are frequently handed off to a third-party logistics provider (3PL). Automobile manufacturer Hyundai Motor America, for instance, uses a 3PL to retrieve reusable components to remanufacture transmissions and other parts. "There are a number of reasons to outsource returns," explains George Kurth, Hyundai's director of supply chain and logistics. "It gets the process out of our warehouse. The third party consolidates parts and ships full containerloads to save transportation costs. Since they serve other auto manufacturers, they bring expertise we don't have."[9]

Although Hyundai uses a third party, Kurth admits that reverse logistics is extremely important in the automotive industry. "We all allow dealers to return parts they cannot use. We sell them to another dealer or put them back in stock. We can use our outbound dedicated delivery service to return parts at little additional cost."

Managing the reverse inventory flow offers a significant opportunity for savings, Kurth adds. Hyundai's goal is to build up returns as a separate demand stream, and to that end the company forecasts the total number of returns. "For example, if our 640 dealers order 100 pieces per month of Part A, and each dealer returns four per month, that's more than 30,000 per year. If we can forecast what's coming back, we can factor it into inventory management." And once Hyundai learns that a return is in the pipeline, it can be entered into the inventory management system, which allows the company to reduce its new parts order.

At a Glance

Reverse Logistics

Reverse logistics is the process of moving returned goods from their consumer destination for the purpose of capturing value or proper disposal. It includes processing returned merchandise due to damage, seasonal inventory, restock, salvage, recalls, and excess inventory as well as packaging and shipping materials from the end user or reseller.

Like Hyundai, specialty retailer Best Buy Co. Inc. opts to use a 3PL rather than develop an in-house proficiency in reverse logistics. When the retailer benchmarked its capabilities, it discovered that becoming best in class in processing returns would involve significant investments in systems, processes, and physical infrastructure. Instead of making that investment, Best Buy decided to align itself with a 3PL that already had that competency. That decision has paid off handsomely, as the retailer's in-house processing costs have dropped by roughly 50 percent, notes John Jordan, Best Buy's director of logistics.[10]

The reverse logistics process begins when a customer returns a defective product to a retail outlet, Jordan explains. Those defective units are consolidated at the stores and then taken to one of 15 consolidation points. Store returns are consolidated into truckload quantities and are then sent to one of the retailer's two return locations. The fact that Best Buy has only two return locations is an illustration of how using a 3PL has become a best practice. With the assistance of the 3PL, Best Buy performed a distribution network analysis that examined both the inbound and outbound components of defective product returns. As part of that process, the retailer was able to phase out two of its four return centers. Now the 3PL receives the defective products at the two remaining return centers, consolidates them, and ultimately submits the returns to the product manufacturer for a return authorization.

Besides lowering Best Buy's return costs, going the 3PL route has allowed the retailer to tighten its supply chain focus. "We used to have an internal team of upwards of 10 people that managed the returns process," Jordan notes, "and now we have just a couple people working closely with the 3PL to monitor returns. We've been able to redeploy and refocus on the many projects that are out there to improve our supply chain." (Learn more about 3PLs in Chapter 12.)

Managing the Relationship

One thing that virtually every company needs is a better way of communicating with its customers. One means to that end has been the adoption of customer relationship management (CRM) software, which integrates all of a company's front-office tasks—sales, marketing, order entry, customer service, and field support. CRM software ties into a central database to determine product status in the manufacturing, warehousing, and shipping processes. Basically, a CRM solution touches and integrates every aspect of a company to make it easier to identify and service the needs of its customers.

At a Glance

Customer Relationship Management

Customer relationship management (CRM) is a customer-centric strategy that uses software tools to optimize profitability, revenues, and customer satisfaction. It ties into all of a company's other enterprise and supply chain systems, with the goal of providing a complete view of a company's operation.

Some examples of companies that have used CRM to improve their customer service operations follow.

- As a diversified manufacturer of various industrial and climate control products, Ingersoll-Rand's global sales force needed a way to effectively exploit cross-sell opportunities whenever they arose. This was no small task given that the company has 30 different operating units, manufacturing a diversified product line that includes golf carts, construction vehicles, refrigeration equipment, and security systems. Using CRM technology, Ingersoll-Rand developed a Web-based call center to support its staff of 2,600 sales professionals. Any salesperson can access the Web site and share sales leads and opportunities (e.g., a golf course manager is in the market for an earth-moving vehicle). Within the first year, the company generated more than $6 million in incremental cross-selling revenue.

- As a supplier of networking and communications devices to more than 25,000 customers, Enterasys Networks Inc. needed to improve the quality of its customer service while empowering its call support staff to make better decisions. Making that task even more difficult is the fact that the company has offices in more than 30 countries, and the product and customer information needed was scattered throughout disconnected databases. Enterasys implemented a self-service portal with on-demand capabilities, which consolidated the various silos of information into a common platform. The company is now better able to detect the early warning signs of when a customer might be dissatisfied. Enterasys can now handle 3,000 cases per month, at a savings of roughly 10 minutes per case, which the company estimates translates into $500,000 in annual savings.

- Although it has more than 450 retail stores as well as a retail Web site, Williams-Sonoma Inc. still mails nearly 300 million catalogs every year to consumers, showcasing its latest offerings of household goods. Any solution that could help the company more effectively target its customers with personalized mailings, and reduce costs at the same time, would offer the retailer a distinct competitive advantage. It would also, inevitably, require a lot more work than just loading up a new software program and flipping the "on" switch. Williams-Sonoma used data mining software, business analytics, and other CRM applications to separate millions of its customers down into several dozen categories. With its customers now segmented into more manageable groups, the retailer is better able to predict how each segment will respond to a specific campaign or mailing and can target its mailings accordingly. By uniting multiple brands and channels, Williams-Sonoma has saved millions in marketing costs.

- Wilson Tool International is an expert at producing punch presses and other tooling solutions for sheet metal manufacturers, but as its 20,000 customers increasingly turned to the Web to place their orders, Wilson Tool needed a way to respond to that demand while reducing the number of order-handling errors that were resulting in too many returns. On top of that, the company's tooling solutions are highly specialized, with 85 percent of its sales coming from configurable products. After implementing a CRM system, Wilson Tool was able to improve the efficiency of its online order management process by 8 percent while reducing order errors and the number of returns. What's more, the CRM system includes an integrated engineer-to-order functionality that allows customers to access an online catalog after they've placed an order, thus streamlining the final product configuration process.[11]

According to analyst firm Gartner Inc., there are four guiding principles for successful customer-centric strategies:

1. Extend the depth and breadth of relationships to achieve a larger share of the customer relationship.
2. Reduce delivery channel costs (e.g., by steering customers toward low-cost channels such as the Internet).
3. Strengthen and reinforce the brand.
4. Create customer satisfaction and loyalty.[12]

Money in the Bank

The book *The Value Profit Chain* relates the story of a manager of a chain of Domino's Pizza outlets who taught his employees to think of the lifetime value of a customer, not just a one-time $8 purchase. If somebody orders one pizza per week for 10 years, that represents a total of $4,000 spent over a decade. The manager told his employees, "Think of the customer as having $4,000 pasted on his forehead, which you peel off $8 at a time. Then act accordingly." To reinforce his message, he would give bonuses to the employees with the fewest number of customer complaints.[13]

While the pizza manager's estimate was based more on his gut than on a spreadsheet calculation, he had the right idea. One of the keys to building successful and long-term relationships with customers is being able to calculate *customer lifetime value*, a metric that attempts to measure how much a customer will spend throughout his or her entire relationship with a company. To arrive at this value, determine how many regular customers you have (let's say it's 1,000), how long they typically remain loyal customers (say it's five years), and your typical net profit over that period of time ($5,000,000). Divide the total net profit by the number of customers and you end up with $5,000. So every one of your regular customers is worth $5,000 in profits over a span of five years.

This rudimentary example illustrates why companies consider a good customer to literally be money in the bank, which is why nurturing and extending the life span of a customer is a trait common to best-in-class supply chains. Variously referred to as "hero customers," "loyalists," and "apostles," these customers have bought into the promises your company offers them and keep coming back for more. It's important that you accurately identify the 20 percent of your customer base that makes up this loyal "hero" base, because these customers produce all of your profits.[14]

As we saw in Chapter 6, Dell has determined that it's much more cost effective to offer customers exactly what they want when they want it, even if that means the computer maker sometimes has to substitute a more expensive part in stock for a less expensive part that has to be ordered. Dell knows that keeping that customer's business, especially spread out over a period of years, will more than compensate for the modest concession it makes every time it offers a slightly better system for the same price as a lesser model. Dell runs its supply chain so well that the incidence of out-of-stocks is quite low to begin with, but if the situation calls for choosing between losing a customer or losing a little bit of margin, Dell and other best-in-class companies will opt for keeping the customer. That's just smart business.

Supply Chain at Your Service

Service parts management is another best practice area where companies can not only reduce their inventory costs but also strengthen their customer relationships. "Significant opportunities and measurable benefits await those who can realize the full potential of an effective service parts management system," observe Joe Parente and Robert Ticknor, directors with consulting firm BearingPoint. "A cutting-edge service parts management system clearly empowers companies in their quest for fully realizing customer lifetime value." Effective service organizations, they observe, can deliver up to twice the profit margin of their product sales counterparts.[15]

For automaker Hyundai's service parts operation, the customer is the dealers who stock the parts. As we saw in Chapter 2, keeping the dealers supplied with parts is a vital link within Hyundai's customer-centric supply chain. If a dealer doesn't have a needed part, then the car owner's level of satisfaction with his Hyundai model is going to suffer. If that experience happens repeatedly, chances are very strong that Hyundai will lose that consumer's business, perhaps forever.

To keep its dealer customers happy, the automaker has implemented an inventory control program called Smart Stock. "We populate our dealer inventory system with part classifications and best-in-class system parameters," explains Hyundai's George Kurth. "The system understands global demand and calculates orders. If the dealers stock product according to our recommendations, we can take back all excess inventory at one time, and then readjust inventory once per quarter." According to Kurth, the program works because "healthy dealers buy inventory that sells. Dealers won't be healthy with excess inventory on their shelves. And we can put their unused parts back into stock and resell it to other dealers."[16]

Those manufacturers that focus on service parts management often find they can eliminate inefficiency while improving inventory turns and delivery times. This streamlined service, Parente and Ticknor point out, benefits both the manufacturer and the customer—the manufacturer by optimizing its inventory investments, and the customer by receiving a higher level of service.[17]

A Culture of Customer Satisfaction

For several decades, J.D. Power and Associates has studied and measured customer satisfaction, honoring those companies that are best at listening to their customers' voices. Companies who reach that exalted best-in-class status consistently do three things:

1. They collect the right information from their customers.
2. They properly analyze that information and ensure that it gets into the hands of the people who are in a position to use it.
3. They properly act upon that information.[18]

Companies have discovered the value in using Web-based surveys and call centers to collect targeted information from their customers. Business analytics and CRM programs are available to crunch through all the mountains of customer data that come in and put that data into some kind of actionable context. But how do you know exactly what to do with that information? J.D. Power suggests every company should be able to answer these four questions:

1. Do you know how satisfied your customers are compared to your competitors' customers?
2. Do you measure how well each individual branch or department in your company is satisfying its customers?
3. Do you understand your customers' needs (i.e., what it takes to make them happy and, more important, get them to do business with you)?
4. Do you know how closely customer satisfaction is tied to your bottom line (i.e., its impact on loyalty, word of mouth, etc.)?

Question 3 is the most important, according to the J.D. Power book *Satisfaction*, because "understanding the needs of your customer provides a filter through which every decision must be screened. Developing a new product or service? Every phase of that process must begin and end with customer needs. Features, options, pricing strategy; they all depend on the wants, desires, and concerns of your customers."

The ultimate best practice, as borne out by countless studies J.D. Power has conducted over the years, is to build a culture of customer satisfaction from the top down, insisting that all employees throughout the organization focus on the customer and then empowering them to do so. As we saw with the Hershey's example earlier, if you fail to keep your customers satisfied, they'll find somebody else who can.

PART III

Supply Chain Strategies

CHAPTER 12

3PLs

When You'd Rather Not Do It Yourself

Flashpoints

Before you consider outsourcing part of your supply chain, you need to figure out what your core competency is.

Using a 3PL will give you the opportunity to focus more on your customers' needs.

A 3PL should be held accountable for its ability to meet your expectations.

Monitor every aspect of your 3PL's operation so that you have full visibility throughout the supply chain.

As one of the world's leading producers of cameras, Nikon wasn't about to be caught short when digital cameras became the latest can't-live-without-one consumer gadget. Ramping up its production facilities in the Far East was a relatively straightforward process; the challenge for Nikon was ensuring that its products were available and replenished whenever needed throughout North America. Nikon had to shorten its supply chain, and to do that, it needed help.

Nikon is headquartered in Tokyo, Japan, and manufactures its products in Japan, Korea, and Indonesia. And yet, for American retailers, distributors, and consumers, the center of Nikon's supply chain universe is actually Louisville, Kentucky. After the basic guts of the cameras are built in Asia, they are shipped direct to Louisville, where the cameras might be kitted with accessories such as batteries and chargers, or they might be repackaged according to the needs of specific retailers.

Kentucky is known for any number of things, horse racing and fried chicken being at the top of the list, but digital cameras certainly isn't one of them. So why would Nikon choose to center its North American supply chain strategy in Louisville? Because that's where United Parcel Service (UPS), Nikon's supply chain partner, is located. And, not coincidentally, that's where UPS's global air operations are located.

UPS handles more than 1 million packages per day at Worldport, based at the Louisville airport, where the package carrier averages 135 in-bound flights per day (or actually, per night, since all UPS flights occur when the Louisville airport is otherwise inactive). The physical operations are quite impressive, as UPS occupies 4 million square feet and more than 100 miles of conveyors in its package system. However, technology makes all the heavy lifting possible. Worldport processes 59 million database transactions per hour, from right there in Louisville, Nikon's North American supply chain hub.[1]

It's no accident, then, that Nikon's product distribution is based in Louisville, where UPS Supply Chain Solutions, a division that offers third-party logistics (3PL) services, operates a 2-million-square-foot campus that is home to more than 70 companies. While the sign outside might say UPS, inside the six nondescript facilities making up the campus you'll find high-tech diagnostics and repair, critical parts deployment, returns management, cross-dock facilities, product configuration and testing, and quality assurance.

A Shift to the Supply Chain Side

What's happening in Louisville is hardly unique. The same story is occurring throughout the United States, typically in medium-size cities like Memphis (TN), Indianapolis (IN), Cincinnati (OH), and Reno (NV) that have access to interstate highways and airports but are spared the congestion and infrastructure constraints of larger cities. According to Robert Lieb, professor of supply chain management at Northeastern University, at least 50 cities in the United States would like nothing better than to establish industry-focused villages in their area.

"If you're trying to run a lean manufacturing or a build-to-order operation, the appeal of having a clustering of related activities around a particular manufacturer is terrific because you're not worried about infrastructure, or being able to handle movement," Lieb points out. The biggest hurdle these budding supply chain villages have to overcome is lack of funding.[2]

Political roadblocks are often more difficult to navigate around than physical ones. To hear some politicians tell it, outsourcing is synonymous with taking jobs away from Americans, but as the Nikon example illustrates, outsourcing can just as easily be credited with bringing jobs *into* the United States. Although the national media, which tends to get preoccupied with doom-and-gloom stories, has yet to notice it, there's been a distinct shift to the supply chain side in the United States, and the emergence of 3PLs is much more than just an interesting sidebar. It's evidence that for best-in-class companies today, competitive advantage comes from knowing when to say "Frankly, I'd rather *not* do it myself."

Letting Somebody Else Do It

As we've seen in previous chapters, many well-known and highly regarded manufacturers today are in fact brand managers, since they no longer do any of the actual making. Dell, Nike, Cisco Systems—these are all examples of product-centric companies that do not make their own products, at least not in the traditional sense. In the same way, companies that used to rely on their own employees to run their warehouses and schedule outbound freight transportation are now relying on 3PLs to do these and similar logistics tasks for them.

At a Glance

Third-Party Logistics Provider

A third-party logistics provider (3PL) is an asset-based or non–asset-based company that manages one or more logistics processes or operations (typically, transportation or warehousing) for another company.

In fact, most companies (roughly 80 percent within North America and at least 70 percent in other industrial regions of the world) are already using an outsourcer for at least one key supply chain task. These outsourcers, known in supply chain circles as 3PLs, have grown within the past decade to become a global market worth $200 billion in 2008, according to market research firm Armstrong & Associates. In fact, major companies such as Ford Motor, General Motors, PepsiCo, Procter & Gamble, and Wal-Mart each use 30 or more 3PLs.[3]

Worldwide, the services most frequently outsourced to a 3PL, according to a 2009 3PL study (http://3plstudy.com) conducted by Georgia Institute of Technology and consulting firm Capgemini, are:

- Domestic transportation (86 percent of responding companies)
- International transportation (84 percent)

- Customs brokerage (71 percent)
- Warehousing (68 percent)
- Forwarding (65 percent)
- Cross-docking (39 percent)

According to Northeastern University's Robert Lieb, the average amount of time a company has worked with its primary 3PL is more than six years. Also, in the true spirit of supply chain management, many companies report that their major suppliers and customers are also served by their primary 3PL. Conversely, 30 percent of the companies surveyed indicated that their use of 3PL services has had a negative impact on their supply chain integration efforts. So clearly, simply signing a 3PL contract is not necessarily a best practice. As we shall see, companies using 3PLs must by definition develop specific best practices in managing those relationships.[4]

Supply Chain Essentials and Nonessentials

The increasing sophistication of supply chains—spanning corporate departments and global boundaries—has made it imperative that supply chain professionals think far beyond the four walls of their companies. At a strategic level, this requires a close study of every task, process, and operation within a company's extended enterprise. Because few companies actually have this expertise in-house, and fewer still are willing to invest resources in nonstrategic areas, a new breed of third-party supply chain specialists has emerged to offer their services to companies that are willing to let somebody else do the actual work.

Much of the motivation behind this trend is that companies are increasingly being challenged to focus on their core competencies. The question constantly being put to them is: How good are you at what you do, in every aspect of your business? Many companies are best in class at designing products, for instance, but are strictly average in the actual building of them. In previous generations, that might have been a black mark against the company, but today the ability to accurately assess your strengths and weaknesses is itself a best practice.

Many of the noncore tasks that manufacturers once routinely performed just because that's the way things got done are now being outsourced to companies that specialize in offering a narrow niche of services. *The World Is Flat* author Thomas Friedman refers to this process as *insourcing*[5] because third-party employees "come right inside your company; analyze its manufacturing, packaging, and delivery processes; and then design, redesign, and manage your whole global supply chain."[6]

As supply chain consultant Jim Tompkins sees it, all of the activities a typical manufacturing company has to perform can be broken down into four categories of essential and nonessential tasks:

1. *Primary core tasks.* Things that differentiate you in the marketplace (e.g., production, product design, production planning, and scheduling)
2. *Secondary core tasks.* Things that need to be done well but are not visible to the customer (e.g., procurement, logistics, human resources, maintenance)
3. *Primary noncore tasks.* Things that if not done well can have a negative impact on your customer relationships (e.g., information technology, finance and accounting, sales and marketing)
4. *Secondary noncore tasks.* Things that need to be done but do not have a significant impact on the success of your business (e.g., real estate, food service, landscaping)[7]

Finding Your Core Competency

Consider the case of Moen Inc., one of the best-known manufacturers of plumbing products. The company considers itself best in class when it comes to sinks and faucets; when it comes to areas outside of its core competency, however, Moen is willing to look elsewhere for help. The company has developed an internal evaluation model that helps it identify when and where it needs help:

- Is this process or function strategic to our organization?
- Does this process or task provide us with a competitive advantage?
- Do we want to upgrade performance in this area to differentiate us from our competitors?

If the answer to any of these questions is no, then Moen will consider outsourcing that process, explains Scott Saunders, the company's vice president of supply chain. For instance, Moen uses a 3PL to design and develop the right kind of packaging to conform to the pallet configuration needs of a major retail customer. Because packaging design expertise wasn't considered a competency that it needed to have in-house, Moen decided to outsource that task.[8]

What it all boils down to is how you answer the question: How good are you at what you do? Whether outsourcing a piece of your supply chain to a 3PL is worth the trouble depends as much on you as it does the 3PL.

"In areas where we don't want to invest, we look to 3PLs to make that investment," Saunders states. "We ask 'Are we the best in the world at that function? Is it a strategic competence area?' If not, we consider outsourcing."

It was the same story, though in a vastly different industry, for PIC USA, a supplier of breeding stock to farms, cooperatives, and others involved in pork production. "Our core competency is swine genetics," observes Ole Torgeson, transport logistics manager. "We used to have our own fleet and drivers, but we realized that transportation was not our specialty and it would probably be better for us to outsource it to someone else."[9]

But choosing a 3PL isn't as easy as consulting a directory and calling around. Most companies today expect considerable value added from their outsourced partners. Saunders, for instance, expects a 3PL to be proactive when it comes to moving Moen's freight—that means suggesting creative solutions, not just mimicking the same processes Moen had done in the past.

"We recognized transportation management wasn't our core competency and thought we could save time and resources by outsourcing the function," Saunders remembers. However, despite being a major player in its niche, Moen didn't have much luck at first when it started looking for the right 3PL. The company's transportation spend wasn't considered large enough to make it worth their while to the major 3PLs who were invited to bid on the business. "The big guys didn't find our business attractive enough, and they didn't offer us enough perceived value to take us to the next level," he says.

Ultimately, Moen did find a 3PL partner, but as Saunders learned, that was just the beginning of the process. Managing a 3PL relationship takes a special knack all its own. It involves skill sets that in many ways are different from those needed to manage the actual task. "It's more like managing a purchasing or sourcing function," he says. "An operations person may not be successful at managing a 3PL relationship."

In the case of PIC USA, the key was to find a 3PL that was as familiar with site selection as it was with transportation management. PIC was shifting its business model from a centralized network that delivered large volumes of lower-priced animals to a decentralized system delivering low volumes of high-priced animals. As a result, PIC searched till it found a 3PL able to perform a site location study as well as a routing and scheduling analysis. The 3PL discovered that PIC needed to revamp its distribution network so that its hubs were closer to the source farms. This led to a reduction in the specialized metric of miles per pig from nine miles to eight, Torgeson explains, which in dollars and cents saved PIC $80,000 per year. (The less time a pig spends on a truck, the healthier it is on arrival.) The reduction in fuel costs due to being closer to the customer has also resulted in significant savings.

Square Pegs And Round Holes

Before you undertake a 3PL relationship, you need to evaluate your own company, Saunders advises. You won't be able to identify if the 3PL is improving your logistics if you never measure your own performance. Look at your own organization with realistic expectations, and make sure you measure the right things internally. If you measure the wrong things, he warns, it will skew your expectations.

Moen uses a 3PL partnership model developed by Ohio State University to measure the effectiveness of its outsourcers. "The model contains a supplier agreement and leads us to spend time with our supplier base developing goals and expectations for both sides. We tie the expectations to scorecards linked to performance. We review those scorecards monthly to gauge performance to expectations," Saunders explains. "And we're willing to reevaluate the relationship and adjust the expectations and the scorecard if we didn't get it right from the start."

The key is finding a comfort level where the customer trusts the 3PL to do its job properly, and the 3PL is confident enough in its abilities that it freely shares the best practices it's learned from other customers and other industries. Reaching that comfort level, however, can be a frustratingly long time in coming.

"Perhaps companies that haven't found a service provider that adds value are trying to fit a square peg into a round hole," suggests Stephen Erb, manager of service parts logistics with truck manufacturer International Truck and Engine Corp. "3PLs tend to specialize in specific competencies and industries. If you want to outsource, specify what you want to achieve, identify the gaps, and use a cross-functional team to evaluate 3PLs. Make sure the provider has the people and processes to support the changes you want to implement."[10]

Think Strategically

Like Moen, network computer maker Sun Microsystems also uses a scorecard to rank its 3PLs in several categories. The high-tech company has very clear expectations for continuous improvement, notes Randy Louie, Sun's director of customer fulfillment. "We set targets for 3PLs every quarter and we measure performance every quarter. The targets get tougher to achieve even as we make improvements." The quarterly scorecard results are discussed, with the emphasis put on identifying the root cause of any problems and steps that need to be taken to correct those problems.

In the scorecard process, the most critical area is cost, Louie explains. Consistent profitability is a paramount goal for the company, so Louie's team assesses market pricing and measures its suppliers against it. Quality is another important consideration. "All products and services provided by 3PLs are measured in the context of the quality of service we receive," Louie states. How many products are damaged in transit? How accurate are the bill of materials and invoices? Sun's 3PLs are held accountable for their ability to meet expectations.

Availability is also a key performance measure. When Sun is paying for three-day service, do the products actually arrive in three days? Sun sets the bar high, expecting 99 percent of all deliveries to meet the specified service levels.

However, Sun also encourages its 3PLs to think strategically. "We bring our strategy directly to the 3PLs," Louie states. "We agree on initiatives or programs we believe will enable us to achieve our objectives." Sun scores its suppliers on goals such as implementing direct shipping in a region. It defines and measures how successful the 3PLs are at meeting those goals and factors that into the performance score.[11]

The Financial Impact of Outsourcing

Just because a company has outsourced some of its logistics or production tasks does not mean it can outsource the ultimate responsibility for those roles. It's quite the contrary: Supply chain professionals at companies need to be tuned in to every aspect of a 3PL's operation so that they know where their products are at every point in the cycle.

Greg Meseck, a senior vice president with risk management consulting firm Marsh, relates the consequences of not keeping a strict eye on the outsourcing process. "A global pharmaceutical company outsourced the production of a key drug to a third party," Meseck remembers. "The pharmaceutical company held the marketing rights to this new drug. The outsourced manufacturer had a major disruption and, as a result, was unable to provide the drug per the agreed-upon terms. Due to the late delivery, both the pharmaceutical company and the outsourced provider suffered significant financial losses in terms of lost market capitalization and reduced revenues."

Most companies, Meseck believes, are unable to model the risks inherent in outsourcing and the corresponding probable results, nor can they map these outcomes to their financial statements. Best-in-class companies, however, have identified ways they can calculate the financial impact of outsourcing. Analyzing supply chains from a risk perspective offers companies a better understanding of the potential sources of a disruption, he notes, and most important, the potential financial impact resulting from a disruption.

Start by constructing a financial framework, Meseck recommends, which identifies key supply chain risk areas as well as critical risk drivers. These drivers include lead times, single-source suppliers, Customs clearance times, material availability, level of customer customization, product returns, financial strength of key suppliers, and port location. The next step, he says, is to assess the percentage of total risk by category, and then to incorporate this information into a financial model.

As Meseck explains, "Mapping the risk categories to the financial statements provides management with a fact-based approach to identifying and quantifying risk." This enables companies to make a 3PL decision based on operational, financial, and risk factors. As a result, he notes, a company will be "fully able to leverage its outsourcing capabilities in order to meet customer demands regarding cost, quality, and timeliness while effectively managing the underlying risks associated with outsourcing."[12]

Staying in Touch

One of the first questions manufacturing companies ask a prospective 3PL is: "How can we stay in touch with our customers if we outsource service to you?" While it may not be the answer you're hoping to hear, a 3PL is entirely within its rights to respond "That's up to you." Just because you outsource some of your supply chain functions doesn't mean you stop interacting with your customer base. If anything, as discussed in the previous chapter, knowing what your customers want and keeping them happy should be one of your company's core competencies, so using a 3PL for other tasks gives you the opportunity to get even closer to your customers.

"It's irrelevant to the customer that we use a third party," says John Mascaritolo, director of global logistics with high-tech manufacturer NCR Corp. "We always try to have NCR exposure to the customer. If we have a set delivery schedule going to 1,000 stores for a retail customer, our project manager oversees that we meet our commitment."

NCR's customers expect on-time deliveries, complete and undamaged—in other words, the "perfect order." (See Chapter 11.) Whether NCR or a 3PL is managing the logistics, ultimately NCR is judged on how well, or poorly, those orders are managed. To stay in tune with its customers' expectations, NCR assigns project managers and sales personnel to regularly meet with its customers after a product has been delivered and installed. In addition, Mascaritolo and his staff frequently meet with the 3PL. "We expect some problems or blips and we bring out-of-scope issues as well as new business challenges to them. Our business and our relationship are always changing. Our partners need to be flexible enough to go along with the changes," he says.

"We have accountability for the performance of our organization even though we outsource the work," adds Gary MacNew, vice president of customer service and logistics with frozen food company Rich Products. "We expect the same or better performance [from our 3PL] than if we did it ourselves." MacNew's staff, like Mascaritolo's, includes people who are directly responsible for overseeing the 3PLs.[13]

Going beyond the 3PL Model

While 3PLs generally assume responsibility for specific services, some companies prefer to outsource even more responsibility to an entity known as a lead logistics provider (LLP), which functions much like a general contractor because it manages all of a company's logistics activities. Since an LLP often acts as an overseer over one or more 3PLs (and since the supply chain field loves to create acronyms), it is sometimes referred to as a fourth-party logistics provider (4PL).

At a Glance

Lead Logistics Provider

A lead logistics provider (LLP) manages all logistics activities for a company, including management of 3PLs. It is sometimes referred to as a fourth-party logistics provider (4PL) because an LLP functions as a third-party overseer of other third parties.

One of the first and best-known LLPs was Vector SCM, a joint venture formed by automaker General Motors and Menlo Worldwide, a 3PL. Vector SCM was designed to "act as the nervous system within the supply chain, providing design and engineering and creative solutions tied to order fulfillment, manufacturing, logistics, and supply chain, end to end," according to Greg Humes, president and chief executive of Vector SCM. Although GM's financial difficulties ultimately led it to reabsorb Vector SCM's logistics capabilities in 2006, at its peak the joint venture integrated all of GM's 3PL relationships and managed more than 80 percent of the automaker's annual $6 billion logistics spend.

An LLP can help make your company more competitive, but you have to be willing to give up some control over your supply chain. For instance, the supply chain of International Truck and Engine includes an LLP, which manages the inbound flow of parts to the 3PLs who directly support the manufacturing plants. As Stephen Erb explains, International is responsible for managing at the strategic level while the LLP manages at the day-to-day operational level. "The LLP brings knowledge from working with other clients, as well as quality resources and project specialists who can look at our process, educate and work with our associates, and identify opportunities," Erb says.

Employees of the LLP often work shoulder to shoulder with International's staff, looking for opportunities to improve processes, he explains. By doing this, the LLP has been able to identify specific ways to improve the truck maker's logistics processes. "When they evaluated our truckload deliveries direct from suppliers, they found some suppliers were underutilizing trailer cube," Erb says, so the LLP worked with those suppliers to improve the way they loaded the trucks.[14]

"It's easier to justify using the 4PL model in a growth environment where the supply chain changes frequently," observes Victor Guzman, director of supply chain and logistics with aerospace manufacturer Honeywell International. For that reason, Honeywell set up a 4PL relationship within a rapidly growing business unit that lacked a logistics infrastructure. "For us, a 4PL sitting on top of 3PLs is the entity that ensures coordination in day-to-day execution," Guzman says. "They also take a step back and analyze our overall activity, identifying opportunities for improvement in customer service and financial performance."

Honeywell rewards its 4PL with financial incentives for projects that lead to better logistics performance. "We pay for returns, not ideas," Guzman notes. "They benefit from projects that work."[15]

Outpacing the Competition

Outsourcing a supply chain process can help a company achieve several benefits, particularly by enabling it to focus on its core business. As William Frech and Ben Pivar, consultants with Capgemini, point out, a third-party outsourcer can also help a company:

- Tap into unrealized cost savings by leveraging spend across the enterprise.
- Accelerate the achievement of results.
- Provide better tracking of key operational functions.
- Add value by converting operations from overhead to competitive strength.

- Decrease supplier costs through leverage of volume discounts, objectivity, and reduced cycle times.
- Improve adherence to policies.
- Improve inventory performance through sophisticated statistical techniques.
- Outpace competition through use of leading-edge technology and best practices methodologies.[16]

CHAPTER 13

Collaboration

Extending the Enterprise

Flashpoints

The key to any successful relationship, supply chain or otherwise, is mutual trust.

Sharing transactional data with suppliers and customers can lead to expanded sales opportunities for everybody.

Recognize that not all of your suppliers are reliable in fulfilling orders on time and complete, and adjust your plans accordingly.

Use performance measures to monitor the overall effectiveness of your collaborative efforts.

When he was head of purchasing for Big Three automaker Chrysler Corp. in the 1990s, Thomas Stallkamp used to think all the time about collaborating with his key supply chain partners. As the nucleus of its own supply chain hub, Chrysler was in a good position to demand whatever it wanted from its suppliers. Like the other major automakers, Chrysler existed in a marketplace where just a few U.S. companies (Chrysler, Ford, General Motors) got to be the king, and all the links to their supply chains occupied progressively lower ranks.

Though it seems archaic, the automotive industry makes no secret of its class system. At the top are the OEMs (original equipment manufacturers), while the major suppliers to the OEMs—companies that deliver finished products such as tires, cooling systems, or chassis—are known as Tier Ones. Manufacturers who sell directly to the Tier Ones rather than the OEMs are called Tier Twos, and so on down the supply chain until you get to the commodity producers (manufacturers of ball bearings, nuts and bolts, etc.).

This class system has been in place for decades, mostly because it works to the advantage of the OEMs, but in the 1990s, when Chrysler was staring down one economic crisis after another, it became clear that a new approach to supplier management was needed. That led Stallkamp to look closely at the approach then up-and-coming computer maker Dell was taking by forming tightly knit partnerships with its most important suppliers, an approach known as the *extended enterprise*. These types of collaborative partnerships are characterized by shared goals and rewards, clearly defined roles and responsibilities, and open lines of communication.[1]

Recognizing the expanding threat of Japanese automakers to the Big Three's status quo, Stallkamp seized on a concept that dates back to the post–World War II days in Japan: the *keiretsu*. A keiretsu is an integrated group of companies that function as a joint partnership—kind of like a supply chain. Stallkamp cites the example of Toyota and its relationship with two Tier One suppliers, Denso and Seiki. "Instead of treating them as distant and independent entities, Toyota shares product planning and proprietary cost information with these two companies," he explains. "Both companies assume complete responsibility for developing the components that they are assigned on a Toyota project," with employees from each of these three companies often working in each other's facilities.

The key, Stallkamp emphasizes, is that Toyota trusts its suppliers to meet their development and production deadlines. "Working jointly and in such close cooperation with its own keiretsu is one way that Toyota is able to leverage its development of new products and come to market more quickly than the domestic American automakers," he observes. Stallkamp introduced that idea of establishing and fostering a closer relationship with Chrysler's own suppliers at his company, where an Americanized version of the keiretsu became known as Chrysler's extended enterprise.

Mutually Beneficial Relationships

"The extended enterprise is a philosophy that we implemented which integrates selected suppliers in the whole supply chain," Stallkamp recalls. "Instead of looking at them as separate links in the chain, we concentrated on the chain itself and on managing that concept. Instead of managing the chain in little segments, we tried to do it holistically."[2]

That led to the formation of Chrysler's SCORE (Supplier Cost Reduction Effort) program. (Not to be confused with the Supply Chain Council's SCOR model, discussed in Chapter 3.) For the automotive industry, SCORE went beyond high concept and actually delivered on what the academics had been punditing about for years—a living-and-breathing model of strategic collaboration with supply chain partners. By seeking cost reduction solutions from its suppliers rather than demanding across-the-board price cuts (a tactic then in vogue at rivals General Motors and Ford), Chrysler not only rebounded from an economic crisis in the early 1990s but in fact achieved cumulative savings of $5.5 billion throughout the decade, thanks to SCORE.

Winning Small Victories

The natural tendency of companies when they get in trouble is to become more adversarial, but the opposite approach—partnering with your suppliers to develop collaborative relationships—is the best course of action, Stallkamp believes.

Many people mistakenly thought that SCORE was just a cost reduction program, he notes. "It was actually an idea generation program." For instance, Chrysler's research and development (R&D) costs were the lowest percentage of sales of any automotive OEM, and yet the company was able to introduce more new vehicles than its competitors. How? By tapping into the R&D capability of its suppliers. Since Chrysler was awarding long-term contracts to suppliers that could meet defined targets, those companies came to view Chrysler as the best company in which to invest their limited R&D resources. It became a win-win situation for all those involved.

How does a company get into a position where collaboration can produce the desired results? "You start off by making sure your senior management buys into this concept," Stallkamp emphasizes. "If you back off a little bit, or you're perceived as being insincere, it'll fail. The only way it can work is if the person at the top of your company buys into collaboration."

After that, you need to proactively build trust among your suppliers and customers through small examples. "You have to work at this daily, winning small victories, and publicizing the success stories that showcase examples of where you listened to your suppliers." Stallkamp remains cautiously optimistic that American manufacturers will change their supplier management style, moving from conflict to collaboration with their supply chain partners. "The model of the old adversarial way is broken," he states, "so I don't think we have any other alternative."

Ironically, Chrysler became a victim of its own success when it was acquired by Daimler Benz, a German automaker whose managers were famously adverse to the collaborative style Stallkamp had championed. Shortly after the merger, the renamed DaimlerChrysler reverted to its adversarial ways of the past, Stallkamp moved on to other ventures, and the Detroit Big Three automakers lost even more market share to Japan's "big three" of Toyota, Honda, and Nissan. The story doesn't end there, though.

In the fall of 2005, hoping to avoid filing for bankruptcy protection, Ford announced its Aligned Business Framework, a series of long-term agreements with several Tier One suppliers based on a familiar concept: collaboration. Ford began offering up-front payment of engineering and development costs in exchange for supplier commitment to bring technology innovations to Ford. A key provision of the framework is that Ford significantly expanded its volume of business with these select suppliers while cutting in half the number of suppliers it used for parts and commodities. Coincidence or not, at this writing (2009) Ford is the only one of the Detroit Big Three automakers that has not declared bankruptcy.[3]

"If the North American automotive industry is to reinvent itself, both the automakers and suppliers must make changes to the way they work with one another," asserts Steve Rose, automotive practice lead at Kotler Marketing Group. Just as the Japanese car makers have traditionally rewarded their suppliers for their contributions to vehicle design, so too should American OEMs consider wholeheartedly adopting the idea of a truly collaborative partnership with their suppliers. For instance, Rose recommends that the Detroit Big Three either "radically revamp" the incentive structure of their purchasing departments, or else do away with it completely. "Better scorecards need to be developed that reward suppliers that bring true value and innovation."[4]

Respecting Your Partners

As Jeffrey Liker explains in his book, *The Toyota Way*, one of the key principles that Toyota follows day in and day out is: Respect your extended network of partners and suppliers by challenging them and helping them improve.[5] (See Chapter 17.) Echoing that philosophy, Robert Handfield, a professor at North Carolina State University, observes that, even during times of recession and economic turmoil, companies need to work with each other, as it's in everybody's best interests that their industries not fail. "Managers of supply chains need to reach out to critical suppliers and work on strengthening their business," Handfield notes, "both to weather the crisis and increase profits for the future."[6]

Research firm Planning Perspectives decided to study exactly which automotive OEMs did best when their suppliers were given a chance to weigh in. In a 2008 survey of nearly 300 Tier One suppliers, Toyota and Honda were far and away the companies suppliers preferred to do business with. Nissan finished third, with Ford receiving the highest marks among the U.S.-based OEMs. GM and Chrysler brought up the rear. Explaining the significance of the rankings, John Henke, Jr., president of Planning

Perspectives, observes that with so much negative attention being focused on the Detroit Big Three, maintaining a cavalier attitude toward suppliers is exactly the wrong message to send. "Now is not the time to take an adversarial approach to working with suppliers," he points out. "The challenges of rampant increases in material costs, poor economic conditions, and increasingly intensive competition require that each OEM works more closely than ever with its suppliers to maximize [their] chances for success."[7]

Henke suggests that OEMs should refocus their efforts in developing meaningful, collaborative relationships with their suppliers. "By putting in place performance metrics that drive the behaviors of the personnel who interface with suppliers, the needed supplier relations will occur," he says. "With the right performance metrics, every OEM can improve its supplier relations to the benefit of both itself and its suppliers."

In any event, it's clear that the evolving role of supplier collaboration will have major implications on the American auto industry for years to come.

A Better Way to Sell Mouthwash

In 1995, while Chrysler's SCORE program was offering a new way for automakers to partner with their Tier One suppliers, retail giant Wal-Mart Stores Inc. was embarking on an entirely separate effort that nevertheless had the same goal: establishing a closer relationship with its vendors. And just like Chrysler, Wal-Mart's initiative was launched out of frustration with the status quo.

Pharmaceutical supplier Warner-Lambert (now part of Pfizer Inc.) had a problem keeping Wal-Mart's shelves stocked with its popular Listerine mouthwash product. It was the classic retail dilemma—the out-of-stock rate was far too high, which forced Warner-Lambert to maintain significant safety stock to satisfy the demand from its retail customers. Jay Nearnberg, Warner-Lambert's director of customer replenishment, was feeling the pressure since the out-of-stock problem was costing his company millions of dollars in lost sales. It was also hurting the company in terms of credibility, both with retailers and with consumers.

Wal-Mart had laid down the law: Warner-Lambert needed to get its in-stock levels up to 98 percent, or else. The "or else" included such dire punishments as the retailer cutting back on shelf space, no longer supporting promotions, and refusing to add new products from the company. So, for Nearnberg, failure to reach 98 percent was not an option.

As Ronald Ireland, information technology manager with Wal-Mart at the time, remembers, Nearnberg consulted with the retailer about its automated replenishment system, Retail Link, and learned that Warner-Lambert, like other suppliers, could use the system to access point-of-sale history as well as a 65-week forecast. Up to that point, Warner-Lambert wasn't using Wal-Mart's Retail Link to develop its own forecasts; for that matter, neither were most of Wal-Mart's other suppliers.

"It was well known that Wal-Mart's demand forecasts and replenishment schedules were inaccurate," Ireland explains. "There also would be challenges in integrating a single customer's forecasts into production planning without additional customers' critical mass also included." Wal-Mart, however, assumed that its trading partners would provide useful feedback that would improve the quality of the forecasts. The real goal, according to Ireland, was for the suppliers to collaborate with the retailer to improve the accuracy of the forecast and replenishment schedules. "The replenishment plan," he explains, "was based on the forecast, so it was imperative to create as accurate a demand forecast as possible. The more accurate the forecast, the more accurate the replenishment schedule would be."[8]

Ultimately, the two companies launched a pilot program called collaborative forecasting and replenishment (CFAR). This project let both companies share and compare sales and order forecasts, with one of the benefits being that Warner-Lambert now knew when Wal-Mart was scheduling promotional events. In the past, not knowing exactly when such promotions would occur, the drug company's strategy was to keep enough inventory on hand to prevent out-of-stocks.[9]

At a Glance

Collaborative Planning, Forecasting, and Replenishment

Collaborative planning, forecasting, and replenishment (CPFR) enables supply chain partners to share historical data and develop plans to manufacture and distribute a product. This shared information is used to forecast needs, establish and alter promotion timelines, and determine when stock or supplies need to be replenished.

By linking customer demand with replenishment needs, the in-stock percentages for Listerine increased from 85 percent to 98 percent. Equally impressive was a sales hike of $8.5 million during the pilot test, which not only convinced Wal-Mart and Warner-Lambert that sharing information with supply chain partners was a good idea but also led in 1996 to a full-scale launch of the slightly renamed collaborative planning, forecasting, and replenishment (CPFR) effort, under the sponsorship of the newly formed Voluntary Interindustry Commerce Standards (VICS) Association.

A Nine-Step Program for CPFR

In the late 1990s, VICS developed a CPFR process model (www.vics.org) that focuses on these nine steps:

1. *Develop a front-end agreement*. The retailer/distributor and manufacturer establish guidelines and rules for the relationship.
2. *Create a joint business plan*. The manufacturer and retailer create a partnership strategy and then define category roles, objectives, and tactics.
3. *Create a sales forecast*, based on the retailer's point-of-sale (POS) data and other information. The sales forecast is then used to create an order forecast.
4. *Identify exceptions for the sales forecast*. The partners identify items that fall outside sales forecast constraints set jointly by the manufacturer and retailer/distributor. They then develop a list of exception items.
5. *Resolve/collaborate on exception items*. The partners then submit an adjusted forecast.
6. *Create an order forecast*. The partners combine POS data, causal information, and inventory strategies to generate a specific order forecast that supports the shared sales forecast and joint business plan. This allows the manufacturer to allocate production capacity against demand while minimizing safety stock. It also gives the retailer increased confidence that orders will be delivered.
7. *Identify exceptions for the order forecast*, based on the predetermined criteria established in the front-end agreement.
8. *Resolve/collaborate on exception items*. As with step 5, the partners then submit another adjusted forecast.
9. *Generate the order*. The order forecast becomes a committed order.

Great Expectations, So-So Results

Being honest with yourself is an important first step on the road to self-improvement, and consumer packaged goods (CPG) giant Unilever was refreshingly forthright about the state of its supply chain when it launched its Path to Growth initiative in 2000. "Rather than arguing about the definition of 'world class,' we decided it was much easier to admit that the supply chain we had wasn't world class," explains Fred Berkheimer, vice president of logistics for Unilever's Home and Personal Care division.[10]

Prior to 2000, Unilever used an internally focused, insular method of forecasting, but that traditional approach was no longer working as customers demanded more service. And when you consider that Unilever's customers include such retail giants as Wal-Mart, Target, and Kroger, having a so-so supply chain just wasn't good enough any more. Throughout the 1990s, the relationship between CPG companies and major retailers became increasingly complex as the manufacturers introduced a plethora of new products to accommodate the merchandising and promotional activities of the retailers. On the logistics front, retailers were adopting zero-inventory policies, which led to the rise of cross-docking at distribution points. (Cross-docking is described in detail in Chapter 8.)

As one of the world's biggest CPG companies, Unilever was challenged to increase its asset utilization, lower its inventories, and improve its customer service. From Berkheimer's perspective, the best place to start was by improving its planning and forecasting processes. And, as Warner-Lambert had learned earlier from its CPFR pilot test with Wal-Mart, there are so many unforeseen factors and unpredictable events in the retail world that a manufacturer's forecasting accuracy could only improve by establishing a collaborative relationship with the retailers. So, as one of the original members of the VICS CPFR committee, Unilever began its own pilot projects to work collaboration into its supply chain relationships.

Berkheimer characterizes the company's supply chain back then as being "like a duck that looks calm above water, and is paddling like crazy underneath." At the time, Unilever did not have a common supply chain planning system for any of the product lines it had acquired, such as the Helene Curtis, Chesebrough Ponds, and Lever Bros. brands. "When you talk about speed-to-market, we were un-speed-to-market. We just couldn't get out of our own way."

High accuracy in replenishment can be achieved only through order forecast collaboration and extended supply chain visibility, Berkheimer explains, and to that end CPFR is a driver for better internal processes, planning, and forecasting. "Companies should be focusing on these goals whether they do CPFR or not."[11]

In its simplest form, CPFR compares two forecasts and decides which one is right, adds Raz Caciula, director of best practice planning for Unilever's Home and Personal Care division. "What's the use of collaborating with a customer and agreeing on a forecast when, internally, you have two or three different forecasts?" Getting to that point required a technology upgrade that would allow the company's logistics and sales departments to share the same information, and then compare that forecast to the forecast of a retail customer.

As one of the first companies to go the CPFR route, Unilever had rather high expectations for its early pilot projects and initially was frustrated at how long it took to realize those expectations. The reality of CPFR, as Caciula came to see, is that the retailer will enjoy benefits before the manufacturer because the retailer will reach critical mass faster (with critical mass identified as between 70 and 80 percent of the forecast). "It's simple mathematics," Caciula explains. During a CPFR project, a retailer will reach critical mass almost instantly on an individual stock-keeping unit; the manufacturer, however, will reach critical mass only after it has established a collaborative relationship with many retailers.

At any rate, though its accomplishments were initially more modest than expected, Unilever achieved a 10 percent reduction in inventory, a 10 percent improvement in forecast accuracy, and a 5 percent increase in sales thanks to better in-stock availability. The company's logistics department also improved its on-time delivery performance and became more efficient at handling its retail customers' promotions. Although by no means a magic bullet, CPFR has proven to be a catalyst for helping Unilever adopt best practices throughout its supply chain.

More Reliability and Better Service

In some ways, CPFR represents the latest in a long tradition of retail-centric efforts to solve a problem that can't really ever be solved but at least can be guessed at more intelligently: How many products are consumers going to buy, and when? Vendor-managed inventory (VMI), for instance, which got its start several decades ago, is a replenishment practice where the manufacturer manages the inventory of its products at a retail location. The retailer provides regular inventory updates to the manufacturer, who's responsible for replenishing that supply as needed. The manufacturer benefits by having more reliable sales data to base its forecasts on; the retailer benefits because it no longer has to maintain its inventory levels.[12]

At a Glance

Vendor-Managed Inventory

Vendor-managed inventory (VMI) involves the supplier, rather than the retailer, taking responsibility for maintaining the retailer's inventory levels based on transactional data shared by the retailer.

Apparel and personal care retailer Limited Brands, for instance, uses VMI to manage stock on hand and to speed products to market. "We are not mass merchandisers," points out Nick LaHowchic, president and chief executive of the company's logistics services operation. "We depend on newness. We need to get out of things quickly and into new things quickly. We need to be out there first and react to what the customer wants."

Limited Brands prepares a weekly report for its suppliers based on transactional information it collects on a daily basis from each of its 3,650 stores. Any unusual activity or exceptions are passed along to suppliers whenever they occur. LaHowchic uses VMI as a means of pushing inventory farther back into the supply chain. "We think about how we can bypass steps or change our manufacturing strategy," he says.

Limited's postponement strategy includes moving product directly from a factory to a store, and in many cases the inventory being held by suppliers is not even close to being a finished product, whether it's uncolored or uncut fabric, or bases and common components for hand creams and soap. "We can pre-position it in the supply chain, and decide later the type of garment or fashion details," he explains.

Limited's use of VMI has improved its reliability and service, LaHowchic notes, but it's also paid off for the suppliers. "VMI offers higher continuity in how the suppliers manage the supply chain," he says. "It gives them more insight into customer likes and dislikes, and they are more aware of consumption."

When properly managed, VMI can be as beneficial to a supplier as it is to the retailer. Another retailer, Ace Hardware, which uses a combination of VMI and CPFR, can point to several success stories involving its suppliers, notes Scott Smith, the company's department manager of inventory. For example, one small manufacturer grew its business from $2 million in sales to Ace to $7 million over a four-year span. "While part of the growth was from better fill rates," Smith says, "by far the majority was because they operated more efficiently in the supply chain than their competition, so it was a no-brainer to increase their volume."[13]

VMI can indeed drive more business, agrees Steve Banker, service director of supply chain management with analyst firm ARC Advisory Group, but he cautions that manufacturers could end up implementing it in a way where it affects cash flow. For manufacturers, "the most advanced forms of VMI involve having a warehouse for your key supplier close to your factory," Banker notes. "Often what happens is there is a line in the factory and the goods come into the factory and they are still owned by the vendor until they cross over that line," negatively affecting cash flow. As a result, the supplier ends up owning inventory for longer periods of time and carrying more inventory risk. That's often the trade-off, Banker says, for getting more business.[14]

Challenges in Supplier Management

This book has looked at the various best practices that companies have developed and adopted in their quest to improve their supply chains. The very nature of supply chain management implies that companies are looking beyond their four walls to improve their processes; they're working closely with their suppliers or their customers, or, better still, both. In reality, human nature plays just as big a role in determining whether a best practice actually will succeed or fail. Let's face it: Nobody wants to feel as if they're being taken advantage of, and as with any partnership, the only way you can attain a mutually beneficial relationship is if all of the parties involved are committed to it.

When analyst firm Aberdeen Group and *Logistics Today* magazine polled supply chain executives about the most challenging issues they face in supplier management, they identified these roadblocks:

- Suppliers aren't always reliable in fulfilling orders on time and complete.
- Suppliers aren't always able to provide accurate, timely information on in-process/in-transit orders.
- It's difficult to integrate electronically to suppliers due to technical capabilities.
- Lead times from suppliers are longer than desired.
- Suppliers aren't always willing to meet manufacturer's guidelines.[15]

As Brooks Bentz, an associate partner with consulting firm Accenture, points out, when it comes to supply chain management, "Each party needs something that the other is hard-pressed (or loath) to deliver. It's the battle of the bottom lines."[16] For instance, logistics managers want to keep their transportation costs as low as possible, while the motor carriers are under constant pressure to raise their rates to keep pace with the ever-growing cost of fuel, the need to attract and pay truck drivers, and a desire to improve their return on invested capital in equipment. Both parties need each other; what's more, they *know* they need each other. But that doesn't mean they're not going to try to get the best deal they possibly can too.

"If divorce is not an option and costs can't fall much further, what happens next?" Bentz asks. "Perhaps it's time for better collaboration—reshaping the relationship so that both parties get more out of it." Collaboration is hardly a new concept, he notes, but it's still largely unknown to many companies, even those that talk a good supply chain game.

Complete harmony probably isn't possible, Bentz admits, but he adds, "Formerly unattainable benefits can and do emerge when parties willingly share information, such as anticipated volumes and capacities, current problems and barriers, and ideas for improving logistical efficiency and developing new customers. We're talking about a cooperative effort to bilaterally remove costs from the relationship, rather than unilaterally cut costs."

How to Get the Most Out of a Relationship

The term *collaboration* means different things to different people, and can be used interchangeably to describe activities that are transactional, tactical, or strategic. To get a better idea of what collaboration actually means in the real world, Accenture teamed up with *Logistics Today* magazine to conduct a collaboration-focused survey of supply chain executives. From that study, a working definition emerged: Collaboration refers to cooperative supply chain relationships—formal or informal—between companies and their suppliers, supply chain partners, or customers, which are developed to enhance the overall business performance of both sides.

The survey also identified the barriers to collaborating with trading partners, which include technology and data hurdles; difficulties in measuring performance; an unclear value proposition; concerns about data security; and a lack of trust.

As the Unilever story relates, not only do collaborative efforts require a lot of time and effort, but the payoff for companies typically lags their biggest customers. That can often lead to a why-even-bother? attitude, which inevitably will doom any collaborative relationship.

So how do you make collaboration work? John Matchette and Andy Seikel, executive partners in Accenture's Supply Chain Management practice, offer these guidelines for getting the most out of a relationship:

- *Fit the relationships to your strategy*. Define the link between overall strategy and collaboration opportunities, identify the purpose of each collaboration, and be prepared to react quickly to changes in strategy or environment.
- *Identify the best partners*. Use a range of competitive and market sources to develop the intelligence to spot and evaluate potential partners.
- *Optimize your relationship portfolio*. Develop systems for timely reporting to enable faster, better-informed decision making about the collaboration. Know how to identify new opportunities based on activity in your current portfolio. Make sensible trade-offs between internal efforts and alliances.
- *Maximize day-to-day performance*. Use performance measures that reflect the organization's overall business objectives so that the people involved in the collaboration will be able to communicate the "why" and "what" of every alliance they form and to share experiences across alliances.

- *Manage the relationship.* Plan to communicate and maintain continuous personal contact with key people at partner organizations. Success on this front makes it possible to develop new opportunities from existing relationships.
- *Capitalize on your collaboration's assets.* Capture and adopt best practices. Share information and leverage collaboration-created assets across the parent company.[17]

CHAPTER 14

Security

Seeking Shelter from Supply Chain Storms

Flashpoints

An effective supply chain security plan requires a strategic view of your
operations as well as that of your supply chain partners.

Risk management contingency programs can help substantially reduce
supply chain disruptions.

The less vulnerable your company is to disruptions, the less susceptible
it'll be to daily market fluctuations as well.

Best-in-class companies constantly train and update their employees on
disruption response procedures.

Everything changed for supply chain managers after the terrorist attacks
of September 11, 2001. Up until then, supply chain security tended to
be parochial, with companies primarily focusing on protecting their goods
from familiar domestic criminal elements: shrinkage, shoplifting, burglary,
arson, and the like. Focusing on theft prevention makes a lot of sense,
since crime costs U.S. companies more than $50 billion per year. The retail
industry alone loses between 1 to 2 percent of its inventory each year to
shrinkage.

However, the events of 9/11 introduced supply chains to a powerful
motivational element that had largely been unknown in the United States:
fear, particularly economic fear. According to a Government Accountability
Office (GAO) report, if a weapon of mass destruction were to be detonated
in the United States, it could result in as much as $1 trillion in costs related

to port closures.[1] To put that number into perspective, $1 trillion is equal to the total amount spent on logistics in the country in a given year.[2]

Given that one bomb exploded in one port could essentially cost the U.S. economy an entire year's worth of supply chain activity, it seems reasonable to assume that significant progress has been made to secure our ports from outside threats. In the years since 9/11, governments throughout the world—and particularly the United States—have added numerous layers of bureaucratic checks and balances designed to make global supply chains safer. The U.S. Department of Homeland Security (DHS), for instance, was created as a cabinet-level agency in 2002 specifically to orchestrate various trade and security efforts. The U.S. Customs Service was reorganized and renamed U.S. Customs and Border Protection (CBP) in 2003. And anybody who has flown on a plane since 9/11 has witnessed firsthand the changes engendered in airport security by the Transportation Security Administration.

At the most obvious level—the protection of America's citizens—the establishment of various security-oriented agencies and initiatives has accomplished its main goal: To date, there have been no full-scale attacks on U.S. soil. However, there is reason to believe that the comfort level felt by most Americans is more illusory than real.

"It'll Never Happen Here"

In the summer of 2005, nearly four years after 9/11, two *Baltimore Sun* reporters examined security efforts at the Port of Baltimore, the nation's eighth largest seaport. What they uncovered was hardly reassuring to a public that had been led to believe adequate procedures were in place to protect the nation's supply chain. As Michael Dresser and Greg Barrett relate, "What appear to be a pair of video cameras guarding one important marine terminal are actually blocks of wood on poles." A high-tech fiber-optic alarm system malfunctions so frequently that it's usually left turned off. At certain times, a bare handful of police patrol the 1,100-acre port, and "two boats that monitor the port's 45 miles of shoreline have been routinely anchored for all but a few hours a day because of manpower shortages."[3]

Lest the reader think these problems are unique to Baltimore, Dresser and Barrett also cite a study conducted by the U.S. Coast Guard and DHS that concludes that 18 percent of the nation's ports (66 out of 359) are "especially susceptible" to terrorist attacks. Seven million ocean containers go through the U.S. ports every year, and yet only about 5 percent of those are inspected.

The Port of Baltimore story should have set off alarms across the country or, at the very least, at those 66 inadequately secured ports, but it was quickly nudged aside in favor of a bigger story that raised even more doubts about the DHS's effectiveness when a devastating attack on the nation's supply chain apparently caught the DHS ill prepared to respond. And unlike al Qaeda's sneak attack in September 2001, Hurricane Katrina's attack on the U.S. Gulf Coast in August 2005 was announced several days in advance.

Katrina was the first big test for the Federal Emergency Management Agency (FEMA) since it was absorbed into the DHS in 2003, and by most accounts FEMA flunked the test. Created specifically to "manage federal response and recovery efforts following any national incident," FEMA was late to react to the storm's potential for damage, was ineffective in coordinating relief efforts, and was stymied by a culture of "It'll never happen here" wishful thinkers in the New Orleans area. As a GAO report notes, "incomplete policies and plans contributed to the lack of clarity in leadership roles and responsibilities in the response to Hurricane Katrina. This problem resulted in disjointed efforts by emergency responders that may have caused increased losses of life and property."[4]

According to the GAO, best practices for program management include developing and utilizing a program management plan, which defines how a program will be planned, executed, monitored, and controlled. However, as of summer 2009, FEMA had not yet established such a program management plan, partly because of the difficulties in coordinating its efforts with other federal departments and agencies.

In any event, although the government's response to Katrina was certainly inadequate at all levels—local, state, and federal—the reaction time of several companies was superlative, as they applied the same type of supply chain best practices to the relief effort that they apply to their daily business activities. Consider, for instance, retail giant Wal-Mart Stores Inc., which responded to the disaster scene promptly and without compromise.

We saw in Chapter 13 how Wal-Mart uses point-of-sale data to strengthen its relationships with suppliers. After Katrina hit, the retailer demonstrated that it could similarly use historical sales patterns from previous hurricanes to determine exactly what products customers would need to recover from the storm. Wal-Mart employs its own meteorologists, and it relied on their forecasts—rather than the government's—to route trucks and supplies to the area. The company's strategy also included setting up "mini–Wal-Marts" in the most devastated areas, where employees handed out clothing, diapers, personal care items, and food.[5]

Similarly, Home Depot Inc., another big-box retailer, reacted quickly to the storm's onslaught thanks to its culture of always being prepared for disasters. The retailer in fact organizes its divisions geographically based on the types of disasters that occur most frequently in a given area, whether it is hurricanes in the South, blizzards in the North, or wildfires in the West.[6]

According to Paul Raines, president of Home Depot's southern division and the retailer's "hurricane honcho," his company manages to stay ahead of storms because they know what to expect (i.e., they pay very close attention to weather forecasts to determine when to close stores and what supplies to stock). For instance, before Hurricane Katrina struck, the retailer preloaded trucks at its distribution centers so it could quickly get products to the areas where they were needed the most.[7]

Perhaps recognizing its own bureaucratic inefficiencies, the U.S. government has become more receptive to the idea of working with private companies like Wal-Mart and Home Depot to deal with emergency relief efforts. Since Katrina, one of the biggest changes has been "government opening its doors to the private sector in general, the recognition that we are part of the collective solution," notes Jason Jackson, Wal-Mart's senior director of emergency management. When preparing for Hurricane Gustav in 2008, for instance, Wal-Mart's transportation division was able to quickly obtain overweight trucking permits that made it possible to carry large power generators to stores in the affected areas.[8]

Customs-Trade Partnership against Terrorism

Whenever government intrudes into global commerce, the moves are generally met with a great deal of resentment from industry, but after 9/11, businesses became highly motivated to cooperate with various security initiatives. While safety protocols and technology are key facilitators of security measures within companies, twenty-first-century supply chain security best practices are increasingly centered on these industry/government initiatives.

In the United States, the best known and most important best practice for supply chain security is the Customs-Trade Partnership Against Terrorism (C-TPAT), which was created shortly after 9/11 by CBP. (There are a couple dozen similar initiatives in other countries, such as Canada's Partners in Protection program, Sweden's StairSec initiative, New Zealand's Secure Export Scheme, and the European Union's Authorized Economic Operator program.) C-TPAT establishes a set of relationships and collaboration between government and industry for companies to implement security practices— both within their own company as well as throughout their supply chain, explains Theo Fletcher, vice president of security and compliance with IBM Corp.'s Integrated Supply Chain. "In return for implementing those security practices and investing in those practices, companies receive benefits from the government," he explains.[9]

One of the main benefits is the assurance that a company's goods will flow more quickly through Customs. Participating companies are also subject to fewer inspections, which allows them to maintain a more predictable global supply chain, which in turn provides a competitive advantage versus those companies that have not adopted C-TPAT.

C-TPAT's role is to certify known shippers through self-appraisals of security procedures, coupled with Customs audits and verifications. To be approved by CBP, participating companies must commit to follow these practices:

- Conduct a comprehensive self-assessment of their supply chain security processes using the C-TPAT guidelines, which encompass these areas:
  - Procedural security
  - Physical security
  - Personnel security
  - Education and training
  - Access controls
  - Manifest procedures
  - Conveyance security
- Submit a supply chain security profile questionnaire to CBP.
- Develop and implement a program to enhance security throughout their supply chain following C-TPAT guidelines.
- Communicate the C-TPAT guidelines to other companies in their supply chain, and work to build the guidelines into relationships with these companies.[10]

Getting Countries to Talk to Each Other

The key to C-TPAT and parallel efforts succeeding is that companies must agree to implement a global common process that includes their supply chain partners, Fletcher explains. "IBM does business in over 160 countries. On a daily basis we ship $70 million of goods. Every day we ship the equivalent of five fully loaded 747 aircraft around the world. What's important for our supply chain is to have a common process." If IBM can operate consistently in a common manner around the world, it can drive efficiencies within its supply chain to further its competitive advantage, he notes. "So it is critical to us that we implement one global process."

The rallying point for industry and government, Fletcher states, should be the World Customs Organization (WCO; www.wcoomd.org) framework on supply chain security and trade facilitation. It's vital to the advancement of supply chain management that there is a common set of global practices and processes. As of summer 2009, 174 countries had adopted the WCO framework, representing over 98 percent of the world's total trade.

The WCO framework is based on four principles:

1. Harmonizing the advance electronic cargo information requirement on inbound, outbound, and transit shipments

2. Applying a consistent risk management approach to address security threats
3. Using nonintrusive detection equipment to effect Customs examinations of high-risk containers and cargo
4. Providing benefits to companies that meet minimum supply chain security standards and best practices

"The WCO requires Customs officials in one country to talk to others, which is a relatively new practice," Fletcher points out. As officials receive the relevant import data and learn what goods are going to be coming into their country within the next few days, if their risk assessment raises any red flags, they can ask the exporting country to inspect those goods before they are shipped. "That creates good relationships between trading partners—good sharing of data, good sharing of knowledge, and a good sharing of trust between trading partners, which previously did not exist—certainly not to the extent that they do within the WCO framework."

Sometimes Low Tech Is as Good as High Tech

In his role as head of security for IBM, Fletcher is responsible for any movement of goods from one place to another, whether it's into the United States, out of the United States, or anywhere else. That requires adherence to best practices in supply chain security. "We've been early adopters of every security program," he points out, "including every government-industry program that's been put in place to help secure supply chains. I also manage an import network, which is a group of import executives in each location where we import goods. They're responsible for ensuring that we import within the laws of the country in which we're importing, and to make sure that our supply chain processes are secure."

Security isn't just about Customs compliance and import/export regulations. It really starts at the most basic levels. "For instance, we do inspections on empty truck trailers," Fletcher notes. "One of our best practices is that when an empty trailer comes in to be loaded, we'll physically measure it both internally and externally to make sure there are no hidden compartments where something could be put into our goods that might have an effect or a disruption somewhere else in the world." And the cost of that best practice? Just a few dollars—enough to buy a tape measure.

"It's just as simple as that," he observes, "and it's a best practice that we worked on with Mexican Customs, which suggested, 'You ought to take a tape measure and measure the outside and the inside of a trailer, or the outside and the inside of a container—whatever your conveyance means is. Measure both to make sure there aren't any secret spaces where something could be put into a shipment before you even pack it.' That's helped us out quite a bit." IBM, like other companies, also uses security seals on all of its trailers and containers, as well as electronic door sensors on its trailers, especially for shipments going between the United States and Canada.

For border crossings, another best practice for U.S. companies is to utilize the Free and Secure Trade (FAST) lanes at the Canadian and Mexican borders. This program, which is a component of C-TPAT, promotes trade "by using common risk management principles, supply chain security, industry partnership, and advanced technology to improve the efficiency of screening and clearing commercial traffic at [the] shared borders." To be eligible for expedited border crossings via dedicated lanes (where available), companies must already be participating in C-TPAT.

The most frequent targets of cargo thieves are consumer electronics, food, and apparel, and more than one-third (39 percent) of all cargo thefts occur at truck stops and highway rest areas, according to a study conducted by the Chubb Group of Insurance Companies. Modal yards managed by trucking companies, railroads, or ocean carriers are targeted by 27 percent of all cargo thieves, and another 25 percent of thefts occur at unsecured locations, such as motel, restaurant, and mall parking lots. "Cargo thieves are opportunists," points out Barry Tarnef, a marine loss control specialist with the Chubb Group, adding that cargo crime in the United States costs businesses several billion dollars per year.

Tarnef suggests that companies follow these seven steps to prevent cargo theft:

1. Thoroughly screen prospective employees.
2. Carefully select transportation partners and intermediaries.
3. Establish a security culture within your company.
4. Factor in security when determining shipment routing.
5. Incorporate counter surveillance.
6. Take advantage of technology, such as vehicle and shipment tracking systems, and high-tech security seals.
7. Conduct periodic security audits.[11]

Taking Responsibility for Your Supply Chain

Effective supply chain security measures require that companies take a strategic, high-level view of not only their own operations, but also the security procedures of their supply chain partners. "Every touch point has to be scrutinized, beginning with the supplier and ending with the final handoff," recommends John Mascaritolo, director of global logistics with high-tech manufacturer NCR Corp. You need to ask specific questions about every one of those touch points, he suggests, such as "Who attaches the cargo security seals? Is there a witness, or are the seals given to the driver? Once the carrier has a shipment, if there's an accident, what is my process and what does my carrier do? What happens if a container arrives with a broken seal?"

Companies need a process for handling all of these situations, Mascaritolo continues. "Achieving C-TPAT certification is one process. Going through the exercises to secure your supply chain is another process. You have to ask yourself what you can and cannot control."[12]

The U.S. government's strategy for supply chain security is basically a two-part approach, notes Greg Aimi, an analyst with AMR Research. The first part is convincing companies to assume responsibility for the security of their own supply chains, through voluntary participation in C-TPAT. The second part, Aimi points out, is focused on the Automated Commercial Environment (ACE), a trade processing system developed by CBP. "Under ACE, importers will be forced to send increasingly detailed information to Customs prior to arrival at border crossings," Aimi explains. "Those [importers] that don't will find significant delays. Those that do it well will eventually be in the fast lane when crossing Customs."[13]

Though currently focused on cargo arriving via motor carriers, the plan is for ACE to provide cargo-processing capabilities across rail, ocean, and air as well. ACE includes information on more than 15,000 users in its portal, and according to CBP, the Food Safety and Inspection Service's ACE portal access detected, detained, and removed from the food chain 1.6 million pounds of ineligible meat, poultry, and egg products in 2006. This represents a 44-fold increase in capabilities for the agency.

Toy manufacturer Hasbro Inc. was in the first wave of companies that signed on to participate in C-TPAT. "We are very proactive with government programs," explains Barry O'Brien, Hasbro's director of global trade and customs. "We have an urgent need to get our products to market, so speed is critical to us." As part of the initial certification process, the company sent its offshore suppliers a lengthy questionnaire asking about security processes at their facilities. "If we thought there was a problem or gap, we went back to the supplier and asked them to correct it," O'Brien says. In addition, Hasbro inspectors pay regular site inspections to their suppliers.[14]

The process has been worth it, O'Brien states, as the company has seen a significant decrease in its import container inspection ratios, dropping from 7.6 percent of all containers entering the United States to 0.66 percent over a three-year period. Initial C-TPAT compliance costs were about $200,000, and the company spends an additional $112,500 every year to maintain its certification; however, Hasbro estimates that it saves $550,000 per year in inspection costs alone. The company's goal is for all of its suppliers, carriers, and third-party logistics providers (3PLs) to also be C-TPAT compliant.[15]

Securing the Supply Chain

The Container Security Initiative (CSI) is another voluntary program orchestrated by CBP that sets security standards for containerized cargo bound for the United States. CSI is designed to increase security of import cargo by providing additional CBP screening capabilities and personnel at overseas ports where those cargoes originate.

As of summer 2009, more than 58 offshore ports had been designated CSI ports by CBP, representing 85 percent of the container traffic coming into the United States. To earn that designation, a port has to meet these standards:

- The port must have regular, direct, and substantial container traffic to ports in the United States.
- Customs must be able to inspect cargo originating, transiting, exiting, or being transshipped through a country.
- Nonintrusive inspection equipment—such as gamma or X-ray—and radiation detection equipment must be available for use at or near the potential CSI port.

CSI ports must also commit to:

- Establishing an automated risk management system.
- Sharing critical data, intelligence, and risk management information with Customs.
- Conducting a thorough port assessment and resolving port infrastructure vulnerabilities.
- Maintaining integrity programs, and identifying and combating breaches in integrity.

By virtue of the rigorous inspection process their shipments are put through before they leave a CSI port, companies will greatly reduce any potential risks to their supply chains while ensuring their goods will be expedited through Customs once they reach a U.S. port. Shipping through a CSI port and participating in C-TPAT will also lower a company's score in CBP's Automated Targeting System (ATS), a decision support tool Customs uses to identify high-risk imports.

C-TPAT currently groups companies into three tiers, which represent a company's progressive commitment to the program:

- Tier 1 companies have submitted security plans and committed to meet minimal security criteria. In addition, companies with clean inspection records (meaning no significant compliance or law enforcement problems) receive expedited inspection service when their containers are pulled for inspection.

- Tier 2 companies have had their plans validated by CBP officials, which improves their ATS score.
- Tier 3 companies have cleared a CBP audit and are judged to be following best practices that exceed requirements. These companies also use "smart boxes," which are containers equipped with tamper and intrusion detection technology.[16]

10+2

As a result of the Security and Accountability for Every Port (SAFE) Act of 2006, the CBP issued new regulations for importers in 2008 known as Importer Security Filing, or informally as 10+2. These rules require importers to electronically file 10 types of data elements at least 24 hours before the cargo is laden aboard a vessel destined for a U.S. port. Ocean carriers also have to file two data elements describing the status of a container and its physical location on board the vessel; hence, the 10+2 designation.

The data elements for importers are:

1. Seller's name and address
2. Buyer's name and address
3. Importer of record/Free Trade Zone applicant ID number
4. Consignee number(s)
5. Manufacturer's (or supplier's) name and address
6. Ship to party's name and address
7. Country of origin
8. Commodity Harmonization Tariff Schedule of the U.S. number
9. Container stuffing location
10. Consolidator's name and address

The additional data elements for carriers are:

1. Vessel stow plan
2. Container status messages

It can be quite expensive for those manufacturers and carriers that do not comply with the 10+2 provisions, with a fine of up to $5,000 assessed per shipment or a "Do Not Load" order being issued.

According to Walt Fountain, director of enterprise security at trucking company Schneider National, "The depth of information needed truly makes the importer responsible for understanding every point in its supply chain."

He suggests that "every importer go to its suppliers and vendors and make sure that each party in the supply chain can provide the needed information within the prescribed time frames." Given that not every company is set up to handle the entire filing process on its own, as well as the high costs of failing to comply, some importers are turning to 3PLs to take on this task on their behalf.[17]

Taking Steps toward Effective Compliance

While there's an ongoing debate over the effectiveness—or lack thereof—of the United States' various homeland security efforts, statistics indicate that a considerable amount of illegal import and export activities is in fact being prevented. In 2008, according to the U.S. Bureau of Industry and Security (www.bis.doc.gov), there were 40 criminal convictions, $2.7 million collected in criminal fines, $800,000 in forfeitures, 56 administrative penalties, and $3.6 million collected from administrative penalties. And it's not necessarily the "bad guys" who are getting punished. Any company transporting, storing, or ultimately responsible for these illicit goods can be subject to fines, penalties, and possible jail time.

In the post-9/11 climate, companies and individuals are obligated to not do business with illegal parties or entities, destinations, and end users, states Larry Christensen, vice president of export controls with JPMorgan Chase Vastera's consulting practice and formerly the director of the Office of Regulatory Policy in the U.S. Department of Commerce. "They are also expected to take steps to ensure they do not commit such violations," he says.

As an expert on security compliance (he helped rewrite the Export Administration Regulations), Christensen offers these best practices that companies should adopt to develop their own compliance programs:

- *Start at the top and obtain board-level commitment.* "Before any compliance program can be successful, buy-in from the board of directors and senior-level staff must be secured," Christensen notes. According to the U.S. Government Sentencing Guidelines, corporate officers and board members must be knowledgeable about the content of their compliance program, exercise reasonable oversight, and give compliance officers direct access to the board.
- *Assess your security processes.* "Hire outside trade experts to perform a compliance gap analysis on your current compliance processes," he suggests. "Then fill the gaps." For instance, look closely at how and where your compliance records are being stored.

- *Compile a list of embargoed countries with which your company is not allowed to trade.* Put effective stop measures in place that ensure items are not shipped to those countries either directly or indirectly.
- *Electronically screen names and addresses in your master customer/partner files against the various government blacklists.* Currently, there are more than four dozen international restricted party lists in existence, Christensen points out, so these lists should be monitored and updated daily. You also need to establish an ongoing name and address screening process. Since governments are continually adding and deleting names from their various restricted lists, you need to be current with list updates and modifications.
- *Collect end-use information from customers and other supply chain partners* to ensure that your product is being purchased for its intended use, Christensen urges. He also suggests you perform diversion risk screening. "Collect information about the nature of your customer's business to determine whether your product or service is consistent with the business of your customer. Make sure that your customer is not diverting your product to another party." To that end, he suggests companies obtain jurisdiction and classification information from each supplier.
- *Write and implement processes and procedures that are part of each business function.* Compliance must be a key concern across a company's entire supply chain and other functional areas, including information technology, research and development, engineering, manufacturing, sales, order entry, fulfillment, shipping, finance, legal, and compliance to ensure that the proper measures are taken to control the export and reexport of goods, technology, and software.
- *Train, train, train.* Don't develop processes and procedures only to file them away in a cabinet, Christensen says. "Procure training for the whole company with different levels of training based upon each job function. Train your staff until they understand how an effective compliance program can make or break a company, and then train them again."
- *Perform annual audits of your compliance procedures.* As Christensen points out, "It is better to be safe than sorry, and every process breaks down over time unless it is audited."[18]

Supply Chains at Risk

Every year, like clockwork, an unpredictable catastrophe will strike somewhere in the world and put supply chains throughout the world to the ultimate test. Tsunamis, earthquakes, hurricanes, SARS (severe acute respiratory syndrome), swine flu, whatever natural disaster might be dominating the news at the time you're reading this book—none of these events could be foreseen, and yet not only reputations and businesses but in fact the lives and livelihoods of thousands of people or more are affected by the ability of a relative few to respond promptly and decisively.

Having a contingency plan in place can help companies respond more quickly to unplanned events, notes Eugene Klein, general manager of warehousing with food distributor SYSCO Corp. Effective risk management programs can also help substantially reduce supply chain disruptions. A contingency management team, Klein suggests, should include representatives from all departments of a company: senior management, operations, distribution and logistics, legal, quality control, engineering, sales and marketing, and public relations. "Eliminating all risk is neither possible nor cost effective, so companies must identify the most vulnerable components of an operation and apply a greater share of resources to the most critical components," he adds.[19]

In *The Resilient Enterprise*, Yossi Sheffi, director of the Center for Transportation and Logistics at the Massachusetts Institute of Technology, suggests that by reducing their vulnerability to disruptions, companies can also reduce their vulnerability to daily market fluctuations and thereby improve their general financial performance. He offers these best practices in vulnerability reduction:

- *Organize for action.* To that end, companies should consider naming a chief risk management officer who would be responsible for security as well as ensuring that the company is flexible enough to recover quickly from a disruption. This flexibility, Sheffi notes, "may involve redesign of operational processes, transformation of corporate culture, changes in product design, organizational changes within the company, and different relationships with customers, suppliers, and other stakeholders."
- *Assess the vulnerabilities.* This involves asking three questions: What can go wrong? What is the likelihood that it will happen? How severe is the possible impact likely to be?
- *Reduce the likelihood of disruptions.* Focus on separating abnormal activities from normal baseline activities, Sheffi advises, such as deciding which containers should be checked, which employees warrant special attention, or how many product failures in a given time period might indicate sabotage. He suggests taking a layered approach to security rather than opting for a single defensive mechanism, which, even if such a mechanism were possible, would be prohibitively expensive.

- *Collaborate for security* with industry associations, citizen watch organizations within a company's community, and government initiatives such as C-TPAT.
- *Build in redundancies.* A too-tight supply chain, Sheffi warns, "may be an indication of danger; when too many 'redundant' employees are let go, when capacity utilization is 'too high,' and when procurement is focused on a single supplier, risk management alarms should go off." Don't abandon your lean business processes, he notes, but be aware of the risk of slicing your supply chain too thin.
- *Invest in people and culture.* Simply put, a company's most important assets are its employees.[20]

An Investment Worth Making

Since 9/11, things have been relatively quiet on the North American continent as far as orchestrated terrorist attacks, which has resulted in a natural tendency toward complacency. For instance, a major effort to thwart security breaches at U.S. ports has been repeatedly delayed, primarily because the $250 million program relies on fingerprint identification technology that has yet to be developed. Although more than 1 million port workers have been issued identification cards since the initiative began in 2002, readers capable of identifying the fingerprints of those workers had not yet been installed by 2009, and it could be 2011 or later when they are finally rolled out to all ports.[21]

Security technology and risk management programs cost a lot of money, which helps explain why, during times of economic slowdowns, they become lower priorities. However, "with exceptional uniformity, the experts report that it isn't a question of whether there will be another terrorist attack on the United States, but when that attack will occur," cautions Rob Housman, counsel to the Homeland Security Practice Group of Bracewell & Patterson law firm, and formerly assistant director of strategic planning in the White House Drug Czar's office. "Over the last 20 years, the United States has seen a consistent growth in terrorism against private-sector companies. Terrorism in the United States didn't start on 9/11 and it won't end there. Companies can ill afford to become complacent in the face of such risks."[22]

"A crisis in one country or region can now ripple very quickly across the world economy, creating tremendous turbulence," adds Sanjeev Nagrath, global leader, supply chain management, with IBM Global Business Services. As supply chains have become more complex, global, and stressed, he notes, supply chain executives "must drive far more intelligence through their supply chains if they are going to anticipate, rather than react."[23]

In an Aberdeen Group study, more than half (58 percent) of the respondents suffered financial losses from supply chain disruptions in 2008. Some of the main reasons for those losses include:

- Supplier capacity did not meet demand
- An increase in the price, or an outright shortage, of raw materials
- Unexpected changes in customer demand
- Shipments that were delayed, damaged, or misdirected
- Fuel price increases or shortages[24]

The Aberdeen study suggests that best-in-class companies are training their employees on disruption response procedures, such as how to communicate delays to customers and how to initiate an urgent purchase order. Bottom line: Companies with risk management programs in place are twice as likely as other companies to suffer no major impact from supply chain disruptions.

CHAPTER 15

RFID

A Game of Tags

Flashpoints

RFID addresses the problem of out-of-stocks by greatly increasing supply chain visibility.

While retailers are enjoying most of the benefits of RFID, some manufacturers wonder if they'll ever see a return on their technology investment.

RFID offers a more efficient means of facilitating product recalls and thwarting counterfeiters.

Battery-powered RFID, in combination with wireless technology, expands the technology's capabilities outside the four walls of a facility.

When your yearly sales are more than the annual gross domestic product of many countries, you can pretty much do whatever you want. That sums up the situation whenever retail giant Wal-Mart Stores Inc. has decided to mandate supply chain improvements from its suppliers. It was the case in the early 1980s, for instance, when the retailer installed point-of-sale scanners in its stores and cajoled its suppliers into affixing bar codes on their products. It was the case when Wal-Mart's suppliers were instructed to start using electronic data interchange (EDI) technology as a way of sending and receiving transactional information, such as orders and invoices. It was also the case when Wal-Mart insisted that its suppliers sign on with the UCCnet global registry, which would allow the retailer to synchronize all of its suppliers' product data.

And that's certainly the case today, as Wal-Mart is the driving force pushing the adoption of radio frequency identification (RFID) technology, which is often described as the next generation of bar codes. Wal-Mart's immediate goal is to have all of its suppliers place RFID tags on every pallet and case shipped to the retailer's distribution centers. The eventual end game, though—and not just for Wal-Mart, but for all retailers as well as the entire U.S. military—is for every product to carry an RFID tag.

Revolutions sometimes take place without a single shot being fired, and that's largely been the case when it comes to the adoption of RFID technology. Although RFID was invented for military applications in the 1940s and has been used for security access and related business tasks since the 1960s, it never really hit the public consciousness until Wal-Mart announced its initiative, which set off a flurry of what-do-we-do-now? reactions from its supply chain partners and suppliers. For many suppliers, dealing with RFID mandates has been remarkably similar to the well-known stages of coping with grief. The first stage, of course, is *denial* ("RFID? You have got to be kidding!"), followed by *anger* ("How dare they try to force us to adopt this untested gimmick!"), then *bargaining* ("Okay, we'll do it, but we'll do the absolute least amount that we can get away with"), then *depression* ("We're going to go broke paying for all these tags"), and if things work out, to the final stage, *acceptance* ("Hey, we're actually a lot more productive now thanks to RFID").[1]

For all the activity and excitement RFID has engendered—entire cottage industries of consultants, analysts, conferences, Web sites, and even political action groups have sprung up in recent years—its purpose and capabilities are still misunderstood, even by companies that have launched pilot programs to satisfy a retailer-driven mandate. As a result, while the technology itself continues to advance, full-scale implementations are still few and far between.

The ABCs of RFID

RFID is a data collection technique that passes product information via radio waves to a receiving unit. This basically requires a tag (an electronic chip with an antenna) and a reader, which receives the data and forwards it on to a computer software application (e.g., a warehouse management system) for processing. There are two general categories of RFID tags: active tags, which include a power source, such as a battery; and passive tags, which do not (the type of tags Wal-Mart is mandating are passive).

RFID is so attractive because it is an enabler of *supply chain visibility*. These tags and labels are designed to locate stuff—whether that stuff is a case of Viagra, a shipment of laptop computers, or an entire 53-foot truck. The big selling point of RFID, however, is not merely that these tags can tell you where stuff is—bar codes and global positioning systems can already do that—but that the amount of information that can be stored in these tags is exponentially greater than what can be stored on the older-generation bar codes. This is possible thanks to an electronic product code (EPC) embedded in the tags, which greatly facilitates the traceability of products, whether it is for product recalls, to thwart counterfeiting and shrinkage, or just being able to locate a case of beans in the back room of a warehouse.

In the late 1990s, a handful of major consumer packaged goods companies, such as Gillette, Procter & Gamble, and Unilever, as well as some big-box retailers, such as Home Depot, Target, and Wal-Mart, joined an RFID think tank at the Massachusetts Institute of Technology with the goal of developing a technology that could track the whereabouts of products anywhere within a warehouse or retail store. Their work led to the creation of the EPC, an important milestone in the development of the technology. (Up to that point, RFID was being used mostly in toll booths, libraries, and building security checkpoints.)

In 2003, encouraged by the results of pilot tests conducted in the United States and abroad, Wal-Mart launched the modern era of RFID when it announced that as of 2005, it expected all of its top 100 suppliers to have an RFID tag on every case and pallet shipped to three Wal-Mart distribution centers (DCs) near Dallas, Texas. That meant each of those companies had to make a major commitment to RFID if they expected to stay on Wal-Mart's good side, and that kind of technology investment wasn't going to come cheap. Analyst group Forrester, for instance, has estimated that a typical supplier can expect to spend as much as $9 million in start-up costs for tags, hardware, software, and related services.[2] Nevertheless, several other retailers announced their own RFID initiatives on the heels of Wal-Mart's dictate, such as Albertson's, Best Buy, Home Depot, and Target, as well as the U.S. Department of Defense.

By 2007, Wal-Mart widened its mandate to well over 1,000 of its suppliers, while in the meantime the retailer installed RFID readers in more than 1,000 Wal-Mart and Sam's Club stores (though installations at the DC level proved to be a more arduous process than expected). However, given that the technology is expensive and that the current enthusiasm for RFID is based mostly on the results of small-scale pilots rather than full-scale implementations, many companies remain skeptical about the chances of their obtaining any real-world value from their investments (other than continuing to be a supplier to a major retailer or military customer). The benefits as promised have been substantial; as delivered, they appear to be more ephemeral.

At a Glance

Radio Frequency Identification

Radio frequency identification (RFID) is a data capture technology that uses radio waves to pass information from a tag to a receiving unit.

Proactive Replenishment

When Wal-Mart put its suppliers on notice that it was launching its RFID initiative, many companies were understandably perplexed. "Why RFID, and why now?" was a typical reaction. The reality of the situation is, despite its having invested millions in various collaborative technologies (see Chapter 13), Wal-Mart still has blind spots in its supply chain, and when you're the biggest retailer in the world, those blind spots can take on the appearance of craters. One particularly annoying technology gap, explains Simon Langford, Wal-Mart's manager of global RFID strategy, is that the retailer has zero percent visibility into its back rooms. For instance, only one out of every four products in stock makes it to a warehouse picking list, Langford says, and only one out of three of those will make it to a retail shelf in a timely manner. "No one has ever sold anything that sat in a back room," he points out.[3]

The promise of RFID, from Wal-Mart's perspective, is that it will provide the retailer with proactive information to replenish its stores more regularly. That, in turn, will allow Wal-Mart to offer its consumers improved customer service, speedier shopping, and fresher product, Langford says. "The stores with the cleanest and best-run back rooms are also the stores with the best in-stock availability," he notes. So for Wal-Mart and any other retailer, by improving visibility into what's in the back room, RFID can help reduce the incidence of out-of-stocks, which not only improves the customer's experience but also directly translates into more sales for the retailer.

Other benefits retailers expect to gain from RFID include:

- Automated receiving will allow retailers to receive and deploy merchandise more quickly, accurately, and inexpensively (i.e., with less labor).
- RFID will also allow more rapid inventory counting. One study from Kurt Salmon Associates projects that it can reduce by as much as 90 percent the amount of time needed to track inventory on the sales floor, in holding areas, and in the back room.

- Retailers will see an immediate reduction in shrinkage, which is a polite way of referring to unpurchased products that leave a store or warehouse in somebody's pocket. Not only can RFID identify when a consumer leaves the store without paying for something, but it can also set off an alert when an employee tries to steal a product from the warehouse or DC.
- RFID will also allow a company to take a full inventory count every day, compared to every four to eight weeks.[4]

"RFID is going to be the enabler that will help us determine very simply if we have merchandise that is in the back room of a store, or if that merchandise has been moved out to the sales floor and what the status of that is," explains Kerry Pauling, director of Wal-Mart's Information Systems Division. That's possible, he explains, by being able to capture the data without having to use traditional line-of-sight technology, a process that is much slower and more labor intensive because it requires a wand or scanner to pass directly over a bar code.[5]

In Search of Payback

All that sounds great for Wal-Mart, the other big retailers, and the U.S. Department of Defense. However, on the supplier side, many consumer goods manufacturers are quietly fearful that it may be years (if ever) before they see a hard dollar's return on investment from their RFID implementations. According to Steve Banker, service director, supply chain management with analyst firm ARC Advisory Group, most manufacturers currently investing in RFID think the payback period will take at least two years. Take the example of a company that ships 50 million cases per year to Wal-Mart. If that company spends 20 cents per tag (the current generation of tags costs between 15 and 20 cents), that would represent $10 million in costs, plus another $1 million in infrastructure costs. Labor added to warehouse processes could add another $500,000 to the total cost. Under this scenario, the shipper would have to generate $11.5 million in new savings to break even, Banker observes.

"They might be able to generate a million dollars in lower chargeback fees, if Wal-Mart cooperates with them, and the other savings bucket could come to, at most, half a million dollars," Banker notes. So at best, this company would be losing $10 million, in a situation that would not noticeably improve until the price of tags drops to the target range of 5 to 10 cents. However, it could be quite a few years before that price point is reached.[6]

One unnamed Wal-Mart supplier told the *Wall Street Journal* that he has yet to see any clear savings from his RFID investment of $200,000 per year.

"[RFID] is a big black box with nothing out there for a return," he says. "A lot of people, if given a true choice, would not [participate]" in the RFID mandate, he observes. Another supplier, apparel manufacturer VF Corp., has put the brakes on its internal development efforts, preferring to take a backseat while other suppliers drive the technology.[7]

In a bid to restore faith in the technology as well as encourage its suppliers to continue in their implementation efforts (the threat of fines for noncompliance apparently not doing the trick), Wal-Mart sponsored a study at the University of Arkansas that would demonstrate how RFID has helped improve inventory accuracy. Based on a pilot study, the university's analysis indicates that an automated, RFID-enabled inventory system can improve inventory accuracy by 13 percent. The study focused on equipping test stores with RFID readers and antennas in backroom locations, such as receiving doors, sales floor doors, and box crushers. The results were compared to an equal number of stores that did not have RFID technology.

"Inventory accuracy, which determines important processes such as ordering and replenishment, is often poor, with inaccuracy rates sometimes as high as 65 percent," observes Bill Hardgrave, director of the university's RFID Research Center. The 13 percent improvement obtained by the test stores in the study suggests that RFID can significantly reduce unnecessary inventory, which Hardgrave estimates could be measured at millions of dollars saved by major retailers and their suppliers.[8]

The ability to have a unique product ID can also have demonstrable advantages. The pharmaceutical industry, for instance, prodded by the U.S. Food and Drug Administration, is incorporating RFID into its businesses to thwart counterfeiters. Pfizer Inc. is shipping every package, case, and pallet of its Viagra product, and every case and pallet of its Celebrex drug, with RFID tags to enhance patient safety. (See Chapter 2.) Similarly, GlaxoSmithKline, another pharmaceutical company, is tagging all bottles of Trizivir (an HIV medicine) distributed in the United States. The tag can be read by wholesalers and pharmacists to verify that the product is authentic. For the entire pharmaceutical industry, it's been estimated that RFID technology is saving companies more than $9 billion thanks to track-and-trace capabilities.[9]

Tagging till the Cows Come Home

One of the chief benefits of RFID is that it offers a more efficient means of facilitating product recalls. According to Wal-Mart's Pauling, with RFID, "you don't have to recall all of your inventory—only the inventory that is impacted from the recall."

"For a food manufacturer, first and foremost, the business is about quality and safety," explains Rick Blasgen, formerly senior vice president of integrated logistics with meat producer ConAgra and currently president of the Council of Supply Chain Management Professionals. According to Blasgen, food companies like ConAgra are especially interested in any technology that can make their supply chains more secure and, just as important, reassure consumers that tainted products can be quickly identified and withdrawn from the marketplace.[10]

Fears of mad cow disease, and the negative impact consumer fears can have on its industry, have led members of the National Cattlemen's Beef Association to adopt an RFID system that can track the whereabouts of cattle on ranches throughout the United States, according to an Associated Press report. "If there is ever a problem with an animal down the line, we can make information available to the agency that needs it," explains Allen Bright, animal identification coordinator with the association. "Source verification is going to become more and more important as we go down the road."[11]

Brandt Beef, a California beef producer, is using an RFID system that can track both backward and forward—backward from a retail site (a grocery store or restaurant) to a specific animal, and forward from a feed lot to a retail site (during a meat recall). Cattle are tagged on their ears and are then scanned as they move from the feed lot to the slaughterhouse. After processing, the beef receives a bar code label that is linked to the animal's ID number.[12]

Similarly, Canadian meat producer Atlantic Beef Products (ABP) uses RFID to enable full traceability of its processed meat products. While discrete manufacturers (e.g., automotive or computer makers) assemble individual components into a finished product, meat producers do the exact opposite, breaking down a whole side of beef, for instance, into various cuts that are sold individually. ABP, like other meat producers, needs to be able to track the pedigree of every one of those cuts of meat back to the ranch where the animal was raised. That's where RFID comes in. As Paul Arsenault, ABP's controller, explains, the benefits of RFID are not solely in the realm of product traceability. Using RFID and bar codes, ABP can also identify what grade and yield it receives from livestock suppliers, along with monitoring shrinkage and tracking worker productivity.[13]

Recalls are also an enormous problem for the automotive industry. Ford became a believer after more than 6 million Firestone tires were recalled because of instances of the tires disintegrating at high speeds on Ford Explorers. Ford has implemented an RFID system that can track the entire life cycle of a tire, from manufacturing to storage and assembly to its mounting on a specific vehicle. Application of technology in this manner not only helps with recalls but can also lead to more timely and accurate orders and shipments.[14]

In the category of a somewhat more fanciful application, imaging products manufacturer Eastman Kodak Co. is working on an edible RFID tag that, when ingested, can provide data on what somebody has eaten. According to Kodak's patent application, the tag would be swallowed like a pill and could be used by physicians to track the pill's progress through a patient's digestive tract. The RFID tag would eventually disintegrate harmlessly into the patient's bloodstream.[15]

Taking RFID Seriously

Inventory reduction is another potential benefit for companies that are willing to take RFID seriously rather than merely adopting a slap-and-ship strategy. Slap-and-ship (also known as wait-and-see) refers to the practice of buying tags to meet the bare minimum compliance requirements of a big-box retailer or military customer. Slap-and-ship is "the simplest way to achieve RFID compliance with minimum investment and implementation complexity," notes Sandip Lahiri, an RFID solution architect with IBM Global Services. "Such an application is either totally separate from or minimally integrated with the business processes and back-end enterprise systems. As a result, such an application offers little or no benefit to the business itself that is implementing this application."[16]

High-tech manufacturer Hewlett-Packard Co. (HP) takes RFID seriously, as its interest in the technology predates the Wal-Mart initiative by at least a year. The company has implemented RFID within its manufacturing and product completion areas as well as its finished goods warehousing and shipping processes, explains Gregg Edds, HP's product manager for global supply chain operations. HP assigns a unique serial number to every one of its printer products and packages the printers one to a box. "Even though we're tagging at the case and pallet level, the fact that we're putting a unique RFID tag with a unique EPC code on a box means, theoretically, we're tracking that unique product at an item level," Edds states.[17]

Since HP outsources many of its warehousing functions to third-party logistics providers (3PLs), the 3PLs have done the lion's share of the RFID tagging on behalf of HP. All of the RFID systems HP has implemented have been done in cooperation with the 3PLs, which use their own shop-floor systems, enterprise software, and warehouse management systems to tie the entire operation together, Edds notes. As discussed in Chapter 12, tapping into the practices of a logistics specialist for noncore tasks is a frequently used best practice of leading supply chains.

The aerospace industry certainly understands the implications of RFID. European airplane manufacturer Airbus, for instance, has tagged every tool and spare part in an effort to simplify inventory and repair management. Every part can be electronically tracked, whether within Airbus's warehouses or as they're installed into airplanes, greatly simplifying maintenance, repair, and operations efforts at Airbus as well as at the airlines. As Carlo Nizam, Airbus's head of value chain visibility and RFID, explains, the use of RFID is helping the company "streamline business processes, cut process cycle times and inventory, eliminate paperwork, and reduce the cost of operations by providing real-time automated tracking of business operations across the life cycle of the product." Airbus is underwriting at least some of the technology costs by providing RFID readers to its suppliers as a way of encouraging their cooperation in tagging products.[18]

For its part, U.S. aerospace manufacturer Boeing Co. is using a new generation of RFID technology known as a real-time locating system (RTLS) to locate tools, parts, and other assets at NASA's Kennedy Space Center. As an active (i.e., battery-powered) RFID system, an RTLS can provide real-time updates on the location of tagged assets via wireless signals within a geographic area, such as a production facility, warehouse, or yard. Boeing has more than 70,000 of its parts in various facilities at the Kennedy Space Center, and thanks to its use of RTLS technology, the company has been able to reduce the number of man-hours previously spent looking for parts and inventorying tools. [19]

Work the Bugs Out

Given that many RFID implementations are still at the pilot stages, examples of tried-and-true best practices are few and far between. Nevertheless, the University of Denver conducted a survey of senior supply chain executives to determine what companies—primarily, suppliers to major retailers or military contractors—ought to be doing to derive the maximum benefit from passive RFID. From those interviews, the researchers compiled a list of recommended practices (we won't necessarily call them "best" practices) concerning RFID:

- Familiarize yourself with RFID, even if you don't plan to use it anytime soon.
- Apply tags upstream, either at your manufacturing facility or at your suppliers' facilities. This will enable you to track tagged products throughout both the production and distribution processes.

- Proceed with extra caution when goods must be repackaged to avoid having to apply tags more than once.
- Take advantage of the capabilities RFID tags offer that traditional bar codes lack, particularly in terms of capturing a much larger volume of data in a shorter period of time.
- Focus first on your highest-value items. With tags costing 15 to 20 cents or more, the more expensive the products being tagged, the easier it is to justify the cost of tags.
- Establish a test lab pilot to work out the bugs in the system before you go live.

Well-known technical problems hinder the effectiveness of RFID, such as its limitations reading through liquids and certain metals, or its operating capabilities in extreme temperatures. As companies are discovering in their pilot tests, the hardware is still evolving, meaning the tags and systems don't necessarily always function as advertised. When it comes to RFID implementations, patience is virtually a best practice.[20]

A Matter of Privacy

In 2003, garment manufacturer Benetton Group placed an order for 15 million passive tags that it planned to fit into its apparel. Almost immediately afterward, however, the company reversed itself and announced that its plans for inserting the tags were put on hold. The reason for the abrupt about-face had nothing to do with the cost of the tags nor their ability to improve Benetton's supply chain processes. What spooked Benetton was the reaction of privacy advocacy groups that accused the apparel maker of adopting "Big Brother"-like tactics and that organized a "Boycott Benetton" movement aimed at stopping the adoption of RFID by the apparel industry in its tracks.[21] Indeed, while today hundreds of companies are using RFID on or in apparel, particularly uniforms and industrial clothing, Benetton's Web site (www.benettongroup.com) to this day includes this statement: "Benetton Group has never used RFID technology nor have microchips (smart labels) ever been present in the 140 million-plus garments produced and sold throughout the world under its brand names."

Thanks to a cottage industry that has dedicated itself to exposing the encroachment of "spychips" (i.e., RFID tags) into our daily lives, there's a perception that by embedding tags into products, large companies and the government will be able to track consumers after they've left a store by using the tags for surveillance purposes. When it was learned, for instance, that a single Wal-Mart store in the Boston area was tagging every Gillette

Mach3 razor (a frequently shoplifted item), the outcry from privacy groups caused Wal-Mart to cancel the pilot test. Gillette ended up moving its pilot test to Germany, where retailer Metro has gone Wal-Mart one better by embedding miniature spy cameras in its smart shelves, which can take a picture of whoever removes a razor from the shelf.

What worries privacy advocates isn't so much what the technology is capable of now but what abuses future generations of RFID could inspire evil-minded people to commit. As Charles Poirier and Duncan McCollum, consultants with Computer Sciences Corp., point out, it's the potential for malicious third parties to hack into or steal your personal data—whether collected via a supermarket loyalty card or captured via an RFID tag— that has privacy groups like CASPIAN (Consumers Against Supermarket Privacy Invasion and Numbering) on edge.[22] Indeed, a report on disruptive technologies compiled by Computer Sciences Corp. states matter-of-factly: "In the future, everyone and everything will be tracked."[23]

While the Orwellian nightmares some of the "spychip" scenarists describe seem pretty loopy (some go so far as to equate RFID tagging with the mark of the Beast, foretold in the book of Revelation), it probably is a good idea to ask retailers exactly *why* they feel the need to embed minicameras in their shelves. If somebody really is watching you all the time, maybe you're not paranoid after all.

In any event, the best argument RFID proponents have at their disposal is the truth: RFID labels sewn inside clothing are there to track the garments *before* they're sold, not after. Also, these RFID tags are designed to be disabled at the point of sale, so once a garment is purchased, the tag is effectively dead. What's more, the tags are tracking the garment, not the person wearing the garment. In a study conducted by the University of Wollongong (Australia), companies were asked to rate the most important and the least important factors when making an RFID investment decision. While data accuracy was rated the most important factor, by far the least important factor to companies when adopting RFID (Benetton Group notwithstanding) is privacy threats.[24]

No Need to Be Passive

While retailers and consumer-oriented companies endeavor to find measurable value from their use of passive RFID tags, the far less publicized active tags have already proven their worth for many companies. NYK Logistics, for instance, maintains a 70-acre distribution facility near the Port of Los Angeles/Long Beach, the nation's busiest port and a key point in retailer Target's global supply chain. NYK uses active RFID tags to track every container in its yard, which encompasses 1,100 parking slots for trucks and 250 dock doors. Activity in NYK's yard includes 50,000 inbound ocean freight containers and 30,000 outbound trailers annually.

The West Coast port lockout in the fall of 2002 convinced NYK it needed a technological boost in its ability to track and trace the comings and goings of each 'of the containers and trailers in its yard. At the end of the 10-day lockout, there was such a backlog of freight that, as Charles Kerr, equipment control manager for NYK, remembers, the first wave of freight basically took all of the trailers and containers back east, and NYK had to wait for the trucks to come back. "When we dug ourselves out of that, we said to ourselves, 'This can never happen to us again.' So we set out to fix it," says Kerr.

That process involved installing small, active radio transmitters affixed via a clamp to every container and trailer that enters the yard. Like Boeing (discussed earlier), NYK uses a real-time locating system (RTLS) as well as yard management software to process and manage all of the incoming signals from the tags. The solution includes 35 wireless locating access points—antennas, basically—mounted around the yard. Previously, NYK personnel had to keypunch the location of every container and trailer into handheld devices, which was a very labor-intensive process. "We were out doing yard checks with clipboards, and checking whether the containers were where the drivers said they had left them," Kerr says. Using RFID has allowed NYK to go to a totally live data environment.

In a traditional yard, Kerr explains, a truck driver arrives at the yard, gets a gate pass from a guard, drops off the container at a specific location, and then goes to a window to get the paperwork signed. If the driver is going to do a double transaction (i.e., a drop-and-hook where he drops off a trailer, unhooks the tractor, and then picks up another trailer), he'll then go to another location in the yard, pick up the load, go to the gate, show his paperwork to the guard, and then drive away. NYK has eliminated several steps in the process thanks to RFID. Now the driver never needs to go to a window.

The streamlined process, Kerr explains, is analogous to a Hertz Gold Club member arriving at an airport's automobile rental lot. "When a trailer or container comes to the gate, the driver knows that he's here for a double transaction. An operator standing in the lanes at the gate has a handheld scanner, tethered to a printer, just like at the airport. The drivers don't have to stop at the window and leave their cabs any more."

The use of active RFID tags has helped NYK reduce the amount of time spent by drivers on-site to complete a double transaction by 66 percent. Just as important, by reducing the number of trailers in its yard at any given time, NYK has freed up 40 to 60 parking spots in the yard, which translates to more productivity and throughput. Other benefits include eliminating 100 percent of the costs associated with manual yard searches and data collection; improving gate personnel productivity by 50 percent; and increasing daily throughput of the yard by 38 percent during the peak fall shipping season.[25]

Associated Food Stores (AFS) also uses active RFID to monitor yard inventory at its 600-acre DC, which includes more than 200 trailers and more than 60 tractors. As a wholesale food distributor keenly focused on maintaining product freshness, it's particularly important that AFS knows exactly where every one of its assets is at all times.

"If you think of the distribution supply chain, it's all about turning that equipment," explains Tim Van de Merwe, internal logistics manager for AFS, who points out that the only time the company makes money is when its trucks are on the road. "We're not making any money when we're loading or unloading a truck, so the trick is to have total visibility of the equipment as soon as it arrives, determine the status of that equipment, and immediately assign and reload it."

AFS has been able to streamline its operations so thoroughly that it's eliminated close to 200 deliveries per week, with a total freight reduction estimated at $2.3 million. However, Van de Merwe doesn't give all of the credit to the technology. "Technology is not going to clean up a sloppy process," he notes. "The process has to be in place, and then the technology can smooth it out and enhance it. But if the process is garbage, then technology isn't necessarily going to save it.[26]

CHAPTER 16

Green Supply Chains
It's Not Easy Going Green

Flashpoints

Most companies are adopting green initiatives to comply with regulations or a customer mandate.

Even so, savings from energy-efficiency programs are proving to be significant.

Companies need to understand and be able to measure exactly what is involved in the manufacturing and distribution of their products.

Sustainability efforts are opening up new revenue opportunities.

Global warming. The greenhouse effect. Natural disasters. Disappearing rainforests. Air and water pollution. Overpopulation. Pestilence and drought. Sounds like the makings of a summer movie blockbuster, but in fact the interest in environmentally friendly business practices has grown at such a rapid pace that the green movement has completely leapfrogged the it's-just-a-fad stage and gone straight to the what's–our–eco-business–strategy–going–to–be? stage.

As *New York Times* columnist Thomas Friedman writes in *Hot, Flat, and Crowded*, "Green is no longer something you do to be good and hope that it pays off in ten years. Green is the way you grow, build, design, manufacture, work, and live because it is just better." It's the smartest, most efficient, lowest-cost way to do things, he states. It's a series of great opportunities cloaked in the guise of insoluble problems.[1]

There's also no denying that the green movement is a veritable holy war, prone to inspiring heights of hyperbole on the farthest ends of the ideological spectrum, from pronouncements that removing every gasoline-powered vehicle from the highways is the sole salvation of the planet to claims that global warming is a hoax concocted by alternative energy producers and shareholders. Rather than discussing the *politics* of green, this chapter focuses solely on the *business* of green, specifically, how to realign your supply chain so that it becomes more cost efficient, more energy efficient, more customer focused, less wasteful, and, ultimately, more productive.

The Elephant in the Room

When it comes to green initiatives, the elephant in the room is that, if left to their own devices, many and perhaps most manufacturers would opt out of participating. To say that some have been dragged kicking and screaming into adopting eco-friendly practices might be only a mild exaggeration. "What's in it for me?" is not an uncommon reaction among supply chain executives given the dictate to start measuring, and then reducing, their company's carbon footprint.

According to a survey conducted by analyst firm Manufacturing Insights, the main reason why companies get involved in green initiatives is to comply with government and/or other regulations (42 percent of responses), and that's by a two-to-one margin over the next closest response. Twenty-one percent say they've gotten into green projects because of a mandate and/or pressure from customers and consumers. Coming in third, with 20 percent of responses, is the opportunity to reduce costs.[2]

The idea of a cap-and-trade market has gained momentum in the United States in recent years, one that would be modeled somewhat on a market adopted by the European Union in 2005 as a result of the Kyoto Protocol. The "cap" refers to a limit imposed on companies on the amount of their greenhouse gas (GHG) emissions. The "trade" refers to a market where companies needing a higher limit than regulations allow can in fact buy credits for additional emissions from companies that are producing far fewer emissions than they're allowed. While the merits of such a plan are subject to debate, it's highly likely that under the Obama administration, the United States will eventually adopt cap-and-trade provisions or some sort of a carbon tax.

As Andrew Winston, an expert on green business, sees it, "climate change regulations are coming and will change business forever. The attack on emissions will affect every aspect of society, from how we power our lives and travel to how businesses source, make, distribute, and sell goods. When governments and markets 'price' carbon, the cost of everything changes, sometimes by a significant margin." As Winston notes, some products in their current forms will become much more expensive to make and ship. That makes it imperative, he says, that companies understand exactly what is involved in the manufacturing and distribution of their products.[3]

At a Glance

Carbon Footprint

The amount of greenhouse gas emissions (carbon dioxide) produced by an individual or an organization, or the amount used in the manufacture and distribution of a product.

Justifying the Cost

A green initiative needs to be cost justified like any other capital expenditure, points out John Davies, vice president of analyst firm AMR Research's sustainability forum. "Manufacturers tend to think that green initiatives are something that is done out of altruism. In fact, a lot of times these programs are great revenue generators and cost-cutters," he says. "Even so, cost is still the driving criteria and will trump any sort of environmental component. In itself there is no advantage in reducing carbon, aside from making a statement. So if you can't make an economic case [for going green], it's hard to get something approved." If done right, however, a company's return on investment can go well beyond improving its public image, he observes.[4]

Taryn Fransen, senior associate with environmental think tank World Resources Institute, suggests that companies take a comprehensive emissions inventory, one that takes into account all of their manufacturing processes, energy use, and transportation infrastructure. "By measuring the emissions that arise from these activities, businesses often realize opportunities to improve efficiency and generate significant cost savings, and in the process reduce energy use and GHG emissions," she notes.

Companies should also take a pragmatic approach to green initiatives, and recognize the inevitability of federally mandated regulations. "Companies that develop and implement climate change strategies now will gain a competitive advantage as the economy adjusts to new policies," Fransen says. What's more, she adds, "developing climate change strategies now will help identify the risks that companies face—and the opportunities for new markets and products—that may result from climate regulations, and a carbon constrained economy."

A strong eco-friendly policy can improve a company's public image by emphasizing corporate social responsibility, she points out. In addition, given the popularity of green initiatives with young people, companies with environmental credibility are being well received on college campuses. It might not show up on a balance sheet, Fransen admits, but the ability to more easily recruit talent because of their green practices is a big plus for some companies, and one that can pay off over the long term.[5]

The key to success with green projects—or any other supply chain project, for that matter—is having commitment from the highest levels of a company. If the chief executive officer (CEO) is solidly behind sustainability efforts, the rest of the company is more likely to be on the same page. "By making it clear to everyone in the company that sustainability is a critical part of the core value of the company, employees are given the freedom to be creative and look at alternatives that they might not have before," AMR Research's Davies says. "That's the differentiator now—whether the leadership is constantly asking you to look again and find ways to reduce emissions."

Look for the Green Label

In July 2009, retail giant Wal-Mart Stores Inc. revealed details of a far-reaching plan that aims to measure the sustainability of every product sold in its stores by its more than 100,000 suppliers. By partnering with universities and creating a Sustainability Index Consortium, Wal-Mart hopes to create a single repository of data for evaluating the sustainability of products—not how long a product will last before it degrades or becomes obsolete (that's the old-school definition of sustainability) but rather how close to "carbon neutrality" that product comes. The database will collect hard data such as GHG emissions, solid waste, water use, and raw materials as well as subjective information such as "ethical production" and "social compliance."

Using a yet-to-be-created set of life cycle analysis metrics, Wal-Mart will eventually roll out a labeling system for every product it sells, grading the products based on the supply chain processes—manufacturing, distribution, and trnsportation—required to bring them to market. The index, says Mike Duke, president and CEO of Wal-Mart, "will bring about a more transparent supply chain, drive product innovation, and ultimately provide consumers the information they need to assess the sustainability of products."[6] If all goes according to plan, sustainability labels should begin appearing on products by 2014.

"This index and the tools that we'll create with it will give us an opportunity to go much deeper into the supply chain and really strip the costs out," adds John Fleming, Wal-Mart's chief merchandising office. Fleming predicts that within 5 to 10 years, when consumers shop in a retail store, they'll find labels assigning a sustainability grade on every product in the store. (The grade might be based on a numerical scale or might be identified by a shade of color; the details haven't yet been worked out.) Consumers would be able to point their smartphone at a product's label and receive specific information about that product's life cycle. Using the example of a cotton T-shirt, Fleming explains that a consumer "would be able to see the field that the cotton came from, even a picture of the farmer that raised the cotton. There would be information about how much cotton was used, and how many product miles were consumed to get that T-shirt into the store." Having that information, he says, "will make a difference in terms of what products customers consider."[7]

The presumption here, of course, is that the buying habits of the typical retail shopper will undergo a radical conversion within the next decade, making decisions based not just on price, look, and feel but also on greenness. While eco-labeling efforts such as the Energy Star program of the U.S. Environmental Protection Agency (EPA) for home and office products have indeed caused consumers to pay closer attention to the fine print, those products have a built-in incentive—they use less energy and thus cost less to operate; hence, consumers will save money over the life of the product. Wal-Mart, for instance, has sold more than 100 million compact fluorescent light bulbs, thanks largely to the EPA's claim that these bulbs use 75 percent less energy, last 10 times longer than incandescent bulbs, and could end up saving a consumer $30 over the bulb's lifetime. Convincing somebody that there's an inherent savings in paying more for a greener box of paper clips or bag of potato chips, though, might be a tougher sell.

"You can design something that is carbon neutral, that does not contribute to climate change, and yet is still detrimental to human health in other ways," observes Arizona State University's Jay Golden, co-chairman of the Sustainability Index Consortium. "So you have to look comprehensively at what sustainability really means."[8]

The Carbon Footprint of a Banana

To understand the difficulty in providing a consumer with a meaningful and accurate sustainability label, consider the carbon footprint of a simple banana. Researcher Edgar Blanco, with the Center for Transportation and Logistics at the Massachusetts Institute of Technology, was commissioned by Chiquita Brands International Inc. to determine the impact that distance traveled has on a banana's overall sustainability score.

"Even a simple product like a banana has a complex supply chain: hundreds of farms with different agricultural practices, a variety of trucks and ocean vessels, multiple logistics flows and distances, varying time spent at refrigerated storage, and multiple sources of electricity at stores and warehouses," Blanco explains. Chiquita's bananas are grown in Central America and are shipped by boat to various U.S. ports, and are then stored in regional warehouses before being shipped on refrigerated trucks to their final retail destination. Naturally, then, a banana sold in a port city like Houston or New Orleans will log many fewer transportation and distribution hours than a banana going to a store in Minneapolis, Chicago, or Kansas City. According to Blanco's research, a banana sold in Minneapolis would have a carbon footprint of 168 g (grams of carbon dioxide equivalent), whereas that very same banana sold in New Orleans would have a much lower carbon footprint of 97 g.[9]

But the logistics journey makes up only one element of the total supply chain of the banana. "Even within one well-defined operation, the number of elements you need to measure is very complex in terms of data and interactions with suppliers," Blanco notes.[10]

A carbon footprint, he points out, has three dimensions: depth, referring to how far back or forward in a product's supply chain you choose to measure; breadth, which takes into account what types of data are measured throughout the supply chain; and precision, which is the degree of accuracy in the measurement of carbon emissions. So the plantation field where a banana is grown has to be factored into the equation, as the process of fruit harvesting can contribute as much as 25 percent of the total carbon footprint of a banana. There's also the fuel efficiency of the various vehicles the bananas are transported in, the energy efficiency of the warehouses they're stored in, and even the cardboard boxes bananas are typically packaged in. (In fact, Wal-Mart has been using a packaging scorecard for its suppliers since 2006.) Companies have to weigh all of these factors to get a full and accurate idea of their total carbon footprint, taking into account even those supply chain processes out of their control.[11]

To that end, many companies have conducted life cycle analysis (LCA) on their products, which documents the entire supply chain life cycle of a product, from raw material production to manufacturing, distribution, transportation, use, and disposal. The LCA is actually a stricter standard than a manufacturing emissions-based footprint, points out AMR Research's John Davies, but it can also open up new revenue opportunities. He cites the example of construction equipment manufacturer Caterpillar Inc., which uncovered a multibillion-dollar business opportunity by expanding its remanufacturing capabilities. For instance, while comparing the carbon impact of remanufacturing a cylinder head versus building a new one, Caterpillar discovered that the remanufacturing process consumes 90 percent less water, uses 80 percent less energy, requires 99 percent fewer materials, occupies 99 percent less landfill, and emits 50 percent fewer greenhouse gases.[12]

Sustainability throughout the Supply Chain

As we saw in the Chiquita example, the carbon emissions of a company's key supply chain partners in such areas as transportation and warehousing can contribute significantly to a product's overall carbon footprint. The same holds true for the sustainability practices of raw materials providers, contract manufacturers, and other contributors—both domestic and global—to the end product.

"Greener products are generally more durable, and their use in your business will lead to fewer losses from damage or returns from customers," notes Daniel Sitarz, director of the Center for Sustainable Business and Technology. "Efforts to source your purchasing from companies that use innovative materials can dramatically reduce the amounts of hazardous or toxic chemicals that your company must handle or dispose of. This can, in turn, reduce insurance rates, disposal and treatment expenses, and legal liability while simultaneously increasing customer satisfaction and employee health and safety."

Sitarz recommends that companies prepare a green supply chain worksheet for each of its suppliers and update it every quarter to track the effectiveness of its green initiatives. Questions to ask every supplier include:

- Are the raw materials used sustainable?
- Does the product contain hazardous or toxic materials?
- Is the product packed in reusable or recyclable material?
- Does the product contain recycled content, and if so, what percent of it is recycled?
- Is the product produced with fair labor standards?
- Is the product traceable with bar codes, RFID, or other labels?
- Is the product produced with renewable energy?
- Is the product shipped energy efficiently?
- Is the product recyclable at the end of its life?[13]

Good to Green

As we saw in Chapter 7, shifting as much of your freight as possible from less-than-truckload to the much less expensive full-truckload mode is a strategic (though traditional) best practice in transportation management. Now, thanks to savvy public relations campaigns, companies adept at managing their logistics costs can point to those very same efforts as environmental innovations.

For instance, consumer products manufacturer SC Johnson & Son Inc. has a program called the Truckload Utilization Project. The company devised a system that combines multiple customer orders and multiple products into as many full truckloads as possible. By optimizing truckloads, SC Johnson found that after the first year of the project, it used 2,098 fewer trucks, cut fuel usage by 168,000 gallons, and saved approximately $1.6 million. But when it came time to publicizing the results, SC Johnson focused on the elimination of 1,882 tons of greenhouse gases.

The company reached these savings the old-fashioned way: By studying its loading dock practices, SJ Johnson discovered that trucks weren't being loaded to their maximum weight capacity. "Loading a truck may seem simple, but making sure that a truck is truly 'full' is a science," explains Pat Penman, the company's director of global environmental and safety actions. "Focusing on consistently hitting a trailer's maximum weight provided a huge opportunity to reduce our energy consumption, cut our GHG emissions, and save money. It illustrates how innovation can drive prosperity and responsibility."

SC Johnson's research indicated that a truckload filled to capacity with cartons of sandwich bags typically was far below a truck's most efficient load weight, while a smaller number of cartons of bottles of window cleaner usually would reach the maximum weight target before all the available space in the trailer was occupied. So by optimizing truckloads, the company is now able to pack multiple products on the same trailer.[14]

Or take the example of office furniture manufacturer Haworth Inc. and trucking company Perkins Logistics, which between them came up with a new packaging procedure that uses reusable protective blankets wrapped around furniture instead of packing them in cardboard containers. This tactic allows Haworth to ship 65 percent more products in the trailers, thereby reducing the number of loads needed while eliminating cardboard waste. The companies estimate that this use of blankets reflects a 20 percent reduction in GHG emissions because there are now fewer trucks on the highway.

"Packaging methods play a significant role in shipping efficiencies, but only after conducting a thorough investigation did we determine that a few fundamental changes in this area could also help reduce one element of the total carbon footprint of our products, taken over their useful lives," says Henry Oosterhouse, Haworth's global transportation manager. "While it took some added effort on our end, our customers said they appreciated avoiding the labor of unpacking boxes and disposing of cardboard waste."

The new packing method actually costs 15 percent more per shipment because of the additional labor and reusable equipment required, but those costs are offset by the ability to ship more items per load, plus the elimination of cardboard boxes and the labor needed to containerize products.[15]

These aren't necessarily green stories at all, in that the motivation for improvements came from fundamental supply chain thinking rather than eco-consciousness, but we've reached that stage where almost any reduction in labor, highway miles logged, fuel consumed, packaging materials used, or excess weight in shipments can be considered not just good supply chain management but green supply chain management.

At a Glance

Green Supply Chain Management

Green supply chain management refers to the alignment of sourcing, manufacturing, distribution, transportation, and remanufacturing/recycling processes with the goal of reducing a company's carbon footprint.

How Big Blue Went Green

In a ranking of the world's greenest manufacturers conducted by RiskMetrics Group, the number-one company is high-tech giant IBM Corp., followed by two other electronics companies, Dell Inc. and Intel Corp. The study indicates that high-tech companies in particular are noteworthy for their product and service innovation, especially when it comes to making their operations, data centers, and product lines more energy efficient. IBM's energy conservation programs, for instance, accounted for nearly $20 million in savings in 2007.[16]

Indeed, IBM has a culture focused on mastering its carbon management, utilizing its integrated supply chain to gain greater leverage and control over carbon emissions. Following are five of the key areas that IBM has focused on, and which other companies can concentrate on as well, in pursuit of a greener supply chain:

1. *Diagnosis and assessment.* Use a carbon diagnostic that evaluates each high-level supply chain component according to a set of carbon statements and key performance indicators. This will help you define your own maturity level, identify gaps, and set target levels.
2. *Carbon asset management.* Areas such as warehousing, machinery, vehicle fleets, and data centers offer the most immediate opportunities for directly reducing carbon emissions because they account for a large percentage of your energy expenditures. By investing in facilities with a low carbon footprint and energy-saving equipment, you'll be able

to have an immediate impact while realizing measurable return on investment.

3. *Functional optimization.* Your ability to reduce GHG emissions generally will be enhanced if you leverage your supply chain early on in the process. Identify where each supply chain functional area can make a specific contribution to reducing your carbon footprint. Make sure you include product design, customer fulfillment, and reverse logistics in the process.

4. *Internal horizontal integration.* Due to the complexity of some types of supply chains, specific functional improvements in certain areas might have a very limited reach. By coordinating your carbon reduction efforts broadly across your enterprise, you'll enjoy better results while gaining greater leverage.

5. *Collaborative, end-to-end optimization.* Be proactive and insist that your supply chain partners work with you and fully participate in your green initiatives.[17]

Eco-Friendly Strategies

As one of the major third-party logistics providers in the United States, Ryder System Inc. has learned firsthand the value of greening its supply chain processes. The company, for instance, has reduced the amount of sulfur emitted from its trucks by switching to ultra-low-sulfur diesel fuel at all of its fueling operations. Ryder also has worked closely with manufacturers on adopting green designs and processes throughout their supply chains, and offers these strategies for developing a more environmentally-friendly supply chain:

Warehousing and Distribution

Integrate energy conservation strategies in the warehouse to reduce reliance on GHG-producing sources.

Set targets for reducing energy consumption and conduct annual audits to ensure progress.

Use low-voltage lighting and install motion sensors or timers on lighting systems.

Conduct regular facility inspections to identify opportunities to upgrade the roofing, doors, and windows, and to repair leaking water pipes and irrigation systems.

Integrate real-time inventory visibility in the warehouse to reduce unnecessary trips and wasteful inventory obsolescence.

Leverage technology to streamline and improve the accuracy of inventory levels.

Create a closed-loop system for reporting and reconciling inventory levels with front-office systems.

Optimize distribution networks to require fewer trips, less idling, and lower overall delivery costs.

Establish regional distribution centers to serve customers based on demand.

Optimize and consolidate routes to reduce the number of loads overall.

Transportation

Align inbound and outbound shipments to reduce carbon emissions with less fuel and to speed up cash-to-cash cycles.

Connect in real-time to customers to synchronize returns with maximized fleet use (i.e., backhauls).

Coordinate supplier shipments to consolidate freight costs and negotiate better rates.

Automate transportation management systems.

Switch to an electronic freight bill, audit, and payment process to reduce or eliminate paper transactions.

Synchronize with warehouse operations to extend efficiency.

Consider a dedicated fleet solution.

Control routes, fuel consumption, and idle time.

Enhance driver training with courses that improve driving skills and performance, and teach drivers simple techniques to reduce fuel consumption.[18]

Low-Hanging Fruit

The vast majority of companies are currently taking steps to reduce carbon emissions, according to a study conducted by consulting firm Accenture. That's not so surprising; what is a bit of a shock is that 37 percent of the supply chain executives surveyed have no idea of the level of GHG emissions in their supply chain network. What's more, only 10 percent of companies are actively modeling their carbon footprints and have implemented successful green initiatives. Most companies, in fact, "are implementing carbon-reduction solutions without understanding their carbon footprint, and are therefore unable to measure the real impact those solutions are having on their emissions," says Jonathan Wright, senior executive in Accenture's supply chain management practice.

However, best-in-class supply chains (which Accenture defines as those that have achieved top-quartile performance in both cost effectiveness and customer service) are much more likely than other supply chains to model their carbon footprints and pursue sustainability projects (20 percent versus

9 percent). These best-in-class companies are successful in linking cost effectiveness, customer service, and sustainable supply chain practices, Wright notes. There is a solid business case for greening the supply chain, he emphasizes, resulting in lower costs as well as environmentally responsible processes.

All told, 86 percent have undertaken some sort of green effort in their warehouses, while 38 percent have pursued green initiatives in their transport fleet, in such areas as streamlining vehicle design, adopting green fuels, and using vehicles with hybrid engines.

Given the propensity of companies to seek out the "low-hanging fruit" when it comes to launching green initiatives, the five opportunities (as identified by Accenture and the World Economic Forum) with the greatest potential for reducing GHG emissions are:

1. Clean-vehicle technologies
2. Slower and optimized transportation
3. Packaging design initiatives
4. Optimized networks
5. Energy-efficient buildings[19]

CHAPTER 17

Continuous Improvement

Lean on Me

Flashpoints

All employees should be empowered with the ability and the responsibility to improve their company.

The Toyota Production System is based on the philosophies of continuous improvement and respect for people.

Lean management is a waste-elimination strategy, not a cost-reduction strategy.

Lean practices need to be tied in tightly with a company's supply chain processes.

Nestled in the mountains of northern Utah, in the small town of Tremonton, Autoliv North America, a Tier One automotive supplier, is a fervent believer in the power of suggestion.[1] Like numerous other companies that have adopted lean manufacturing practices, Autoliv relies heavily on input from its employees—*all* of its employees, at every level and in every department—to offer recommendations on how to do things better. Over the past decade, however, the suggestion box at Autoliv has been rendered obsolete as the number of individual suggestions has grown from a little more than 200 in 2002 to well over 15,000 in 2007. The number of formal continuous improvement workshops, involving teams of employees focused on specific projects, went from zero workshops in 2003 to roughly 160 in 2007. And, fittingly enough, the impetus for these efforts came when a major customer suggested that Autoliv needed to get better at manufacturing its products.

Autoliv's workshops, known as *kaizen* events, involve employees diligently poring through production data to identify bottlenecks and other problem areas, with the goal of eliminating waste in the manufacturing process while improving productivity.[2] The key to success for these workshops is getting everyone on the team involved in applying lean manufacturing principles, explains plant manager Mark Newton. He offers as an example a time when the plant needed to add capacity because of additional business but did not have the available capital to create six large work cells to accommodate the new business. A kaizen work team was given the assignment to increase capacity on the existing production lines by making key improvements.

"For the first two hours," Newton recalls, "the cross-functional engineering team went in circles, basically saying it couldn't be done. The team leader reiterated, 'There is a way, and we will not leave until we figure it out.'" Working together, the team applied lean principles and other out-of-the-box thinking until it came up with a solution, which resulted in 1.4 lines of increased capacity for less than half the cost of a new line. "The hundreds of kaizens that were generated by this team and the involvement of our hourly operators have made this a home run gain," Newton says.[3]

Lean principles and kaizen events are both central concepts in the drive for continuous improvement, which aims at "improvement in small, incremental, continuous steps that can be placed in the context of a number of tactical initiatives," explain Terence T. Burton and Steven M. Boeder, authors of *The Lean Extended Enterprise*. "Daily improvement in small amounts carried out in every job and function of the business eventually accumulates into very large gains."[4]

At Autoliv, the kaizen teams are encouraged to look for ways to reduce waste, eliminate scrap, reduce inventory, and identify and solve safety issues. Safety in particular is a major concern because the Tremonton plant's main product is airbag initiators, which require the use and manufacture of large amounts of pyrotechnic materials (basically, the initiator generates an explosion to inflate the airbag). As Newton explains, "With pyrotechnics, we must avoid friction, heat, impact, and static discharge. Any of these can cause combustion."

Not surprisingly, then, many of Autoliv's kaizen workshops have been dedicated to safety and productivity improvements. One of these workshops, for instance, led to the adoption of the slurry loading process, a manufacturing process based on the principle that handling pyrotechnic chemicals is safer when they're wet than when they're dry. The company saved over $1 million from this new process, thanks in part to 67 percent fewer safety incidents and cost savings of 59 percent.[5]

From Push to Pull

Autoliv's biggest overall continuous improvement initiative is its development and use of what it calls the Autoliv Production System, which is based on the Toyota Production System (TPS), the granddaddy of all lean manufacturing models. Back in the late 1990s, Toyota Motor Corp. determined that the production processes of its main supplier of airbags—namely, Autoliv—were not quite up to the Japanese automaker's standards. Autoliv asked Toyota for help, and was rewarded with a two-year mentoring program led by one of Toyota's top production experts, Takashi Harada. (Toyota's extremely close relationship with its key suppliers (*keiretsu*) is discussed in Chapter 13.)

As a result of Harada's instruction, visitors to any of Autoliv's plants today "see a clean, organized, and visual workplace where they can clearly see and identify normal from abnormal," Newton says. What's more, since 2003, the Tremonton plant has tripled its inventory turns, improved its on-time delivery performance to 99.6 percent and achieved a 96.5 percent reduction in external customer quality defects.

The *visual workplace*, one of many ideas Autoliv learned from Toyota, makes it easy to spot a problem wherever it exists in a plant and allows for easy manager updates, Newton explains. By walking the floor, anyone with practice can determine in about 10 minutes how well the plant has done over the previous 12 hours. "The visual aspect means being able to look at the process, a piece of equipment, inventory, or information or at a worker performing a job and immediately see the standard being used to perform the task and if there is a deviation from the standard," adds consultant Jeffrey Liker, author of *The Toyota Way*.[6]

Autoliv is far from being the only company that has a production system based on the Toyota Production System, and the influence of the TPS goes well beyond the automotive industry. For instance, there's the Bosch Production System, the Canon Production System, the Danaher Business System, the Eaton Business System, the Ford Production System, and so on throughout the alphabet. Each company puts its own spin on the Toyota model, based on its own needs and goals, but when it comes to the full package of lean principles, the TPS is in a class of its own. "What is unique about Toyota is how pervasive lean manufacturing is across every process at all of its plants, as well as all of its first-tier suppliers," Liker points out. While other companies might be good at preventive maintenance, or employee engagement, or mistake-proofing, "at Toyota all of these elements of lean are used together in its TPS."[7]

Although vestiges of the TPS date back to the 1920s, when Toyoda Automatic Loom Works invented a loom that would automatically stop itself whenever a thread broke, it was in the 1950s that the TPS as we know it came to be. Taiichi Ohno, an executive with Toyota Motor Corp., came to the United States to study how American automakers built their cars. As it happened, Ohno's epiphany came not within an automotive plant but in fact in a supermarket, a concept largely unknown in Japan at the time. The ability of American shoppers to self-select whatever groceries they wanted, in whatever quantities, inspired Ohno to develop an analogous pull system at Toyota where each production line would serve as a kind of supermarket for the next succeeding line, replacing only the items that were selected.

All of these events and concepts were combined, refined, and ultimately streamlined into the Toyota Production System. Some of the best-known elements of the TPS include:

- Eliminating waste (*muda*) from every process and activity the company is involved in; these wastes include overproduction, waiting, transportation, motion, inventory, space, and defects.
- Empowering workers with the responsibility of shutting down the production line if and whenever necessary (*jidoka*).
- A visual management system known as *5S*—sort, straighten, shine, standardize, and sustain—which aims at maintaining a clean, well-organized facility.
- Implementing a pull system, based on color-coded index cards (*kanban*), that signals when a product needs to be replenished (just in time).

At its heart, the TPS is based on two core philosophies that are deeply ingrained in the Toyota culture: continuous improvement and respect for people. "Under a push system, there is little opportunity for workers to gain wisdom because they just produce according to the instructions they are given," explains Teruyuki Minoura, a senior managing director of Toyota Motor Corp. In contrast, he notes, a pull system asks the workers to decide what needs to be built and how quickly that has to happen. "An environment where people have to think brings with it wisdom, and this wisdom brings with it continuous improvement." The greatest strength of the TPS is its ability to develop people, he notes, and for that reason, Minoura says the "T" in TPS can also stand for "thinking."[8]

The Toyota Way

Obviously, nobody would pay much attention to what Toyota was doing if it hadn't proven to be tremendously successful. As it so happens, the TPS is largely responsible for the conversion of a once-obscure company into the biggest and most respected automaker in the world. In *The Toyota Way*, Jeffrey Liker explains point-by-point the 14 management principles Toyota follows in its pursuit of continuous improvement and respect for people. He summarizes these best practices in this way:

1. Base your management decisions on a long-term philosophy, even at the expense of short-term goals.
2. Create continuous process flow to bring problems to the surface.
3. Use pull systems to avoid overproduction.
4. Level out the workload.
5. Build a culture of stopping to fix problems, to get quality right the first time.
6. Use standardized tasks as the foundation for continuous improvement and employee empowerment.
7. Use visual control so that no problems are hidden.
8. Use only reliable, thoroughly tested technology that serves your people and processes.
9. Grow leaders who thoroughly understand the work, live the philosophy, and teach it to others.
10. Develop exceptional people and teams who follow your company's philosophies.
11. Respect your extended network of partners and suppliers by challenging them and helping them improve.
12. Go and see for yourself to thoroughly understand the situation.
13. Make decisions slowly by consensus, thoroughly considering all options; implement decisions rapidly.
14. Become a learning organization through relentless reflection and continuous improvement.[9]

Don't Settle for Occasional Improvement

When asked about their implementation of strategic practices, 76.9 percent of U.S. manufacturing companies named continuous improvement programs as their primary initiative, according to the 2007 *IndustryWeek*/MPI Census of Manufacturers. (By point of comparison, only 47.4 percent of Chinese manufacturers said they were involved in a lean/continuous improvement initiative.) The popularity of lean in general, however, does not necessarily mean that all companies are following through with the management principles that lean proponents espouse, particularly if the company's main goal is to cut costs. "Lean management is not a quick solution for cost reduction," points out Jim Womack, founder of the Lean Enterprise Institute.

"It's a fundamentally different system than traditional management for organizing and managing employees, suppliers, customer relationships, product development, production, and the overall enterprise."[10]

Some companies look at continuous improvement as some kind of "silver bullet" solution so they engage in numerous *kaikaku* (radical change) events in pursuit of a dramatic turnaround, observes Ralph Keller, president of the Association for Manufacturing Excellence trade organization. "Meanwhile, some of the most respected companies in lean manufacturing continue on their steady course of improvement using lots of mini-kaizens performed continuously by small teams of value-adding operators right at their worksites. While it's nice to have some quantum leap improvements from kaikaku events, it's the steady continuous improvement kaizens that will yield lasting performance increases," Keller notes. "It's also the only way to get lasting culture change in the organization and to get everyone's buy-in on 'that's how we do things around here.'"[11]

According to lean consultant Rick Pay, there are four major reasons that companies fail to achieve benefits from their continuous improvement programs:

1. Senior management is not committed to or doesn't understand the full significance of lean.
2. Senior management refuses to accept that cultural change is necessary for lean to be successful.
3. The company does not have the right people in the right positions.
4. The company chose lean when a different process improvement program—or none at all—would have been the better choice.[12]

Before adopting lean or any other continuous improvement program, corporate management must ask itself: Will this initiative directly contribute to our business strategy? The answer, Pay suggests, is not always obvious. "Some companies' strategic focus, for example, is on competitive market positioning through new product development. In these companies, process improvement and productivity measures may not be perceived as contributing directly to their competitive advantage. You can bet that in these companies senior management may not support a lean initiative if waste reduction on the shop floor is the focus. And, without the full support of top management, the likelihood of success of any process improvement program is jeopardized. Top management," Pay insists, "needs to fully understand the various stages of implementing lean so they won't be tempted to pull the plug before results are achieved. In short, they need to accept lean as part of their overall operations and business strategies and support it all along the way."

Lean Principles

As noted, lean is not a quick fix. When 771 managers and executives were asked by the Lean Enterprise Institute (www.lean.org) to identify the biggest obstacle to implementing lean at their companies, nearly half (48 percent) said it was "backsliding to the old ways of working." It's also revealing to note that when asked how far along they were with their lean implementations, more than half (53 percent) characterized their companies as being in the early stages. So while a lot of lip service is being paid to the idea of lean manufacturing, there remains a sizable gap on the execution end.

At a Glance

Lean Manufacturing

Lean manufacturing is a management philosophy focused on eliminating waste, reducing inventory, and increasing profitability.

As a result, companies continue to seek guidance in exactly how a lean operation should be set up and, just as important, how to maintain it. Mandyam Srinivasan, a professor with the University of Tennessee, has identified 14 principles that companies should follow to build and manage lean supply chains:

1. Measure any improvements in subsystem performance by weighing their impact on the whole system.
2. Focus on improving the performance of the lean supply chain, but do not ignore the supply chain's business ecosystem.
3. Focus on customer needs and process considerations when designing a product.
4. Maintain inventories in an undifferentiated (unfinished) form for as long as it is economically feasible to do so.
5. Buffer variation in demand with capacity, not inventory.
6. Use forecasts to plan and pull to execute.
7. Build strategic partnerships and alliances with members of the supply chain, with the goal of reducing the total cost of providing goods and services.
8. Design products and processes to promote strategic flexibility.
9. Develop performance measures that allow the enterprise to better align functions and move from a functional to a process orientation.

10. Reduce time lost at a bottleneck resource, which results in a loss of productivity for the entire supply chain. Time saved at a nonbottleneck resource is a mirage.
11. Make decisions that promote a growth strategy and focus on improving throughput.
12. Synchronize flow by first scheduling the bottleneck resources on the most productive products, then schedule nonbottleneck resources to support the bottleneck resources.
13. Don't focus on balancing capacities—focus on synchronizing the flow.
14. Reduce variation in the system, which will allow the supply chain to generate higher throughput with lower inventory and lower operating expense.[13]

Lean, Mean Flying Machine

When aerospace giant Boeing committed itself to lean manufacturing, it sent teams of workers to various automotive plants around the world to learn the best manufacturing practices from companies such as Porsche and Volkswagen. The aerospace industry is considerably more parts intensive and labor intensive than the automotive industry—a typical jet has more than 3 million parts—but Boeing still learned plenty about job scheduling and just-in-time manufacturing. Those lessons have been put to good use in streamlining what is arguably the most complex manufacturing supply chain in the world.[14]

Boeing has been devoted to lean principles since the early 1990s, and one of the company's key goals has been to eliminate waste and the costs associated with it, whether it's wasted time, wasted production materials, wasted labor, or wasted money. To reach that goal, the company has substantially reduced its supply base (down by 65 percent since 2000) and now partners only with those suppliers that can provide the best in terms of capability, quality, delivery performance, and collaboration, explains Norma Clayton, vice president of supplier management for Boeing's Integrated Defense Systems group.[15]

Boeing's lean consultants work directly with suppliers and train them so they can implement lean on their own, Clayton notes. Additionally, suppliers are encouraged to attend lean conferences and symposiums as well as participate in manufacturing extension partnerships where available. Through a process known as value stream mapping, Boeing has been able to reduce its procurement costs while helping its suppliers identify areas where they can drive out costs as well. With value stream mapping, a company begins by defining the current state of how a process is being done. Then it focuses on where it wants to be and identifies areas of improvement that will bring about that desired state. Using this process, one cable supplier to Boeing has been able to cut assembly time by 44 percent while increasing productivity by 27 percent. It's all part of Boeing's program goal of keeping the flow of information, requirements, products, and services free of waste. In that situation, everybody in the supply chain ends up a winner.

Beginning with the Boeing 737 project in 1999, and continuing on to current projects, the airplane manufacturer has focused its lean production initiatives through a program it calls the Nine Tactics, according to consultant John Black, formerly director of lean manufacturing research and development for Boeing's Commercial Airplanes Group:

1. *Value stream mapping* helps everyone involved to visualize the production processes.
2. *Work balancing* allows the work on the production line to be more predictable and standardized.
3. *Standardization* results in finding and documenting the simplest, fastest, and most easily repeatable way to perform a task.
4. Putting *visual indicators* in place (*andon systems*) helps employees track production progress and problems.
5. *Point-of-use staging* means everything necessary to complete a job is kept where it will be used.
6. *Establishing feeder and supply lines* helps reduce overall flow time, how often a part is handled, and how many parts come into final assembly.
7. *Redesign of major processes* is accomplished through the use of breakthrough concepts. In fact, Boeing has a collaborative group, known as the Moonshine Shop, dedicated to coming up with pushing-the-envelope ideas.
8. *Converting from a stationary line to a pulse line* involves moving (pulsing) everything on a production line from one station to the next at a pre-set time. This is an intermediate step to Tactic 9.
9. *Converting to a continuously moving line.*[16]

At a Glance

Value Stream Map

A value stream map is a chart that lays out in sequence all of the steps a manufacturer takes to bring a product from order to final delivery.

The Value of Teamwork

To Tom McMillen, formerly director of global logistics with automaker General Motors (GM) and currently vice president of purchasing and supply chain with GM Europe, implementing lean practices is a continuing adventure. The company is constantly coming up with new ways to optimize its supply network and remove waste in the process of moving parts from its suppliers to a GM assembly plant. "Throughout our organization, lean practices allow us to reduce inventory in plants and streamline business practices. The benefit is more efficiency and productivity in our supply chain."[17]

The supply chain view is the approach Toyota has taken all along, but it's a difficult lesson for many American manufacturers. In the past, too many companies have looked on the TPS model as a departmental solution suitable only for the plant floor and the production line, observes Jim Matheson, a professor with Stanford University.[18] What's more, this shortsighted thinking comes despite Toyota's insistence that lean should be embraced at the enterprise level to guide future growth from senior management levels on down.

In terms of best practices, companies should have lean teams that will determine the best manufacturing processes, document those processes, train each other on those processes, and then implement a plan where they all agree to follow those processes. Running lean throughout the supply chain requires evaluating every step within the manufacturing cycle. At United Technologies Electronic Controls (UTEC), for instance, teamwork is critical to launching and sustaining continuous improvement projects.[19] When UTEC, a manufacturer of controls for the heating, ventilation, and air conditioning industry, decided to implement certification procedures on critical production processes, "several teams were formed to understand the best ways to reduce variation within the process and how to effectively monitor its performance," explains Kelly Raugh, manufacturing manager. "The teams included manufacturing engineers, process engineers, technicians, and operators specific to each critical-to-quality process."

However, while the teams were fully informed as to their project objectives, operators on the production floor found themselves left out of the loop. "Operators had a difficult time understanding the importance of control plans and control charts to their process. Therefore, the operators were not always completing the actions they needed to ensure their process was robust," Raugh notes. This convinced UTEC that not just hand-picked employees but in fact *every* employee at the plant should be trained on process certification fundamentals, with the training customized for each particular group. As a result, the purchasing department learned how important procurement and sourcing are to the quality of the product, while factory technicians learned the relationship between proper equipment maintenance and ensuring high quality products. "When you can show an employee how a change impacts their job and why it is beneficial," Raugh points out, "their buy-in is much stronger and the results are more consistent."[20]

Leaning in the Right Direction

Jim Womack, one of the United States' leading proponents of lean, believes that U.S. companies need to transition from merely using lean tools to fully embracing lean management principles. "Companies today understand that you need to have quality at the source, that you need to put things into continuous flow, that pull is better than push in terms of scheduling, that the correct way to maintain machines is proactively rather than reactively. They understand lots of things," Womack acknowledges. "The real question now is, can they implement a lean management system that can use the tools most effectively on a continuing basis? In most businesses there's a complete disconnect, for example, between the metrics they're using and the lean methods they're deploying."

For instance, if your company is telling the purchasing department to beat down suppliers to get the lowest price, then you're not leaving yourself much of an opportunity to collaborate with your suppliers, Womack points out. Instead of aiming for consistently brilliant performance, you're settling for a short-term gain, which will soon evaporate when your suppliers decide they can no longer afford to work for you.

"There's a whole lot of curiosity about what it's going to take to change the way companies are managed, to actually get the full benefits from lean on a sustainable basis," he says, "but it's going to require both experimentation and a fair bit of change in what managers do, and in what they think management is. Most managers think that their greatest contribution to the business is doing workarounds on broken processes rather than doing the hard work to get the process right so it never breaks down and you don't need to do workarounds."

The biggest change needed in management thinking, Womack believes, is developing the ability to step back and say "Gosh, the reason why we're fighting fires all the time is we don't have any fire marshals around here. We're brilliant at fighting fires, but not adept at all at preventing fires." What Toyota has done so well, he asserts, is to put bulletproof processes in place for product development, fulfillment, order delivery, and supplier management so that things work and get done. Too often U.S. companies settle for an attitude of "we'll get back to you in a few days with an answer."[21]

Analyst firm Aberdeen Group recommends managers adopt these five best practices to achieve top performance through lean principles and inventory management:

1. Develop standardized information flows from the supply chain organization to manufacturing, and vice versa.
2. Establish a bidirectional information flow between the supply chain and manufacturing.
3. Determine optimal inventory levels to ensure the reduction of wasted inventory by establishing optimal safety stocks at various buffers within the supply chain.
4. Incorporate demand and production variability, inventory levels, and supplier lead time as part of the schedule creation process.
5. Develop lean techniques that support kanban variations suitable for supplier and internal operations.[22]

"At the end of the day," observes AME president Ralph Keller, "continuous improvement is about delighting your customers and setting a new standard of customer service in your industry. It's the focus on speed in satisfying your customer's needs, resulting from continuous improvement and operational excellence, that will make you the preferred supplier in your industry. This status will allow you to grow your revenues with existing customers and to acquire business from your competitors' customers without having to resort to price wars and the resulting margin reductions that price wars produce. That's not a bad place to be in this globally competitive world."[23]

CHAPTER 18

The Supply Chain Profession
What Keeps You Up at Night?

Flashpoints

Top-performing companies have top-performing supply chain people working for them.

Effective supply chain managers must be able to measure the right things rather than everything.

Every company should consider appointing a chief supply chain officer.

The time is now to start developing the next generation of supply chain talent.

In today's business climate, just managing to get through an entire workday without a major crisis has become a core competency for supply chain professionals. Whether a company looks on supply chain management as the be-all and end-all of its corporate strategy, or whether it chooses to outsource most of its warehousing and transportation processes to a third party, its supply chain specialists always seem to be in the middle of one contentious situation after another. Maybe that's just the nature of the job.

Up to this point, this book has looked at best practices as they relate to tasks, processes, and technology, but with this final climactic chapter, it's only fitting that we reveal the ultimate secret to supply chain success: *you.* That's right, for a company to truly have a fighting chance at transforming its supply chain and achieving consistent best-in-class performance, it's going to be up to you to help lead that effort.

Throughout this book we've looked at the supply chain through practitioners' eyes because supply chain management isn't a dry study of theories and spreadsheets—it's the daily alignment of the right people in the right

227

tasks to run their companies as efficiently and profitably as possible. Despite the numerous different job classifications and titles within the supply chain profession (e.g., logistics manager, supply chain director, procurement manager, vice president of distribution, operations manager, director of global trade), these professionals all share common goals and face similar challenges.

Fortunately, there is a solid sense of fraternity within the supply chain community based on a shared need to learn from each other. The sense that "we're all in this together" has helped foster a spirit of continuous improvement that motivates supply chain professionals to attend and participate in numerous industry events to share their experiences while learning the best practices of their peers.

In fact, travel itself is a frequent activity for supply chain professionals. According to a 2007 career patterns study conducted by Ohio State University, 50 percent of all logistics professionals spend at least one week per month on the road, and 25 percent say they're spending at least one week per month traveling internationally. Not surprisingly, when asked how they allocate their time, logistics professionals say they're engaged in transportation activities 27 percent of their workday, with the next closest response being warehousing, at 16 percent. They're also a well-educated group; half of the respondents spend between two to four weeks per year on continuing education and training. All survey respondents have at least an undergraduate degree, and 55 percent have a postgraduate degree as well.[1]

The number-one best practice when it comes to managing your supply chain is to have best-in-class people in positions of responsibility throughout your organization. Learning how to identify these people, how to train them, and how to develop them into productive employees has become increasingly important—as well as much more difficult—as supply chains have gone global. If it sometimes seems like companies tend to make it up as they go along when it comes to developing their supply chain groups—if they even have a supply chain group—there's some truth in that. Managing the people within a supply chain is every bit as challenging as managing the functional processes.

Talent Search

To begin with, where are you going to find these top-notch people? Mark Wilson, director of recruiter relations and technology at Ohio State University, one of the nation's leading supply chain breeding grounds, suggests that many of the best supply chain minds are currently completing degrees at colleges and universities and haven't even entered the job market yet.

Recruiting these candidates into entry-level positions can be an overwhelming task for firms that have little to no college campus recruiting experience, Wilson admits. First of all, if your company isn't in the Fortune 1000, chances are most college students have never heard of you, especially if you've never recruited at their school in the past. Second, college recruiting is rarely a skill possessed by direct-line managers, who tend to be unfamiliar with the on-campus recruiting cycle. And, frankly, "Most employers lack a plan for organizing their recruiting efforts," Wilson observes.

Fortunately, as supply chain programs grow in popularity, it's becoming easier to find quality candidates. "Whether your plan is for an ongoing recruiting program or a program for just-in-time hiring," he says, "there are some simple steps you can take to improve your odds for achieving success." Wilson offers this advice:

- *Get to know the people who work in career services.* "These professionals can be your resource for gaining insight into how and when to recruit on-campus," he explains. "They can help you understand the cycle and timing for interviewing college candidates, average salary offers, and when to make offers of employment. They can also help you understand what students are looking for in written descriptions of the job and your company."
- *Get to know the top candidates by seeking them out directly.* Many supply chain programs have professional organizations for students. "The student leaders of the organizations are typically leaders in every category of life, and tend to be highly regarded by college faculty, students, and employers," Wilson points out. "Invite these student leaders to lunch and ask them which firms recruit effectively and how you can help their student logistics organization. You are likely to find many valuable nuggets of information to assist you in your recruiting efforts."
- *Establish an on-campus presence with a few select schools.* This could involve corporate sponsorship programs, working with student organizations, and facilitating information sessions for top candidates.
- *Develop a connection with the supply chain faculty at these schools.* "Before or during your visit to conduct interviews on campus, take the time to meet with a faculty member and ask how you and your firm might be of help and get involved with their work," Wilson suggests. "This can lead to assisting with research and to classroom access, where you will find the candidates you are seeking. Plus, faculty can point you in the direction of their top performers."[2]

APICS (www.apics.org), a trade association for operations management, offers certification programs to train supply chain professionals, and to that end has developed what it calls a multitiered "supply chain manager competency model." While some of the tiers focus on basic foundational skills (e.g., effective communicator, team oriented, possesses interpersonal skills), the model also breaks down what technical competencies a supply chain manager should have and what skills a hiring organization should look for from a candidate:

- Site selection/ability to locate facilities
- Distribution
- Warehousing
- Logistics
- Global trade regulations
- Strategic sourcing/supplier relationship management
- Customer relationship management
- Knowledgeable in lean and Six Sigma tools

The best supply chain programs at U.S. universities, according to analyst firm AMR Research Inc., are offering their students ample opportunities to participate in the core supply chain activities in various ways, such as simulation, timed projects, cooperative projects, and internships. Based on a 2009 study of the best-known university programs, AMR Research has determined that the top five supply chain programs are:

1. Penn State University
2. Michigan State University
3. Arizona State University
4. Ohio State University
5. Massachusetts Institute of Technology (MIT)[3]

In a separate study of more than 200 global manufacturers and retailers, the Supply Chain Council undertook to identify which supply chain skills were at the top of companies' "need to have" lists. For the year 2010, companies identified hiring or developing staff with strategic and change management skills as their top supply chain priority, not surprising given the recessionary climate when the survey was conducted in late 2008. The second greatest need for supply chain talent in 2010 will be in the area of planning and forecasting. "As the saying goes, adversity is the mother of invention," notes Ken Cottrill with the MIT Center for Transportation and Logistics, "and there is more than enough adversity to require a reinvention of the skills needed to run a supply chain and steer a course toward profitability."[4]

Hiring Problem Solvers

Just because students do well in school doesn't mean they'll prove to be as capable on the job. How can you predict whether a job candidate will be a proactive problem solver once he or she joins your firm? Harry Joiner, an executive recruiter with SearchLogix, a firm that specializes in placing supply chain personnel, suggests using a seven-step checklist that projects how well or poorly a candidate will do when confronted with a real-world supply chain problem at your company. Start the process by asking the candidate to describe a specific challenge he or she has confronted in a previous work situation. Good problem solvers should demonstrate an ability to:

1. *Define the problem.* "Have the candidates identify what went wrong by including both a cause and an effect in the definition of the problem they solved," Joiner says.
2. *Define the objectives.* They should be able to articulate the outcome they achieved after solving the problem.
3. *Generate alternatives.* Pay close attention to how many alternatives the candidates came up with, Joiner suggests. "Did the quality of the alternatives vary greatly? Was there a significant difference in the hard (and soft) costs associated with each idea? This is the area in which the candidates can demonstrate their creativity and resourcefulness as problem solvers."
4. *Develop a detailed action plan.* Have the candidates recap their action plan, and observe whether they specify who did what and by what dates. The devil is in the details, Joiner notes, and detailed problem solvers are usually more effective than generalists.
5. *Troubleshoot.* You want to see if the candidates were aware of worst-case scenarios and what steps they took to ensure the plan would work.
6. *Communicate.* "Getting information to the right people is key for getting the buy-in to make it a success," Joiner observes. He suggests you have the candidates address which individuals or groups affected the success of their action plan. "The most effective executives are those who can leverage their time and talents by getting things done through other people. This is your opportunity to build your company's management bench."
7. *Implement.* It's important that the candidates be able to identify who carried out the plan and monitor its implementation. You want to find out whether, as a manager, the candidates will be "hard on the issues and soft on the people."

The more you can drill down into real-world examples of how candidates have solved problems in the past, the better an idea you'll get of how well they'll solve problems at your company, Joiner points out. "Think in terms of the quality, consistency, and costs of their solutions. During the interview, you must get the candidates to be specific about their problem-solving experience. Minimize the chances of being duped by getting the candidates to recap in vivid detail exactly what happened in a given situation. If you don't challenge them during the interview process," he adds, "you may pay a steep price later for your lack of persistence."[5]

Training the Next Generation

With the goal of developing top supply chain talent, some companies actually start the training process even before they hire an employee. Toy manufacturer Hasbro Inc., for instance, hires an intern every year within its logistics group, with a good crop of students to choose from throughout New England. New hires will spend their first three months in training with senior executives in all core supply chain areas. Their training will then be tailored to the specific role for which they were hired. "New hires in logistics who will have people management responsibility might attend a five-day people management curriculum," explains Kim Janson, Hasbro's vice president of organizational effectiveness. Those who are being groomed for senior-level positions will attend the company's global leadership program, which was designed in partnership with Dartmouth College's Tuck School of Business.

That program is paying dividends in how Hasbro's various business units are being run. "There's a degree of collaboration never before seen across the business units and around the globe," Janson observes. The overall objective is to foster community within Hasbro as well as in the outside communities and throughout the supply chain. The toymaker also offers e-learning as well as more traditional skills development options through tuition reimbursement.

Bernard Hale, principal with Hale Logistics Consulting, notes that general training needs for any supply chain hires should focus on these areas:

- Develop and enhance their communication skills. Managing the supply chain means managing relationships.
- Help them develop problem resolution skills, so they can learn to turn potentially bad situations into positive experiences.
- Teach them how to delegate effectively.

- Effective managers need to be able to measure performance, and just as important, they must be able to measure the right things rather than everything.
- Provide effective and timely performance evaluations.[6]

Computer giant IBM Corp.'s Integrated Supply Chain (ISC) group offers a mentoring program, which includes a shadow program that allows any employee to observe and accompany an IBM executive for a day. Within the first year of the program's introduction, hundreds of employees had participated and learned what a day in the life of an executive is really like, notes Patricia Lewis-Burton, vice president of human resources with the ISC. "We encourage employees to identify people they would want to have as a mentor—role models from whom they can benefit." That includes looking for leaders with broad backgrounds and experience in various supply chain departments. Key leaders throughout the ISC participate, having recognized the value of developing future leaders. "We view this as a company best practice, not something that should be left to human resources alone," Lewis-Burton explains.[7]

Optimizing the Workforce

As a global organization employing 325,000 people in 75 countries, IBM not only needs to be able to recruit and develop the best people it can find, but it also needs to be able to effectively deploy its human resources so that the right people are matched up with the right opportunities. The problem, as Mark Henderson, manager of IBM's Workforce Management Initiative (WMI), describes it, is very much akin to finding a needle in a haystack. For instance, the company discovered it had more than 13,000 different job descriptions for all of its employees, which made it nearly impossible to effectively identify where it was lacking in certain skills.[8]

The company's ISC group developed the capability to identify where its parts and systems are all over the world, but being able to identify where it had, say, Spanish-speaking Java programmers with a background in Voice over Internet Protocol proved to be an even more challenging task, because a system that could track human resources in such a manner would have to be built from scratch.

A company needs to be able to link its labor strategy to its business strategy, Henderson notes, and that requires being able to deploy "a common and consistent skills taxonomy to assess skills and talent across internal, external, and subcontracted personnel." IBM's goal is no less than to manage the supply chain of its intellectual capital. "An on-demand workplace requires flexibility, agility, and resiliency," he notes, so to that end Big Blue set out to create "a comprehensive ecosystem for tracking skills and job opportunities, and matching those skills with current and future work opportunities."

For instance, the WMI developed a Hot Skills Index, which functions much like a temperature gauge. Any IBM employee, whether a manager or an employee, can access the index to identify where job opportunities are, anywhere in the world. That became possible after the company reduced the total number of job descriptions from 13,000 to a more manageable 500. So now, if there is a huge need for Spanish-speaking Java programmers in Ireland, any IBM employees interested in moving to the Emerald Isle can start brushing up on their language or programming skills to take advantage of that opportunity. As the company has discovered, making this skills-and-opportunities information available allows its employees to reinvent themselves to match current job demand.

According to Henderson, the WMI has produced more than $1 billion in cash savings—$100 million in travel savings alone—and a 5 to 7 percent improvement in employee utilization. In addition, the WMI has greatly improved the company's ability to rebalance skills, significantly sped up staffing in growth areas, and enabled IBM to quickly adapt its workforce to the typical ups and downs of the high-tech industry.

What Keeps You Up at Night?

Basing his conclusions in part on the success IBM has had in steering its entire company toward supply chain proficiency, Forrester analyst Navi Radjou suggests that like-minded companies should consider appointing a chief supply chain officer (CSCO), who would be responsible for integrating enterprise-wide supply chain strategy into their business strategy. This senior-level executive would also promote the company's supply chain proficiency to Wall Street analysts by reporting on the positive impact of its supply chain transformations.[9]

Very few business cards actually have a "CSCO" imprinted on them, but nevertheless, many professionals feel the weight of their entire supply chain rests on their shoulders. With that kind of enterprise-wide responsibility, it's only natural that supply chain professionals—no matter what their title—would want to be able to compare their situation with others in similar positions of authority at other companies.

Logistics Today magazine conducts an annual salary survey of industry professionals and in the process compiles a portrait of the typical supply chain manager. This person has the title of logistics manager, is male, 45 years old, lives in the Midwest, has 17 years of supply chain experience, has worked for his current company for the past 10 years, and earns just under $78,000 per year.[10]

The magazine also asks its readers the question: "What keeps you up at night?" Perhaps some of these responses sound familiar:

- Finding quality people to get the job done right
- The costs of having to constantly train new hires
- Managing customer compliance issues and challenging chargebacks from customers
- Government intrusion into logistics business processes without regard to the costs it layers onto private companies
- Rising fuel, insurance, and transportation costs, and continually trying to find cost reductions to offset those rising costs
- Finding and retaining qualified drivers
- Export restrictions, security requirements, and Customs clearance issues
- Top management dragging its heels on adopting new technologies
- Whether the trucks have picked up the scheduled loads and will deliver to the customer's schedule
- The hidden costs (payoffs and kickbacks) of doing business offshore
- How to get truckload freight moved on unwanted lanes
- Increases in fuel and security fees, and peak surcharges for ocean imports from the Far East
- Determining the best metrics to measure operations and bottom lines
- Having too much to do and too little time to do it in[11]

Gray Matters

While no company in its right corporate mind would ever refer to it as a best practice, one of the most frequently used tactics to initiate a quick turnaround is workforce reduction. Supply chain professionals, especially senior-level CSCO-type executives, are learning the sad truth: With healthcare costs skyrocketing beyond all reason, some companies are concluding that an experienced (read: older) supply chain expert will cost more in salary, healthcare, and other benefits than a less experienced (read: younger) person. The fact that Wall Street tends to reward massive layoffs with an immediate hike in the share price only perpetuates the ritual.

This short-term mentality ends up costing a company in the long run when it discovers key supply chain operations aren't being managed as efficiently anymore. Companies lose a wealth of business wisdom when they lay off seasoned professionals, and they're just as myopic when they don't consider these professionals for job openings, notes Lynn Failing, vice president of executive search consulting firm Kimmel & Associates. The push toward outsourcing noncore supply chain activities to third parties (see Chapter 12) also means that the positions that used to manage these jobs are being eliminated, Failing adds.[12]

Bruce Cutler knows what it feels like to be laid off in midcareer from a high-ranking supply chain position.[13] After 16 years with high-tech manufacturer Compaq Computer Corp. and in his mid-40s, Cutler was laid off when Compaq was acquired by Hewlett-Packard Co. Despite his experience as the director of logistics operations with a major global corporation, it took him nearly a year to land a comparable position with Star Furniture. He offers this advice to other seasoned supply chain professionals who find themselves looking for another job:

- Personal networking is essential but not sufficient. "Find a way to match available job openings—or companies likely to be hiring—with inside contacts," he suggests.
- Honestly assess your weak areas, then work on improving them.
- Take a broad perspective of your capabilities, and tailor your resume to match. Cutler's experiences in the high-tech industry might not seem much of an asset for a furniture retailer, but it wasn't knowledge of the end product that mattered to his new employer—it was his experience with Asian imports.
- Conduct a nationwide job search, because volume matters. The more resumes you send out and contacts you establish, the better your odds of finding a job that fits you.

The Secret to Supply Chain Success

Here's a happy statistic to close this chapter as well as this book: In a 2007 poll of more than 2,500 supply chain professionals conducted by *Logistics Today* magazine, 79 percent said they were satisfied with their jobs. So that's very good news.[14]

However, a lot of work still needs to be done before executives at every company truly understand the importance of key supply chain processes to their company's mission. This situation is gradually improving, according to the 2007 Ohio State career patterns survey, as more than half of the companies studied have named a CSCO-level executive within the past decade.

In addition, as global business activities increase, the role (some might say "the burden") of supply chain professionals is expanding to address the need for companies to have strategic thinkers able to manage global trade effectively. "The prices and availability of oil, the financial markets and availability and cost of working capital, competitors/competition, and commodity prices are examples of rapidly changing external forces," the Ohio State study reports. "The forecasted changes in the supply chain and the ability to remain flexible create unprecedented needs for supply chain management skills."[15]

When asked by *Logistics Today* to describe their job situations and how they feel about their profession, here's what some supply chain people had to say:

Generally, logistics is underestimated in companies and so are the salaries, but this is nothing new. Companies do not recognize the importance of logistics and see it in most cases as only costs. Otherwise my biggest satisfaction in the job is the feeling of improvement, moving things forward, making things better.

> —Operations manager at a wholesale distributor

Moving hazardous goods is becoming more difficult on a daily basis and the job now requires much added effort to complete hazardous shipments via air or ocean. Many of the shipping lines are now refusing to carry our products, making it virtually impossible to move shipments on a timely basis. It makes the job much less enjoyable than it was two or three years ago.

> —Global trade manager with an industrial products manufacturer

Logistics is that place that has a rock on one side and a hard place on the other. To succeed you have to be able to think quick, act fast, and get things moving when they have to be there.

> —Fleet manager with a transportation services company

Executives in general have little if any understanding of supply chain activities. They seem to be totally consumed with sales and finance outcomes and not on other areas that don't have apparent immediate impact on financial reporting.

> —Production/materials manager with an industrial products manufacturer

This is a career choice that is not suitable to all individuals. Anyone looking for a 9-to-5 job need not apply. However, if you enjoy hard work, long hours, and being on call 24 hours every day, then this can be a very fulfilling field.

> —Operations manager with a 3PL

Most of us are looked upon as cavemen because there is little recognition. Very few people actually understand what it takes to move a product from point A to point B.

> —Logistics manager with a wholesale distributor

In the past several years, as part of an overall cost-cutting measure, my company has been reorganizing such that the supply chain is more decentralized. We no longer have a vice president of supply chain or director of supply chain. However, we have continued with our supply chain managers supporting individual businesses.

—Supply chain manager with a chemical manufacturer

I have always enjoyed the fact that no two days are the same. There are always new challenges to be met and new products to solve.

—Logistics manager in the transportation services industry

As our executive management continues to ignore the importance of our company's logistics efforts, I suggest we outsource their positions— directors through CEO—and see how much we can save on those salaries and benefits. After all, reduced head count is a good thing, no matter how empty those heads are.

—Traffic manager for a retailer

Successful execution is all about managing relationships. It is based more on experience, knowledge, and hard work versus new information or technology. Collaborative relationships take time to mature but pay off in the long run, especially when times get tough. That's a true competitive advantage.

—Logistics manager with a chemical manufacturer

I have been in various aspects and at increasing levels within the entire global supply chain discipline for the past 30 years. I derive a tremendous amount of satisfaction from my job because of how all supply chain disciplines have gained such tremendous growth in responsibility and recognition within all industries over the past 15 years. I love what I do and love the company I work for. Challenge and job satisfaction are by far the biggest rewards.

—General manager with a wholesale distributor[16]

Clearly, in some companies, senior management has yet to be convinced that the supply chain is the "straw that stirs the drink." Depending on the company and the executives, there still lingers a mind-set that supply chain management is just a fad, or that it's too disruptive, or that it takes too long to derive any benefits, or that it's a bottomless pit of expensive technology solutions that don't solve anything. Or maybe no reason at all is given for disdaining supply chain programs, other than the old standby, "not invented here."

This book is offered as evidence to the contrary, having as its theme that the best-run companies in the world have the best supply chains and employ the best supply chain managers. Rather than only focusing on the "whats" and the "hows," this book has, I hope, opened up a realization that the "whos" make the difference. Without exception, top-performing companies have top-performing people working for them. That's the competitive advantage supply chain professionals offer their companies, and it's the secret to long-term and long-lasting success.

Notes

Chapter 1: If Supply Chain Is the Answer, Then What's the Question?

1. Council of Supply Chain Management Professionals, www.cscmp.org.
2. Forrester spells out many of his theories in the book *Industrial Dynamics* (Cambridge, MA: MIT Press, 1961).
3. David Blanchard, "Moving Past the Problems Can Be Problematical," *Chief Logistics Officer* (October 2003): 5.
4. Porter actually uses the term "value chain" rather than supply chain, but the difference is mainly one of semantics.
5. Michael Porter, *Competitive Advantage: Creating and Sustaining Superior Performance* (New York: The Free Press, 1985): 39–43.
6. Ibid., 318–319.
7. Carol Hymowitz, "Mind Your Language: To Do Business Today, Consider Delayering," *Wall Street Journal*, March 27, 2006, B1.
8. Blanchard, "Moving Past the Problems Can Be Problematical."
9. Debra Hofman, "The Secret to Supply Chain Excellence Is Balance," *AMR Research Alert Highlight* (April 22, 2004): 1.
10. Karen Butner, "Scoring High on the Supply Chain Maturity Model," presentation delivered at Supply Chain World, Dallas, TX, March 27, 2006.
11. Peter Heckmann, Dermot Shorten, and Harriet Engel, "Supply Chain Management at 21," *Chief Logistics Officer* (August 2003): 19–24.
12. J. Paul Dittmann, "What's On the Minds of Supply Chain Professionals Today?" www.IndustryWeek.com, June 1, 2009.

Chapter 2: Anatomy of a Supply Chain

1. Jill Jusko, "Building a Better Supply Chain," *IndustryWeek* (August 2009): 26–28.
2. www.seattlepi.com/boeing/787/787primer.asp.
3. John Teresko, "The Boeing 787: A Matter of Materials," *IndustryWeek* (December 2007): 34–38.

4. Stephen C. Rogers, *The Supply-Based Advantage* (New York: Amacom, 2009): 144–148.

5. Perry A. Trunick, "Sum of Many Parts," *Logistics Today* (March 2004): 1, 16–17.

6. Helen L. Richardson, "Staying on Track," *Logistics Today* (July 2004): 42–45.

7. Helen L. Richardson, "Inventory in the Balance," *Logistics Today* (May 2004): 1, 16–17.

8. Helen L. Richardson, "Building a Better Supply Chain," *Logistics Today* (April 2005): 17–25.

9. Tim Clark, "Driving at the Speed of Demand," *Consumer Goods Technology* (October 2005): 14–17.

10. David Blanchard, "Inbound for Glory," *Supply Chain Technology News* (April 2003): 1, 11.

11. Dale Buss, "Case Study: Land O'Lakes and Collaborative Logistics," *CIO Insight* (May 2003). Downloaded from www.cioinsight.com.

12. "The 25 Most Influential People in the Supply Chain," *Supply Chain Technology News* (April 2002): 14.

13. Roger Morton, "Making It There, Moving It Here," *Logistics Today* (December 2003): 33–34.

14. Rick Dana Barlow, "Drug Makers Fight Back against Counterfeiters," *Logistics Today* (February 2004): 9.

15. David Blanchard, "Tower of Babble," *Logistics Today* (February 2006): 7.

16. Lisa M. Kempfer, "RFID Helps Secure Drug Distribution Chain," *Material Handling Management* (July 2005): 1, 8.

17. Roger Morton, "Doctors of Speed," *Transportation and Distribution* (March 2003): 20–24.

18. "Working It Out," *Supply Chain Technology News* (December 2002/January 2003): 14.

19. Jennifer S. Kuhel, "The Science of Retail," *Supply Chain Technology News* (November 2001): 28.

20. Ken Cotrill, "Best Buy's Customer-Facing Supply Chain," *Supply Chain Strategy* (December 2005–January 2006). Downloaded from http://hbswk.hbs.edu/archive/5175.html.

21. www.microsoft.com/dynamics.

22. Video posted to www.bestbuyinc.com.

Chapter 3: Supply Chain Metrics: Measuring Up to High Standards

1. John Thorn, "Sabermetrics," *Total Baseball,* 3rd ed. (New York: Harper-Perennial, 1993), 620.

2. Jennifer S. Kuhel, "Bad Sport," *Supply Chain Technology News* (April 2001): 1.
3. David Blanchard, "The Software Vendor and the Shoemaker," *Supply Chain Technology News* (April 2001): 5.
4. David Blanchard, "Chain Reactions," *Logistics Today* (March 2004): 6.
5. David Blanchard, "Moving Past the Problems Can Be Problematical," *Chief Logistics Officer* (October 2003): 5.
6. David Blanchard, "What Exactly Is a Supply Chain, Anyway?" *Material Handling Management* (June 2009): 48.
7. Helen L. Richardson, "How Do You Know Your Supply Chain Works?" *Logistics Today* (June 2005): 30–33.
8. Helen L. Richardson, "Building a Better Supply Chain," *Logistics Today* (April 2005): 17–25.
9. David Blanchard, "The Trouble with Benchmarking," *Logistics Today* (June 2005): 7.
10. Ibid.
11. Sarah R. Sphar, "A Supply Chain Check-up," *Supply Chain Technology News* (October 2001): 34.
12. David W. Morgan, "What Have You Done for Me Lately?" *Logistics Today* (June 2005): 23–24.
13. Peter Bolstorff and Robert Rosenbaum, *Supply Chain Excellence: A Handbook for Dramatic Improvement Using the SCOR Model,* 2nd ed. (New York: Amacom, 2007), 2–3.
14. Shoshanah Cohen and Joseph Roussel, *Strategic Supply Chain Management* (New York: McGraw-Hill, 2005), 186–187.
15. Peter Bolstorff, "Supply Chain Management for Dummies," *Supply Chain Technology News* (October 2000): 51–53.
16. Peter Bolstorff, "Keeping Your Focus," *Supply Chain Technology News* (December 2000): 43–48.
17. Mike Ledyard and Kate Vitasek, "Don't Measure What You Won't Change," *Logistics Today* (June 2004): 37–38.
18. Richardson, "Building a Better Supply Chain."

Chapter 4: Planning and Forecasting: Headed for the Future

1. Lora Cecere, Eric Newmark, and Debra Hofman, "How Do I Know That I Have a Good Forecast?" *AMR Research Report* (January 2005): 9.
2. Laurie Joan Aron, "Nobody's Perfect," *Supply Chain Technology News* (September 2001): 13–15.
3. Scott Berinato, "What Went Wrong at Cisco?" *CIO Magazine*, August 1, 2001. Downloaded from www.cio.com.

4. Helen L. Richardson, "Keep Plenty of Flex in Your Supply Chain," *Logistics Today* (February 2005): 17–19.
5. David Blanchard, "High-Tech Companies Look to High-Tech Solutions," *Supply Chain Technology News* (June 2001): 5.
6. David Blanchard, "Food for Thought," *Logistics Today* (June 2006): 1, 12.
7. Yossi Sheffi, "Creating Demand-Responsive Supply Chains," *Supply Chain Strategy* (April 2005): 1–4.
8. Richardson, "Keep Plenty of Flex in Your Supply Chain."
9. Helen L. Richardson, "Shape Up Your Supply Chain," *Logistics Today* (January 2005): 26–29.
10. Blanchard, "Food for Thought."
11. Richardson, "Shape Up Your Supply Chain."
12. Author interview with Joe DiPrima, October 24, 2005.
13. www.sas.com; www.informationbuilders.com; www.cognos.com.
14. Dean Takahashi, "Crunching the Numbers," *Electronics Supply & Manufacturing*, November 11, 2004. Downloaded from www.my-esm.com. Cisco's Jim Miller also spoke at the Council of Supply Chain Management Professionals' annual meeting, October 25, 2005, in San Diego, CA.

Chapter 5: Procurement: Go Right to the Source

1. Jennifer S. Kuhel, "Motorola Rings Up Big Savings," *Supply Chain Technology News* (June 2002): 1, 7.
2. Larry Paquette, *The Sourcing Solution* (New York: Amacom, 2004), 8.
3. Michael Hugos, *Essentials of Supply Chain Management* (Hoboken, NJ: John Wiley & Sons, 2003), 64.
4. Patricia E. Moody, *The Big Squeeze* (Richmond, VA: The Oaklea Press, 2005).
5. Dave Nelson, Patricia E. Moody, and Jonathan R. Stegner, *The Incredible Payback* (New York: Amacom, 2005), 54–55.
6. Perry A. Trunick, "Why Do Companies Overspend for Logistics?" *Logistics Today* (July 2004): 1, 10.
7. Dave Nelson, Patricia E. Moody, and Jonathan Stegner, *The Purchasing Machine* (New York: The Free Press, 2001), 35.
8. "Ten Best Supply Chains of 2003," *Logistics Today* (December 2003): 21.
9. Author interview with Greg Shoemaker, October 31, 2005.
10. Ibid.
11. Mary Pat Flaherty and Gilbert M. Gaul, "Lax System Allows Criminals to Invade the Supply Chain," *The Washington Post*, October 22, 2003, A1. Downloaded from www.washingtonpost.com.

12. Walt Bogdanich, "Heparin Find May Point to Chinese Counterfeiting," *New York Times*, March 20, 2008, www.nytimes.com.

13. Rick Dana Barlow, "FDA Prescribes a Cure for Counterfeit Drugs," *Logistics Today* (January 2004): 1, 16–17.

14. Christine Blank, "Pharma Industry Expands Electronic Tracking of Drugs," *Drug Topics*, June 12, 2009. Downloaded from www .modernmedicine.com.

15. Rick Dana Barlow, "Drug Makers Fight Back against Counterfeiters," *Logistics Today* (February 2004): 9.

16. Daniel G. Jacobs, "Winning the War on Complexity," *Supply Chain Technology News* (June 2003): 22.

17. Nelson, Moody, and Stegner, *The Incredible Payback*, 242.

18. David A. Taylor, *Supply Chains: A Manager's Guide* (Boston: Addison-Wesley, 2004), 170.

19. David Blanchard, "Covisint Follows the Road Less Traveled by," *Logistics Today* (September 2005): 14.

20. Stan Liebowitz, *Re-thinking the Network Economy: The True Forces That Drive the Digital Marketplace* (New York: Amacom, 2002), 211.

21. Nick Zubko, "Online Marketplaces Are Back in Play," *IndustryWeek* (April 2008): 34–36.

Chapter 6: Manufacturing: Supply Chain on the Make

1. David Blanchard, "It's Not Easy Being Lean," *Logistics Today* (October 2003): 7.

2. Christopher Calnan, "Dell's Retail Store Strategy Yet to Compare with Online Sales," *Austin Business Journal*, May 22, 2009. Downloaded from http://austin.bizjournals.com.

3. Daniel G. Jacobs, "Anatomy of a Supply Chain," *Supply Chain Technology News* (March 2003): 20–22.

4. Jennifer S. Kuhel, "Balancing Act," *Supply Chain Technology News* (June 2001): 23–27.

5. James P. Womack and Daniel T. Jones, *Lean Solutions: How Companies and Customers Can Create Value and Wealth Together* (New York: The Free Press, 2005), 161–162.

6. Author interview with Nick Donofrio, March 17, 2003.

7. Wikipedia Contributors, "Digital Supply Chain," *Wikipedia, The Free Encyclopedia,* http://en.wikipedia.org/w/index.php?title=Digital_supply_chain&oldid=318849816.

8. C. J. Wehlage, "How the Digital Supply Chain Made Apple No. 1 on the Supply Chain Top 25," July 25, 2008. Downloaded from www .amrresearch.com.

9. Jennifer S. Kuhel, "A Solution Worth a Thousand Pictures," *Supply Chain Technology News* (May 2002): 12–14.
10. www.oracle.com/agile; www.sap.com; www.softech.com.
11. Jill Jusko, "Acronym Alert: P&PLM," *IndustryWeek* (August 2007): 44.
12. Alan Larson, *Demystifying Six Sigma: A Company-Wide Approach to Continuous Improvement* (New York: Amacom, 2003), 9.
13. Ibid., 42–43.
14. Helen L. Richardson, "Inventory in the Balance," *Logistics Today* (May 2004): 1, 16–17.
15. Steve Minter, "Six Sigma's Growing Pains," *IndustryWeek* (May 2009): 34–36.
16. Simon Harris, Brad Mackay, Floyd D'Costa, and Victoria Eavenson, *The Global Networked Value Circle: A New Model for Best-in-Class Manufacturing* (Edinburgh, UK: University of Edinburgh Business School/ Capgemini, 2009), 6–16.
17. David Blanchard, "Compete or Retreat," *IndustryWeek* (January 2007): 7.
18. David Blanchard, "The Face of American Manufacturing," *IndustryWeek* (June 2007): 27–31.

Chapter 7: Transportation: Logistics à la Mode

1. Pipelines are a highly specialized mode specific to the transportation of oil, natural gas, and other commodities. However, their use represents less than 2 percent of the U.S. total transportation spend, so they are not directly addressed here.
2. According to statistics compiled by Rosalyn Wilson in the Council of Supply Chain Management Professional's *2009 State of Logistics Report*, total transportation costs in the United States in 2008 were $864 billion. Breaking it down by mode, it looks like this:

Trucks: $680 billion
Rail: $63 billion
Maritime: $33 billion
Domestic Waterway: $6 billion
Domestic Air: $24 billion
International Air: $16 billion
Forwarders (Air): $32 billion
Oil Pipelines: $10 billion

3. *Logistics* traditionally refers to both transportation and distribution, but in some circles the term is used interchangeably with *supply chain*.

Rather than adding to the confusion, this chapter focuses on transportation and the next chapter on distribution and warehousing.

4. Gerhardt Muller, *The Supply Chain Handbook*, edited by James A. Tompkins and Dale Harmelink (Raleigh, NC: Tompkins Press, 2004), 304.

5. David Blanchard, "Owens Corning to Launch Fuel Reimbursement Program," *Logistics Today* (November 2005): 1.

6. David Blanchard, "Buddy, Can You Spare a Driver?" *Logistics Today* (July 2005): 1.

7. Jill Dunn, "Driver Shortage Turns to Surplus," *e-Trucker*, January 9, 2009. Downloaded from www.etrucker.com.

8. David Blanchard, "If You're Not Collaborating with Your Carriers, What Are You Waiting For?" *Logistics Today* (March 2006): 5.

9. Mateusz Perkowski, "Trucking Companies Hit the Brakes," *Capital Press*, November 13, 2008. Downloaded from www.capitalpress.info.

10. David Blanchard, "Get Inside the Mind of the Carriers," *Logistics Today* (March 2006): 1.

11. Mike DuVall and Mark Beischel, "Six Ways to Achieve Sustainable Carrier Savings," *Logistics Today* (March 2005): 20–21.

12. Beth Enslow, "Best Practices in Transportation Management," *Aberdeen Group Report* (June 2005): 3.

13. Roger Morton, "All the Right Answers," *Logistics Today* (May 2005): 36–39.

14. Roger Morton, "Rating the Carriers," *Logistics Today* (January 2004): 12–13.

15. Roger Morton, "Tracing the Track to Transportation Success," *Logistics Today* (March 2008): 26–29.

16. Roger Morton, "TMS Right Now," *Logistics Today* (May 2007): 32–34.

17. David Blanchard, "Portrait of Best-in-Class Transportation Management," *IndustryWeek* (October 2008): 56.

Chapter 8: Distribution and Warehousing: Going with the Flow

1. Lisa Terry, *2008 Third-Party Logistics: Results and Findings of the 13th Annual Study* (Atlanta: Georgia Institute of Technology/Capgemini U.S., 2008), 13. In Europe and the Asia-Pacific region, the percentage of companies that outsource warehousing is even higher, at 73 percent and 75 percent, respectively.

2. Helen L. Richardson, "Out in the Open," *Logistics Today* (February 2004): 32–35.

3. Helen L. Richardson, "Execution at the Dock," *Logistics Today* (April 2004): 31–33.

4. Perry A. Trunick, "Time Is Inventory," *Logistics Today* (April 2005): 26–27.

5. Ken Ackerman, *Warehousing Tips* (Columbus, Ohio: Ackerman Publications, 2002), 105.

6. Cross-docking can also be applied to less traditional situations, such as transferring a load from an inbound ocean container directly onto a truck. This tactic is becoming more popular as a way of circumventing congestion at the ports, particularly on the U.S. West Coast.

7. Trunick, "Time Is Inventory."

8. Richardson, "Execution at the Dock."

9. Roger Morton, "Wireless in the Warehouse," *Logistics Today* (May 2006): 44–45.

10. *2008 Cross-Docking Trends Report* (Lakeland, FL: Saddle Creek Corp., 2008), 7–8.

11. David Blanchard, "Full Circle," *Supply Chain Technology News* (May 2003): 7.

12. Edward Frazelle, *World-Class Warehousing and Material Handling* (New York: McGraw-Hill, 2002), 1.

13. Ibid., 8–11.

14. Clyde E. Witt, "Cutting Costs with Cutting-Edge WMS," *Material Handling Management* (April 2005): 14–15.

15. Ackerman, *Warehousing Tips*, 80.

16. David Blanchard, "Listen Up!" *Logistics Today* (March 2005): 1, 14.

17. Patti Satterfield, "Everybody's Talking," *Supply Chain Technology News* (July/August 2002): 32–35.

18. Ian Hobkirk, "Warehouse Management Software: Five Key Capabilities for Every Distribution Center," *Aberdeen Group Report* (December 2007): 9–10.

19. "Ace Beverage Goes Mobile and Wireless to Eliminate Distributor Overtime," *Material Handling Management*, April 1, 2008, www.mhmonline .com.

20. Jonathan Katz, "Going Down to the Wireless," *Supply Chain Technology News* (March 2003): 1, 8–9.

21. Richardson, "Out in the Open."

22. Perry A. Trunick, "Putting a Fresh Face on an Old DC," *Logistics Today* (October 2005): 36–39.

23. Helen L. Richardson, "Eight Ways to Prevent Overloading Your Warehouse," *Logistics Today* (October 2004): 21–22.

24. Ibid.

25. Perry A. Trunick, "How to Design a Regional Warehouse," *Logistics Today* (May 2004): 31–36.

Chapter 9: Site Selection: Location, Location, Location

1. Perry A. Trunick, "How to Design a Cost-Effective DC," *Logistics Today* (May 2005): 42–45.
2. Roger Morton, "Adapting to an Adaptive Supply Chain," *Logistics Today* (September 2004): 14–15.
3. Author interview with Greg Shoemaker, October 31, 2005.
4. Kevin O'Marah, "Design for Supply Chain Starts with Supply Chain Strategy," *AMR Research Alert*, December 11, 2003. Downloaded from www.amrresearch.com.
5. David Simchi-Levi and Edith Simchi-Levi, "Finding the Right Balance," *Chief Logistics Officer* (December 2003): 16–19.
6. James A. Tompkins and Dale Harmelink, *The Supply Chain Handbook* (Raleigh, NC: Tompkins Press, 2004), 82–83.
7. Bill King, "America's Most Logistics-Friendly Cities," *Logistics Today* (November 2007): 34–46.
8. Perry A. Trunick, "Sites under Construction," *Logistics Today* (November 2005): 22–24.
9. David Blanchard, "How to Build a Lean-Green Warehouse Network," *IndustryWeek* (March 2008): 64–65.
10. Author interview with Louise Knabe, November 30, 2005.
11. "A Comparative Operating Cost Analysis for Distribution Warehousing," The Boyd Company Inc., www.bizcosts.com.
12. Perry A. Trunick, "How to Put the 'Where' in Warehouse," *Logistics Today* (February 2005): 24–26.
13. Perry A. Trunick, "The Power of a Positive Attitude in Site Selection," *Logistics Today* (July 2004): 30–35.
14. Perry A. Trunick, "Think Inside a Bigger Box," *Logistics Today* (September 2004): 27–28.
15. Jonathan Katz, "A Quick Guide to Strategic Siting," *IndustryWeek* (May 2008): 14–16.

Chapter 10: Globalization: It's a Not-So-Small World

1. David Blanchard, "Shipping Out, Not Shaping Up," *Supply Chain Technology News* (December 2002/January 2003): 11.
2. Author interview with Louise Knabe, November 30, 2005.
3. Perry A. Trunick, "Ten Things to Consider When Establishing a Global Distribution Network," *Logistics Today* (September 2005): 26–28.
4. Robert B. Handfield and Ernest L. Nichols Jr., *Supply Chain Redesign: Transforming Supply Chains into Integrated Value Systems*

(Upper Saddle River, NJ: Financial Times, Prentice Hall, 2002), 233–234.

5. Jean-Francois Arvis et al., *Connecting to Compete: Trade Logistics in the Global Economy* (Washington, D.C.: The World Bank, 2007), 26–33.

6. The World Bank study omits some countries, largely due to political considerations (e.g., Iraq, Cuba, North Korea).

7. James Canton, *The Extreme Future* (New York: Plume, 2007), 304.

8. David Blanchard, "The Cost of Doing Low-Cost Business," *IndustryWeek* (November 2007): 7.

9. Perry A. Trunick, "Breaking the Global Logjam," *Logistics Today* (May 2005): 1, 11.

10. "Too Many Companies Fall Short of Effective Offshoring," *Logistics Today* (April 2005): 9.

11. Shoshanah Cohen et al., *Global Supply Chain Trends 2008–2010* (Boston: PRTM Management Consultants, 2008), 4–7.

12. Thomas L. Friedman, *The World Is Flat: A Brief History of the Twenty-First Century* (New York: Farrar, Straus and Giroux, 2005), 118–123.

13. David Blanchard, "Heroes and Villains," *IndustryWeek* (September 2008): 7.

14. James McGregor, *One Billion Customers: Lessons from the Front Lines of Doing Business in China* (New York: The Free Press, 2005), 188.

15. "China Logistics: Challenges and Opportunities," EFT Research Service (January 2006): 20–25.

16. "Better Forecasting Needs to Build Stronger Supply Chains," *Logistics Today's Supply Chain Report*, May 2, 2005, www.logisticstoday.com.

17. Simon Ellis, "Profitable Proximity: Product Decisions in the Modern Supply Chain," *Manufacturing Insights: Supply Chain Strategies: Market Overview* (July 2008): 6–7.

18. J. Michael Kilgore and Jeff Metersky, "Overseas Manufacturing May Be Costing Your Firms Millions," *Chainalytics Supply Chain Strategy* (July 2003): 1–3.

19. Laird Carmichael, "How to Configure Success through Outsourcing," *Logistics Today* (June 2004): 40–41.

20. Douglas Long, *International Logistics: Global Supply Chain Management* (Norwell, MA: Kluwer Academic Publishers, 2003), 13–14.

21. Trunick, "Ten Things to Consider When Establishing a Global Distribution Network."

22. Long, *International Logistics*.

23. Carmichael, "How to Configure Success through Outsourcing."

24. Adrienne Selko, "Global Hot Spots," *IndustryWeek* (August 2007): 26–30.

25. Ian Coleman and John Hawksworth, *Balancing Risk & Reward* (London: PricewaterhouseCoopers, 2008), 3.
26. Nick Zubko, "The Low-Cost Learning Curve," *IndustryWeek* (August 2008): 32.
27. Helen L. Richardson, "Out in the Open," *Logistics Today* (February 2004): 32–35.
28. Noha Tohamy, "Can India Parlay Its IT Services Success into Manufacturing Outsourcing?" March 31, 2009, www.amrresearch.com.
29. Jonathan Katz, "Welcome Back U.S. Manufacturing," *IndustryWeek* (August 2008): 35–38.

Chapter 11: Customer Service: Keeping the Customer Satisfied

1. David Blanchard, "The Joys and Sorrows of ERP," *Supply Chain Technology News* (October 2002): 1, 7.
2. David F. Carr, "Hershey's Sweet Victory," *Baseline* (December 2002): 68–73.
3. Edward J. Marien, "The Customer's Bill of Rights," *Logistics Today* (February 2005): 20–22.
4. Robert B. Handfield and Ernest L. Nichols Jr., *Supply Chain Redesign: Transforming Supply Chains into Integrated Value Systems* (Upper Saddle River, NJ: Financial Times, Prentice Hall, 2002), 73–74.
5. Ibid., 76.
6. David Blanchard, "Moving Forward in Reverse," *Logistics Today* (July 2005): 1, 8.
7. Helen L. Richardson, "Point of No Returns," *Logistics Today* (June 2004): 20–25.
8. David Blanchard, "Moving Ahead by Mastering the Reverse Supply Chain," *IndustryWeek* (June 2009): 58–59.
9. Richardson, "Point of No Returns."
10. Blanchard, "Moving Forward in Reverse."
11. www.oracle.com; www.salesforce.com; www.sas.com; www.sap.com.
12. Scott D. Nelson, "Ten Secrets for Creating a Customer-Centric Enterprise," *Gartner RAS Core Research Note*, December 22, 2005, 2.
13. James L. Heskett, W. Earl Sasser Jr., and Leonard A. Schlesinger, *The Value Profit Chain: Treat Employees Like Customers and Customers Like Employees* (New York: The Free Press, 2003), 53.
14. Ibid., 74.
15. Joe Parente and Robert D. Ticknor, "Hidden Potential," *Logistics Today* (September 2004): 38–41.
16. Helen L. Richardson, "How Do You Know Your Supply Chain Works?" *Logistics Today* (June 2005): 30–33.

17. Parente and Ticknor, "Hidden Potential."
18. Chris Denove and James D. Power IV, *Satisfaction: How Every Great Company Listens to the Voice of the Customer* (New York: Portfolio, 2006), 232–239.

Chapter 12: 3PLs: When You'd Rather Not Do It Yourself

1. The author visited UPS Worldport in September 2004.
2. David Blanchard, "It Takes a Supply Chain Village," *Logistics Today* (November 2004): 9.
3. Adrienne Selko, "3PL Market at $200 Billion in 2008," Industry Week.com, April 6, 2009.
4. David Blanchard, "How to Win at Outsourcing," *Logistics Today* (November 2004): 1, 21.
5. Analysts, consultants, and business writers apparently believe that the *3PL* term lacks a certain elegance. Friedman opts for insourcing, while other terms such as logistics service provider (LSP) and transportation service provider (TSP) are occasionally suggested as substitutes. However, within the supply chain field, 3PL is the most widely used and recognized acronym for logistics outsourcing.
6. Thomas L. Friedman, *The World Is Flat: A Brief History of the Twenty-First Century* (New York: Farrar, Straus and Giroux, 2005), 144.
7. James A. Tompkins, Steven W. Simonson, Bruce W. Tompkins, and Brian E. Upchurch, *Logistics and Manufacturing Outsourcing: Harness Your Core Competencies* (Raleigh, NC: Tompkins Press, 2005), 41.
8. Helen L. Richardson, "How to Maximize the Potential of 3PLs," *Logistics Today* (May 2005): 19–21.
9. Roger Morton, "Why Is This Pig Smiling?" *Outsourced Logistics* (August 2008): 14–16.
10. Helen L. Richardson, "The Pros and Cons of 3PLs," *Logistics Today* (October 2005): 17–18.
11. Helen L. Richardson, "Measure for Success," *Logistics Today* (October 2005): 18.
12. Greg Meseck, "Risky Business," *Logistics Today* (August 2004): 34–41.
13. Helen L. Richardson, "3PLs at Your Service," *Logistics Today* (September 2004): 47–50.
14. Richardson, "How to Maximize the Potential of 3PLs."
15. Helen L. Richardson, "What Are You Willing to Give Up?" *Logistics Today* (March 2005): 27–29.
16. William Frech and Ben Pivar, "Riding the Outsourcing Wave," *Supply Chain Technology News* (June 2003): 13–15.

Chapter 13: Collaboration: Extending the Enterprise

1. Thomas T. Stallkamp, *SCORE! A Better Way To Do Business* (Upper Saddle River, NJ: Wharton School Publishing, 2005), 97–101.
2. David Blanchard, "Conflict of Interests," *Logistics Today* (May 2005): 5.
3. "Ford Plans to Cut Its Supplier Base in Half," *Logistics Today's Supply Chain Report*, October 10, 2005, www.logisticstoday.com.
4. Steve Rose, "Fixing Detroit's Broken Business Model," *Detroit Free Press*, May 8, 2009, www.freep.com.
5. Jeffrey K. Liker, *The Toyota Way* (New York: McGraw-Hill, 2004), 199.
6. Robert Handfield, "United They'll Stand," *Wall Street Journal*, March 23, 2009, R6.
7. Nick Zubko, "Tier Ones Say Toyota Is Tops in Supplier Relations," *IndustryWeek* (October 2008): 26–27.
8. Ronald K. Ireland with Colleen Crum, *Supply Chain Collaboration: How to Implement CPFR and Other Best Collaborative Practices* (Boca Raton, FL: J. Ross Publishing, 2005), 37–40.
9. Dirk Seifert, *Collaborative Planning, Forecasting, and Replenishment* (New York: Amacom, 2003), 30–31.
10. Jennifer S. Kuhel, "Building a Better Supply Chain," *Supply Chain Technology News* (December 2001): 28–31.
11. Mary Aichlmayr, "Is CPFR Worth the Effort?" *Chief Logistics Officer* (February 2003): 27–30.
12. David A. Taylor, *Supply Chains: A Manager's Guide* (Boston: Addison-Wesley, 2004), 48.
13. Helen L. Richardson, "The Ins and Outs of VMI," *Logistics Today* (March 2004): 19–21.
14. Traci Purdum, "VMI: Size Matters," *IndustryWeek* (March 2007): 19–20.
15. Beth Enslow, "How to Communicate Better with Your Suppliers," *Logistics Today* (September 2004): 52.
16. Brooks A. Bentz, "Can This Marriage Be Saved?" *Logistics Today* (May 2004): 42–45.
17. John Matchette and Andy Seikel, "How to Win Friends and Influence Supply Chain Partners," *Logistics Today* (December 2004): 40–42.

Chapter 14: Security: Seeking Shelter from Supply Chain Storms

1. "Container Security: Expansion of Key Customs Programs Will Require Greater Attention to Critical Success Factors," U.S. General Accounting Office, July 2003, 8.

2. Rosalyn Wilson, "20th Annual State of Logistics Report: Riding Out the Recession," Council of Supply Chain Management Professionals, June 17, 2009, 1.

3. Michael Dresser and Greg Barrett, "Port Security Gaps Pose Threat," *The Baltimore Sun*, July 10, 2005. Downloaded from www.baltimoresun .com.

4. "National Preparedness: FEMA Has Made Progress, but Needs to Complete and Integrate Planning, Exercise, and Assessment Efforts," U.S. General Accounting Office, April 2009, 9.

5. Michael Barbaro and Justin Gillis, "Wal-Mart at Forefront of Hurricane Relief," *The Washington Post*, September 6, 2005, D1.

6. Justin Fox, "A Meditation on Risk," *Fortune*, October 3, 2005, 50–62.

7. Julia Boorstin, "Rapid Response," *Fortune*, October 3, 2005, 80.

8. Ann Zimmerman, "Wal-Mart's Emergency-Relief Team Girds for Hurricane Gustav," *Wall Street Journal*, August 30, 2008, A3.

9. Author interview with Theo Fletcher, October 4, 2005.

10. Descriptions of U.S. Customs and Border Protection programs and relevant statistics cited in this chapter are available at www.cbp.gov.

11. David Blanchard, "Seven Steps to Prevent Cargo Theft," *IndustryWeek* (December 2008): 54.

12. Helen L. Richardson, "Think Supply Chain Security—Think Strategy," *Logistics Today* (September 2005): 17–19.

13. Greg Aimi, "Securing the Global Supply Chain," *AMR Research Alert*, April 20, 2006. Downloaded from www.amrresearch.com.

14. Lisa H. Harrington, "Securing the Borders," *Logistics Today* (December 2003): 1, 42–43.

15. Ben Worthen, "Peering into Your Supply Chain," *CSO* (April 2006). Downloaded from www.csoonline.com.

16. Perry A. Trunick, "Increase Security, Reduce Delays," *Logistics Today* (February 2006): 28.

17. Roger Morton, "Calming the Waters on 10+2," *Outsourced Logistics* (January/February 2009): 18–21.

18. Larry E. Christensen, "Twelve Steps to an Effective Compliance Program," *Logistics Today's Supply Chain Report*, February 16, 2006, www .logisticstoday.com.

19. Helen L. Richardson, "Is Your Supply Chain at Risk?" *Logistics Today* (April 2006): 1, 14.

20. Yossi Sheffi, *The Resilient Enterprise: Overcoming Vulnerability for Competitive Advantage* (Cambridge, MA: The MIT Press, 2005), 270–278.

21. Thomas Frank, "$250M Effort to Secure Ports Lags," *USA Today*, April 15, 2009, www.usatoday.com.

22. Rob Housman, "Crunch Time for Maritime," *Logistics Today* (December 2003): 36–41.

23. David Blanchard, "Better, Faster, Cheaper... and Smarter," *Industry-Week* (April 2009): 40–42.
24. David Blanchard, "Portrait of Best-in-Class Risk Management," *IndustryWeek* (February 2009): 44.

Chapter 15: RFID: A Game of Tags

1. David Blanchard, "The Five Stages of RFID," *IndustryWeek* (January 2009): 50-53.
2. David Blanchard, "Aww, Geez, Not Another RFID Article," *Logistics Today* (May 2004): 7.
3. David Blanchard, "RFID Is Off and Running at Wal-Mart," *Logistics Today* (February 2005): 1, 10.
4. "Moving Forward with Item-Level Radio Frequency Identification in Apparel/Footwear," Kurt Salmon Associates, 2005, 2–4.
5. David Blanchard, "Countdown to RFID-Day," *Logistics Today* (December 2004): 1, 11.
6. Blanchard, "RFID Is Off and Running at Wal-Mart."
7. Gary McWilliams, "Wal-Mart's Radio-Tracked Inventory Hits Static," *The Wall Street Journal*, February 18, 2007, D6.
8. David Blanchard, "Wal-Mart Lays Down the Law on RFID," *Industry-Week* (May 2008): 72–74.
9. V. Daniel Hunt, Albert Puglia, and Mike Puglia, *RFID: A Guide to Radio Frequency Identification* (Hoboken, NJ: John Wiley & Sons, 2007), 60–64.
10. Blanchard, "Countdown to RFID-Day."
11. "System of Tracking Farm Cattle May Help Energize U.S. Market," *The Wall Street Journal*, November 30, 2005, B2B.
12. Claire Swedberg, "Brandt Tracks Its Beef," *RFID Journal*, March 31, 2006. Downloaded from www.rfidjournal.com.
13. Perry A. Trunick, "From Stable to Table," *Logistics Today* (March 2007): 18.
14. Charles Poirier and Duncan McCollum, *RFID Strategic Implementation and ROI: A Practical Roadmap to Success* (Fort Lauderdale, FL: J. Ross Publishing, 2006), 124.
15. Marc L. Songini, "Open Wide: Kodak Looks to Patent Edible RFID," *Computerworld*, February 27, 2007. Downloaded from www.computerworld.com.
16. Sandip Lahiri, *RFID Sourcebook* (Upper Saddle River, NJ: Pearson/IBM Press, 2006), 145.
17. Roger Morton, "RFID Compliance: Year Two," *Logistics Today* (January 2006): 1, 8–9.

18. "Airbus Plans Transformational RFID Roll-Out Across End-to-End Supply Chain," *Supply Chain Digest*, April 23, 2008. Downloaded from www.scdigest.com.
19. Claire Swedberg, "Boeing Tracks Assets at Kennedy Space Center," *RFID Journal*, November 13, 2008. Downloaded from www.rfidjournal.com.
20. Paul Nuzum and Carol J. Johnson, "RFID—Lessons Learned," *ProLogis Supply Chain Review* (October 2005): 1.
21. David Blanchard, "Fears of 'Big Brother' Sidetrack Benetton's Smart Tag Initiative," *Transportation & Distribution* (July 2003): 20.
22. Poirier and McCollum, *RFID Strategic Implementation and ROI*, 17–29.
23. Paul Gustafson and William Koff, *Digital Disruptions* (Falls Church, Va.: Computer Sciences Corp., 2008), 39.
24. Samuel Fosso Wamba et al., *RFID Adoption Issues* (Wollongong, NSW, Australia: University of Wollongong, 2009), 11–12.
25. David Blanchard, "RFID at the Gates," *Logistics Today* (September 2004): 1, 16.
26. Jonathan Katz, "Going Down to the Wireless," *Supply Chain Technology News* (March 2003): 1, 8–9.

Chapter 16: Green Supply Chains: It's Not Easy Going Green

1. Thomas L. Friedman, *Hot, Flat, and Crowded* (New York: Farrar, Straus and Giroux, 2008), 170-177.
2. Kimberly Knickle and Bob Parker, "Attitudes and Trends Toward Greening Manufacturing and the Supply Chain in North America," *Manufacturing Insights: Emerging Agenda: Customer Needs and Strategies* (December 2008): 5–6.
3. Andrew S. Winston, *Green Recovery* (Boston: Harvard Business Press, 2009), 25–27.
4. Nick Zubko, "Does the End Justify the Green?" *IndustryWeek* (June 2008): 26–28.
5. Brad Kenney, "The 'What, Why, How, and When' of Carbon Footprinting," *IndustryWeek* (May 2008): 48–55.
6. David Blanchard, "How Green Is Your Supply Chain?" *Logistics Today* (September 17, 2009): 10–12.
7. Mary Aichlmayr, "The World in a Grain of Sand," *Material Handling Management* (August 2009): 4. The entirety of John Fleming's remarks are posted as a video at www.walmartstores.com/Video/?id-1379.
8. Miguel Bustillo, "Wal-Mart to Assign New 'Green' Ratings," *Wall Street Journal*, July 17, 2009, A4.
9. Aichlmayr, "The World in a Grain of Sand."

10. William Pentland, "Here Comes Carbox," *Forbes*, July 3, 2008. Downloaded from www.forbes.com.
11. Edgar Blanco et al., "Chiquita and MIT Center for Transportation and Logistics Aim High on Defining Carbon Footprint Measurement," *Distribution Business Management Journal* 8 (2009): 80–81.
12. Kenney, "The 'What, Why, How, and When' of Carbon Footprinting."
13. Daniel Sitarz, *Greening Your Business* (Carbondale, IL: EarthPress, 2008), 173–182.
14. David Blanchard, "SC Johnson Finds a 'Greener' Way to Load Trucks," *IndustryWeek* (February 2008): 64–65.
15. David Blanchard, "Haworth Rolls Out a Greener Way to Move Its Freight," *IndustryWeek* (December 2008): 54–54.
16. David Blanchard, "Green Is the New Black," *IndustryWeek* (March 2009): 46–48.
17. David Blanchard, "How IBM Limits Its Greenhouse Gas Emissions," *IndustryWeek* (July 2008): 63.
18. David Blanchard, "How to Green Your Supply Chain," *IndustryWeek* (May 2008): 74.
19. David Blanchard, "Green Supply Chain Movement Hits a Speed Bump," *IndustryWeek* (April 2009): 42.

Chapter 17: Continuous Improvement: Lean on Me

1. The author visited Autoliv in November 2007 and January 2008.
2. *Kaizen* is a Japanese term that, loosely translated, means "continuous improvement." Short-term projects are known as blitzes, while long-term projects are called events. Japanese terms are plentiful within lean circles due to the central role Japanese automaker Toyota has played in developing and promoting many of the concepts.
3. Mark Newton, "Autoliv North America Continues the Improvement Process," *IndustryWeek* (November 2008): 72.
4. Terence T. Burton and Steven M. Boeder, *The Lean Extended Enterprise* (Boca Raton, FL: J. Ross Publishing, 2003), 72–73.
5. David Blanchard, "The Power of Suggestion," *IndustryWeek* (January 2008): 36.
6. Jeffrey K. Liker, *The Toyota Way* (New York: McGraw-Hill, 2004), 152.
7. Peter Strozniak, "Toyota Alters Face of Production," *IndustryWeek* (August 13, 2001): 46–48.
8. "The Toyota Production System." Downloaded from www.toyotageorgetown.com/tps.asp.
9. Liker, *The Toyota Way*, 37–41.

10. David Blanchard, "Lean, Green, and Low Cost," *IndustryWeek* (October 2007): 37–39.
11. Ralph Keller, "Silver Bullets Only Exist in Hollywood," *IndustryWeek* (October 2008): 12.
12. Rick Pay, "Everybody's Jumping on the Lean Bandwagon, but Many Are Being Taken for a Ride," *IndustryWeek* (May 2008): 62.
13. Mandyam M. Srinivasan, *Streamlined: 14 Principles for Building and Managing the Lean Supply Chain* (Mason, OH: Thomson, 2004), vii–viii.
14. Christopher Trunk, "Keep 'Em Flying," *Supply Chain Technology News* (April 2003): 9.
15. "Embracing Lean," *All Systems Go: Journal of Boeing Integrated Defense Systems* 2, no. 3 (2004). Downloaded from www.boeing.com.
16. John Black, *Lean Production* (New York: Industrial Press Inc., 2008), 47–54.
17. Helen L. Richardson, "Forever Lean," *Logistics Today* (March 2006): 32–34.
18. John Teresko, "Learning from Toyota—Again," *IndustryWeek* (February 2006): 34–41.
19. The author visited United Technologies Electronic Controls in November 2008.
20. David Blanchard, "Achieving Competitive Excellence," *IndustryWeek* (January 1, 2009): 44.
21. David Blanchard, "Lean on Me," *IndustryWeek* (December 2007): 53–54.
22. Nari Viswanathan and Matthew Littlefield, "Lean Manufacturing," Aberdeen Group (April 2009): 24.
23. Ralph Keller, "What's Continuous Improvement Worth?" *IndustryWeek* (August 2008): 12.

Chapter 18: The Supply Chain Profession: What Keeps You Up at Night?

1. Bernard J. La Londe, James L. Ginter, and James R. Stock, "The Ohio State University 2007 Survey of Career Patterns in Logistics," The Ohio State University, 10–14. Downloaded from www.cscmp.org.
2. Mark D. Wilson, "Best Practices in College Recruiting," *Logistics Today* (March 2004): 13.
3. David Aquino and Bob Kraus, "Leading U.S. Supply Chain Programs, 2009," June 15, 2009. Downloaded from www.amrresearch.com.
4. Ken Cottrill, "Wanted: Leaders with a Talent for Change," *MIT-CTL Supply Chain Strategy* (October 2008): 1, 12.

5. Harry Joiner, "Seven Steps to Successful Problem Solving," *Logistics Today* (August 2004): 33.
6. Helen L. Richardson, "Have New Employee, Will Train," *Logistics Today* (August 2004): 24–30.
7. Clyde E. Witt, "IBM Builds a Successful Mentoring Program," *Material Handling Management* (December 2005): 24.
8. David Blanchard, "How Big Blue Manages Its Human Assets," *Logistics Today* (June 2006): 1, 14. IBM's Mark Henderson also spoke at the Supply Chain World annual meeting, March 27, 2006, in Dallas, TX.
9. Navi Radjou, "IBM Transforms Its Supply Chain to Drive Growth," *Forrester Best Practices*, March 24, 2005, 14–15.
10. David Drickhamer, "Going for the Green," *Logistics Today* (February 2007): 1, 26–29.
11. David Blanchard, "What Keeps You Up at Night?" *Logistics Today* (September 2004): 5.
12. Madeleine Miller-Holodnicki, "Help Wanted: Experienced in Everything," *CLM Logistics Comment* (January/February 2004): 1–3.
13. Bruce J. Cutler, "Landing a Job Takes Skill and Perseverance," *CLM Logistics Comment* (March/April 2004): 11. Ironically, Cutler ultimately accepted a job in the same town he was already living in—Houston—via a blind ad in the local newspaper.
14. Drickhamer, "Going for the Green," 1, 26–29.
15. La Londe et al., "The Ohio State University 2007 Survey of Career Patterns in Logistics," 7, 19–20.
16. Several hundred more comments like these from supply chain professionals can be found at www.logisticstoday.com: search "salary survey."

About the Author

DAVID BLANCHARD is an award-winning journalist and the editorial director/associate publisher of Penton Media's Supply Chain Group. He previously served as editor-in-chief of several Penton magazines, including *Supply Chain Technology News*, *Logistics Today*, and *IndustryWeek*. He has also launched and edited numerous print and online newsletters covering the supply chain, transportation, manufacturing, and computer industries. He is a frequent speaker at major supply chain industry events. He lives in a suburb of Cleveland, Ohio.

Index